A LATTER-DAY SAINT ODE TO JESUS

A LATTER-DAY SAINT ODE TO JESUS

Praise to the Most Influential Person Who Ever Lived

Edward K. Watson

Brainy Books

Copyright © 2019 by Edward K. Watson

All rights reserved. No part of this publication may be reproduced, stored in a retrieval system, or transmitted, in any form or by any means, electronic, mechanical, photocopying, recording, or otherwise, without the prior written permission of the author.

ISBN: 9781097346912

Nestle-Aland, Novum Testamentum Graece, 28th Revised Edition, edited by Barbara and Kurt Aland, Johannes Karavidopoulos, Carlo M. Martini, and Bruce M. Metzger in cooperation with the Institute for New Testament Textual Research, Münster/Westphalia, © 2012 Deutsche Bibelgesellschaft, Stuttgart. Used by permission.

Cover Design by Edward K. Watson using Adobe Stock File #: 136364712 (Standard License)

Adobe Stock (Standard License) for File #81841371; #259338615; #2357118; #42161953; #187997069.

All other illustrations and author photo copyright © 2019 Edward K. Watson.

Distributed by Brainy Books

Printed in the United States of America

www.edwardkwatson.com

All biblical quotations within ***A LATTER-DAY SAINT ODE TO JESUS*** are paraphrased text and came from this author's ***THE GOD WHO WASHES FEET*** (Brainy Books), which is a comprehensive examination of fifty-five (55) specific doctrines about Jesus that when put together, shows the New Testament has a core message, a single soteriological cosmology centered on Jesus Christ.

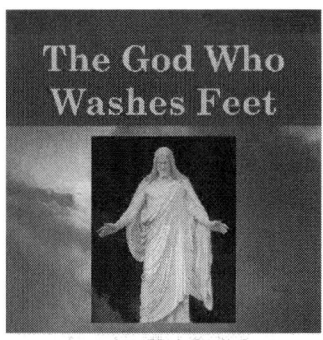

THE GOD WHO WASHES FEET demonstrates that the New Testament is *the world's only frameless, unharmonized, correlative anthology*—a stupendous accomplishment without parallel in literature, and the only empirical evidence that gives a very high probability that something supernatural was involved in its creation.

A LATTER-DAY SAINT ODE TO JESUS also extracts, and in some cases, modifies portions of ***THE GOD WHO WASHES FEET*** due to discussing the same subject.

The Holy Bible's Core Message or "Gospel"

God's only Son, Jesus Christ, the Creator of the universe who is "God" by nature – obeyed his Father's will and became human flesh. He then suffered and died to annul the Fall – the establishment of death, sin, weakness, and trials on humanity.

He rose from the dead to destroy death itself and make all humans immortal physical beings. He conjoined the divine and human natures so that his grace allows <u>some</u> humans to become perfect by being "adopted" by God, share ultimate glory, and participate in God's very nature, mutual indwelling, and oneness.

All who come unto him, repent of their sins, get baptized in his name, strive to live his teachings whereby the Holy Spirit within them constantly refines and purifies them, and endure to the end will be rewarded with eternal bliss in his kingdom.

Table of Contents

INTRODUCTION — 1

Why Is Jesus Christ Important?... 1
The Atonement of Jesus Christ is the Most Important Event in the History of the Universe 7
How Can You Know the Holy Bible is True and Credible?.... 11
How Can You Know the Book of Mormon is True and Credible?.. 17
Latter-day Saint Theology is Christian and Basic Trinitarian. 36
My Witness 45
The Exalted Children of God 46

ODE TO JESUS HYMNS — 53

Prologue 54
1. The Pre-Existence of Jesus................................. 56
2. Jesus Mutually Indwells With the Father................... 58
3. Jesus is the Creator 60
4. Jesus Became Human Flesh................................... 62
5. The Atonement of Jesus 64
6. The Resurrection of Jesus.................................. 66
7. The Glorification of Jesus 68
8. Jesus Creates the Children of God.......................... 72
Epilogue 76

STANZA CLARIFICATIONS — 79

Clarification of the "Prologue" Stanzas 81
Clarification of the "1. The Pre-Existence Of Jesus" Stanzas 86
Clarification of the "2. Jesus Mutually Indwells With the Father" Stanzas 101
Clarification of the "3. Jesus is the Creator" Stanzas 107
Clarification of the "4. Jesus Became Human Flesh" Stanzas 112

Clarification of the "5. The Atonement of Jesus" Stanzas ... 117
Clarification of the "6. The Resurrection of Jesus" Stanzas 122
Clarification of the "7. The Glorification of Jesus" Stanzas.. 129
Clarification of the "8. Jesus Creates the Children of God" Stanzas 137

CONCLUSION 147

APPENDIX: PROOF THE BOOK OF MORMON CONTAINS ARGUMENTATIVE AND PERSUASIVE ESSAYS 149

Alma 32 150
Alma 33 158
Alma 34 164
Alma 36 171

SCRIPTURE REFERENCE GUIDE 181

Old Testament 181
New Testament 183
Book of Mormon 190
Doctrine and Covenants 193
Pearl of Great Price 195

INDEX 197

INTRODUCTION

This book is the Latter-day Saint version of *Ode to Jesus* – a work containing ten interrelated hymns or poems centered on the most important and most influential person in history: Jesus Christ. The eight core hymns reveal fundamental biblical doctrines and are bookended by the Prologue and Epilogue hymns.

Ode to Jesus grounds the reader on what's truly important in life. It gives knowledge and comfort. It helps one be grateful, stay humble, and be charitable—by giving a constant reminder that we owe so much to him who suffered and died for us. It gives stability and certitude to those who doubt or who face challenges and obstacles.

> *Most of all, it reveals the magnificent Lord Jesus Christ, the glorious Only Begotten Son of God, who is both God and Man.*

By merely reading or singing these lyrics, one is provided with the Holy Bible's real teaching concerning Jesus Christ—that simple faith that changed the world and improved the lives of everyone.

> *Anyone can now understand the Bible's actual teachings concerning Jesus without confusion, filters, or distortion.*

Each stanza has scripture references for verification, and the reader is encouraged to use their own bibles or online parallel versions to confirm the stanzas are accurate. Also, each stanza is further explained in the Stanza Clarifications section of this work.

Why Is Jesus Christ Important?

In some ways, it does not matter if the biblical message concerning him is true – that is, he is the Son of God made human flesh who annulled the Fall and allows us to enjoy eternal bliss if we strive to follow him. His influence on the world can be seen by the actions of his followers – those who were directly involved in the recognition of every "inalienable" natural right[1] mankind enjoys

---

[1] From an ethical standpoint, we have natural rights – rights that are inherent in us as human and do not come from any government. Consequently, they cannot be ethically taken away by anyone provided we do not violate the natural rights of others or break the Social Contract where we knowingly and willingly make these rights subject to a human law.

today and who influenced the formation of virtually every technology that makes our life better.

> *Jesus Christ's impact for good on the world cannot be overstated since every human today is positively affected in one way or another by ideas and products that can be shown to owe a debt to Jesus and his followers.*

Belief in Jesus was the glue that resulted in hundreds of tribes and nations merging into the modern nation states of Europe and the Americas (and some parts of Africa and Asia). Christianity's mindset and milieu allowed for the establishment of modern Science, Technology, Engineering, and Mathematics (STEM). Its ethical and social practices became the ideal in virtually all contemporary countries today.

Thanks to Christ's followers, we enjoy and take for granted:

- ✓ Recognition of our natural rights
- ✓ All humans are equal regardless of race, religion, gender, or sexual orientation
- ✓ All humans have inherent dignity
- ✓ Civil rights, women's rights, children's rights
- ✓ Government leaders bound by law
- ✓ No religion can dominate or veto a government
- ✓ Criminalization of rape and sex with children

Because we are human, we have a natural right to:

1. Life
2. Liberty
3. Physical Security
4. Pursue Happiness
5. Freedom of Speech
6. Freedom of Religion
7. Equality
8. Fair Trial
9. Property
10. Vote for a Representative Government Within a Social Contract (for citizens only)

- ✓ Abolition of slavery, infanticide, human sacrifice, and torture
- ✓ Monogamy
- ✓ Sexual exclusivity in marriage by *both* partners
- ✓ Welfare program
- ✓ Universal literacy and public/private education
- ✓ The scientific method, universities, universal standards, degrees
- ✓ Hospitals and public health care
- ✓ Many, many others

Without Christianity, the foundations of modern STEM could've never been made since of the four major world religions, it was only Christianity's theology, cosmology, and cultural practices that allowed for its establishment—and eventual spread across the world. Christianity's birth to modern STEM and support of it is why we enjoy the highest standard of living in human history.

When the framers of Western civilization developed our code of ethics, forms of government, and the Common Law and Civil Law legal systems, they used teachings from Aristotle, Moses, Cicero, and Jesus Christ in crafting their arguments and inventions.

While the influences of Aristotle, Moses, and Cicero played a part in the development of Western civilization, their teachings were *justified* by Jesus Christ's moral teachings of empathetic morality and human equality.

THE WEST

ARISTOTLE	MOSES	CICERO
Representative Government	Absolute Authority of the Law	Supremacy of Natural Law

JESUS CHRIST
Empathetic Morality & Human Equality

The West's ethics and recognition of our natural rights are built on teachings that originated from Jesus Christ, such as:

> "Do unto others what you want to be done to you." (Matthew 7:12)
>
> "Whatever you did to the most unimportant of my brothers and sisters, you did it to me ... Whatever you did not do to the most unimportant of my brothers and sisters, you did not do it to me." (Matthew 25:40,45)
>
> "Love your neighbor as you love yourself." (Mark 12:31)
>
> "Love one another." (John 12:34)
>
> "There is no Jew or Gentile, slave or free, or male or female: You are all one in Christ Jesus." (Galatians 3:28)

This is why societies that followed Christian ethics became the most attractive in history. Serving God meant having genuine love and charity towards others. It meant serving each other and taking responsibility for the welfare of others. It meant swallowing one's pride and tolerating differences. Moral discipline (the action of obeying rules and doing "good") and bodily self-control (the deferment or rejection of selfish pleasure) became *internal* instead of externally enforced by the state or by another authority figure.[1]

Most people in the West believe we possess inherent rights and assume that recognition is normal everywhere. It isn't – one only needs to live outside the West to see that not every nation has the same ethical values.

Our natural rights are not self-evident because they go against the default of human nature, which has invariably been: *"Powerful insiders are always more valuable than weak outsiders"* and *"Might makes right."* People in positions of power tend to want to keep that power and even increase it. What then justifies the Western ethics of the innate worth and equality of all humans?

---

[1] This is why the true follower of Jesus Christ does not keep money they saw fell out of a pocket of an "enemy" because their internal moral code tells them that it is "wrong." They do not need to be externally forced by the state to return the cash on pain of punishment.

It is that internal moral code that made the West the most attractive and successful civilization in history.

The teachings of Jesus Christ. Without this foundation, there would be no objective justification for this ethics.[1]

This is why regardless of our religious views, we must never lose sight of what made our civilization great: **Jesus Christ's teachings of empathetic morality and human equality**. Any attempt to remove the Christian foundation of the West removes the justification for the innate worth and equality of all humans. And if that removal succeeds, it will result in calamity for the vast majority of us.

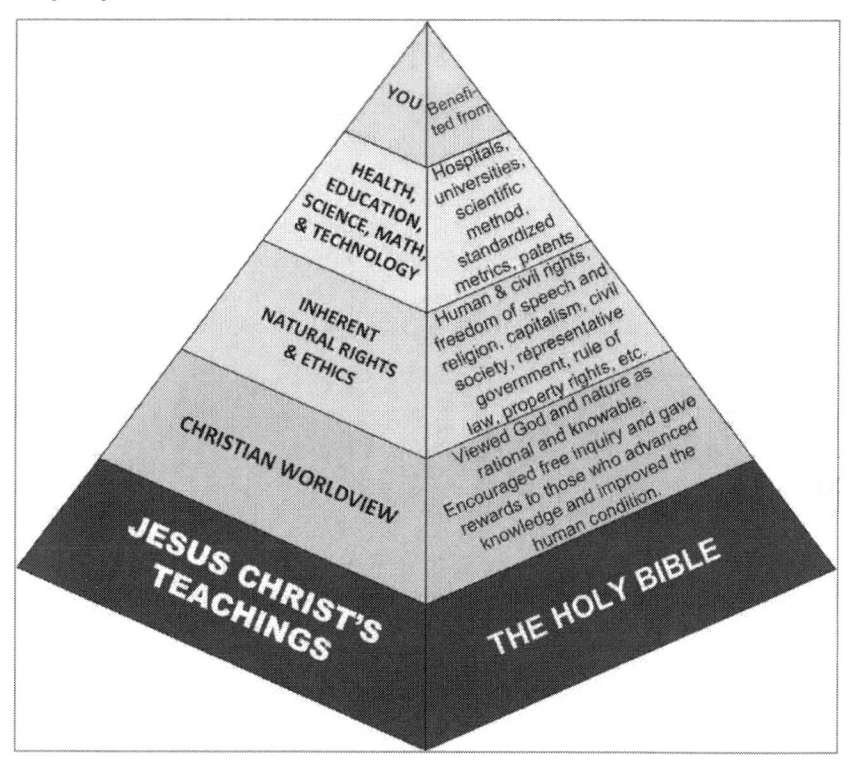

Pyramid diagram:
- **YOU** Benefited from
- **HEALTH, EDUCATION, SCIENCE, MATH, & TECHNOLOGY** — Hospitals, universities, scientific method, standardized metrics, patents
- **INHERENT NATURAL RIGHTS & ETHICS** — Human & civil rights, freedom of speech and religion, capitalism, civil society, representative government, rule of law, property rights, etc.
- **CHRISTIAN WORLDVIEW** — Viewed God and nature as rational and knowable. Encouraged free inquiry and gave rewards to those who advanced knowledge and improved the human condition.
- **JESUS CHRIST'S TEACHINGS** / **THE HOLY BIBLE**

These facts should give any Christian immense joy and gratitude in being a Christian. Even today, millions annually migrate to nations founded on Christian principles, to give themselves and

---

[1] For example, where did atheists get the idea all humans have equal worth regardless of race, wealth, social status, appearance, and sexual orientation? This is not self-evident in nature or outside Christian ethics.

their children better lives and better futures. Actions always speak louder than words.

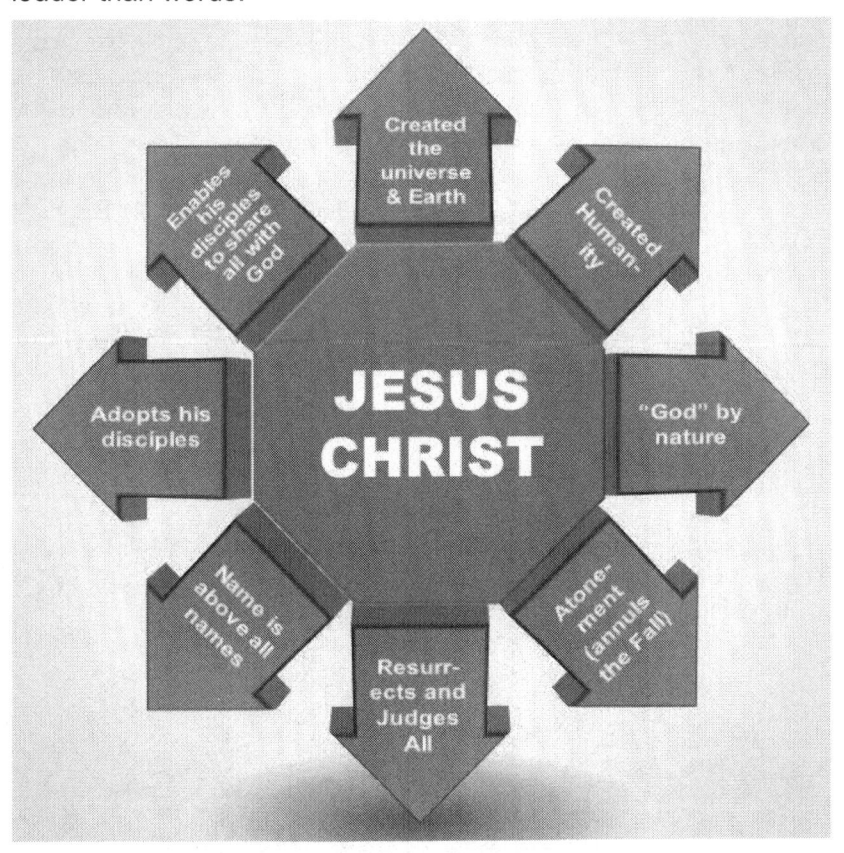

Diagram: JESUS CHRIST — Created the universe & Earth; Created Humanity; "God" by nature; Atonement (annuls the Fall); Resurrects and Judges All; Name is above all names; Adopts his disciples; Enables his disciples to share all with God.

Moreover, if the Bible's core message is true, then Jesus also played the most vital parts in every aspect of our reality because he:

- ✓ Created the universe and keeps it together
- ✓ Saves mankind from the consequences of sin by suffering and dying for our sins – *if* we believe in him and *strive* to obey him
- ✓ Gives all mankind the gift of immortality by physically rising from the dead
- ✓ Helps us overcome our moral weaknesses and tolerate trials and hardship
- ✓ Receives the universe as his inheritance

- ✓ Functions as the only way to God the Father and is his gatekeeper
- ✓ Replaces the earth with a new and better world
- ✓ Judges all mankind and gives eternal rewards/punishments
- ✓ Conjoined the God and human natures together, so that some humans can share the divine nature he shares with the Father by "adoption" and become the "Children of God"

The Bible's message is a phenomenally powerful worldview. One loses nothing important by believing in it and gains the infinite. <u>Even if it wasn't true</u>, belief in it gives tangible benefits to a person, both internally, and in a positive influence on others and on society.

The Atonement of Jesus Christ is the Most Important Event in the History of the Universe

If the Holy Bible's message about Jesus Christ is true, then he was the entity who created the universe.[1] He became human flesh two thousand years ago to conjoin the divine and human natures together and perform an infinite Atonement on our behalf.

The Atonement—the substitutionary suffering and death of our God for our sakes—annulled the Fall (the introduction to humanity of death, sin, weakness, and trials).

The Atonement was infinite – it covers all humans for all time. There is no sin and no negativity that humans will ever experience that it didn't include. It was also infinitely painful and infinitely terrifying. Jesus Christ, as the only entity who is fully "God" and fully "Man" was the only one capable of performing it. It changed the very nature of the cosmos when Jesus resurrected. The universe was dominated by death, but it will now be dominated by immortal life.[2]

---

[1] John 1:3,10,14; Colossians 1:13-17; Hebrews 1:8-10; Hebrews 2:10 cf. 1 Corinthians 8:6; Hebrews 1:2-3; Revelation 3:14.

[2] Human life for sure, but perhaps also other immortal life forms.

The Atonement of Jesus Christ

The *Pivot* Event of the Universe

Big Bang → **Creation of Earth** → **Atonement** ← **Final Judgment**

<4.5 billion years - present
Mortal Life Exists

After the General Resurrection – infinite future
Glorified Immortal Life Exists

TRIUMP OF DEATH | **ANNULMENT OF DEATH**

The Atonement saves and perfects those who strive to follow Christ after conversion. It makes bad people good and good people better.[1]

---

[1] A slight rephrase of President David O. McKay's saying, in the film *Every Member a Missionary*, as quoted by Elder Franklin D. Richards in Conference Report, Oct. 1965.

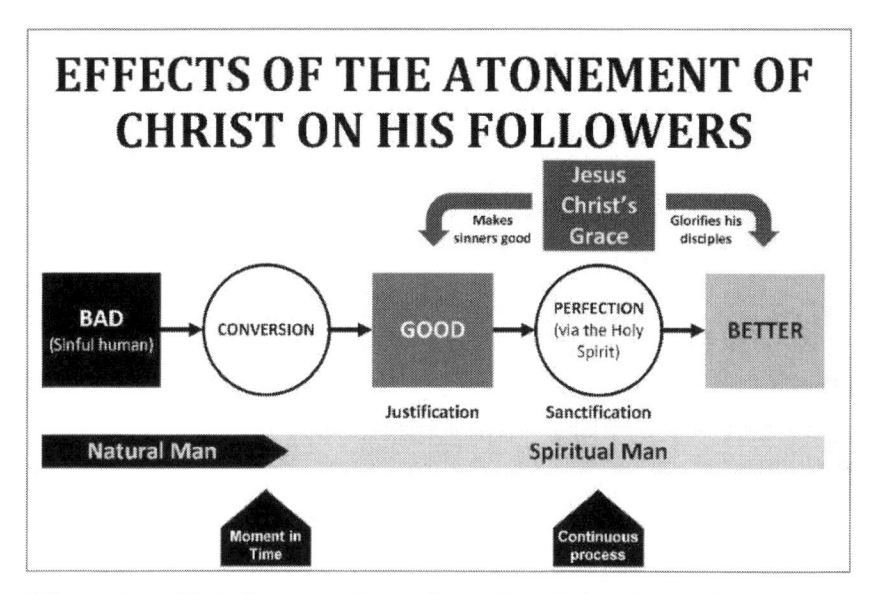

EFFECTS OF THE ATONEMENT OF CHRIST ON HIS FOLLOWERS

Jesus Christ's Grace
- Makes sinners good
- Glorifies his disciples

BAD (Sinful human) → CONVERSION → GOOD → PERFECTION (via the Holy Spirit) → BETTER

Justification — Sanctification

Natural Man → Spiritual Man

Moment in Time — Continuous process

When the Christian receives the gift of the Holy Spirit after conversion and strives to follow Christ, the Holy Spirit uses the Atonement to perfect the person as he or she continuously has faith, repents, and walks the narrow path that leads to eternal life. The Christian can also pray to the Father to have Christ's Atonement help them overcome a moral weakness or tolerate a

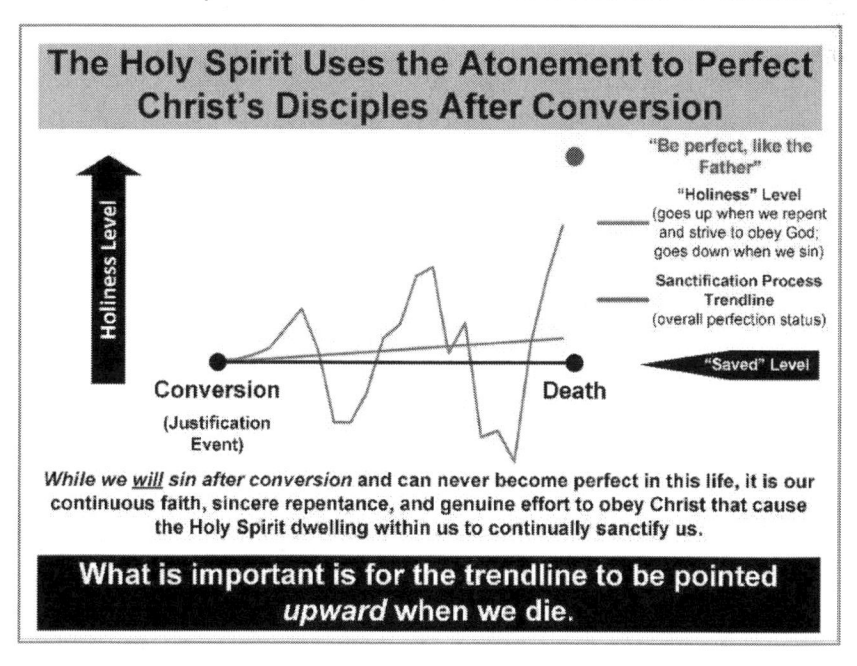

The Holy Spirit Uses the Atonement to Perfect Christ's Disciples After Conversion

- "Be perfect, like the Father"
- "Holiness" Level (goes up when we repent and strive to obey God; goes down when we sin)
- Sanctification Process Trendline (overall perfection status)
- "Saved" Level

Holiness Level

Conversion (Justification Event) — Death

While we will sin after conversion and can never become perfect in this life, it is our continuous faith, sincere repentance, and genuine effort to obey Christ that cause the Holy Spirit dwelling within us to continually sanctify us.

What is important is for the trendline to be pointed *upward* when we die.

trial so that they continually become more "perfect" after conversion (to fulfill Christ's command in Matthew 5:48).

Christ's true disciples – those who prove themselves by their constant striving to obey and follow him no matter what – are "adopted" by his Father[1] as the "Children of God" and become his heirs and his Son's fellow-heirs over the universe.[2]

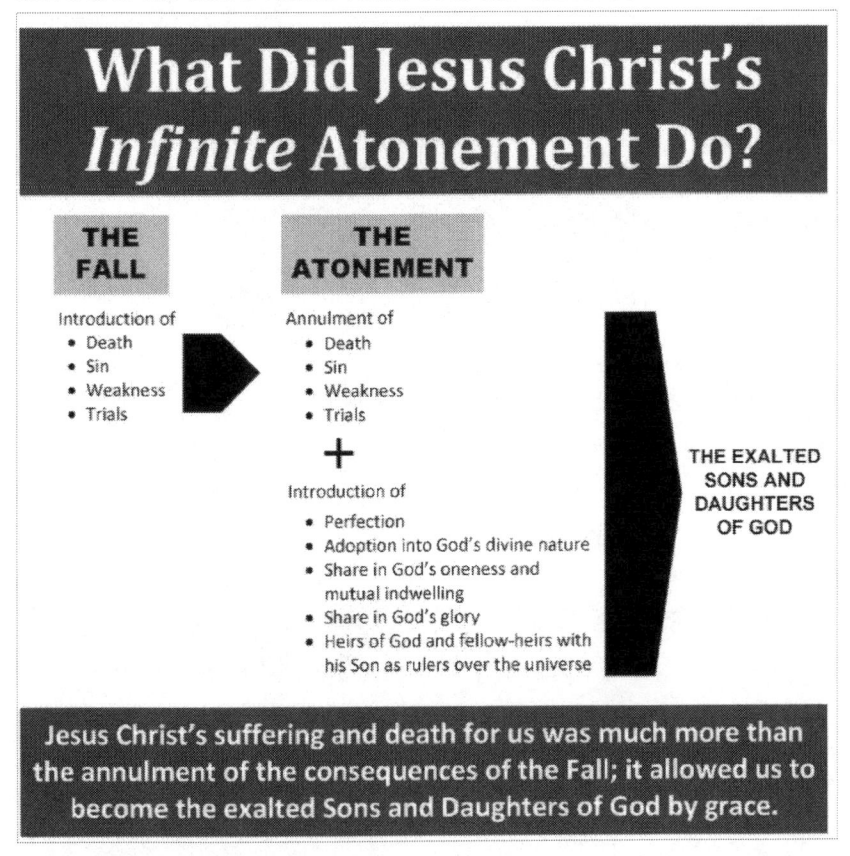

What Did Jesus Christ's *Infinite* Atonement Do?

THE FALL
Introduction of
- Death
- Sin
- Weakness
- Trials

THE ATONEMENT
Annulment of
- Death
- Sin
- Weakness
- Trials

+

Introduction of
- Perfection
- Adoption into God's divine nature
- Share in God's oneness and mutual indwelling
- Share in God's glory
- Heirs of God and fellow-heirs with his Son as rulers over the universe

THE EXALTED SONS AND DAUGHTERS OF GOD

Jesus Christ's suffering and death for us was much more than the annulment of the consequences of the Fall; it allowed us to become the exalted Sons and Daughters of God by grace.

Christ's Atonement was infinite – infinite in the sense that it covers all humans for all time and infinite in the sense of value, where an

---

[1] Romans 8:15,22-23; Galatians 3:26-4:7; Ephesians 1:4-5.

[2] John 1:12-13; 1 John 2:29-3:3; 1 John 3:9; 1 John 5:1-5; Revelation 21:7; Romans 8:14-21; Galatians 3:26-4:7; Hebrews 2:10-17; Acts 20:32; Acts 26:18; Ephesians 1:11-18; Colossians 1:12-13; Colossians 3:24; Titus 3:7; Hebrews 1:14; Hebrews 9:15; James 2:5; 1 Peter 1:3-5.

entity of infinite worth substituted himself for beings of finite worth. This infinite/finite substitution justifies the exaltation of those who become the Sons of Daughters of God by Christ's grace – those who will reign with him over the universe for all eternity. No one can ever credibly contend that justice was cheated because all claims over us have been paid in full.

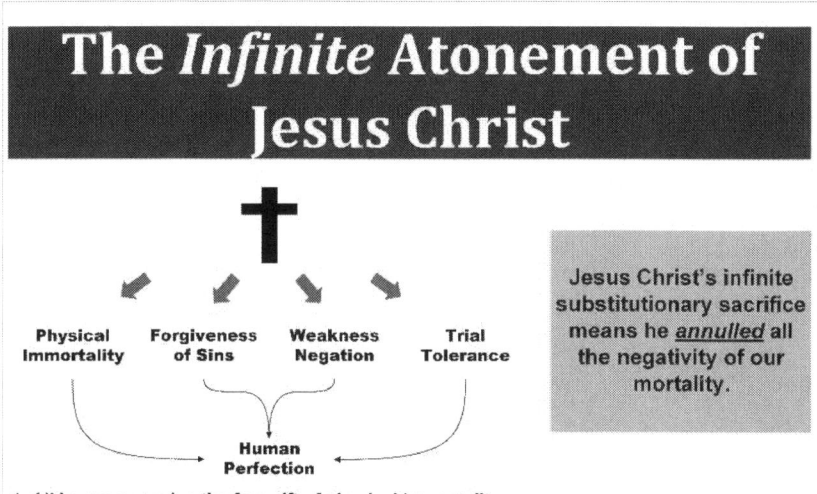

The *Infinite* Atonement of Jesus Christ

†

- Physical Immortality
- Forgiveness of Sins
- Weakness Negation
- Trial Tolerance

→ Human Perfection ←

Jesus Christ's infinite substitutionary sacrifice means he *annulled* all the negativity of our mortality.

1. All humans receive the free gift of physical immortality.

2. All who have genuine faith in Christ, sincerely repent, and strive to follow him have their sins forgiven (the "saved" justification event at conversion and sanctification process afterwards).

3. All who sincerely ask God to have his Son's sacrifice help them tolerate or overcome a weakness (temptation, addiction, personal flaw) or trial (such as a loss, pain, depression, hurt, misery) will find relief (the fortification process).

The Holy Spirit uses the Atonement to perfect Christ's true disciples after conversion (the sanctification or purification process) for eventual eternal oneness and mutual indwelling with God by divine adoption.

The infinite Atonement is the most important thing to have ever happened in the history of the universe. It changed *everything*.

How Can You Know the Holy Bible is True and Credible?

1. Subjective Evidence: The Holy Spirit Tells You

Millions convert to Christianity every year because they feel the Holy Spirit within them as they read the Holy Bible. His presence gives them comfort, peace, joy, warmth, and a desire to do good and stop sinning. As they pray and ask God to teach them the truth and reveal his will, the Holy Spirit witnesses to them of the truthfulness of Jesus as God's Only Begotten Son and the only way for salvation.

This witness is subjective – no one can independently confirm in a lab that the Holy Spirit—that is, "God," communed with that person. But it is the most powerful and convincing witness to the person – and the genuineness of the experience is seen by how the Christian changes his or her life to follow the pattern set by Jesus himself. To this day, thousands of Christians are killed every year for refusing to deny the Holy Spirit's witness.

It is this subjective witness that caused Christians in the past half millennium to change the world and usher in our technological civilization.

2. Objective Evidence: The New Testament is the Only Known Frameless, Unharmonized, Correlative Anthology

The New Testament (NT) is an astonishing triumph to those who understand the difficulties involved in creating correlative anthologies like textbooks or major project execution plans and RFP response proposals.

Somehow, the NT, a collection of 27 books written by no less than nine people over a period of 50 years, has a single coherent cosmology. This is despite no single book or author describes the entire worldview.

The New Testament is the only known frameless, unharmonized, correlative anthology. This isn't seeing something that isn't there since a straight linguistic and conceptual translation of the text shows the pieces of the whole are valid, making the whole valid as well.

So improbable is this accomplishment that this author, as one with over 70,000 hours of experience with correlative anthologies, estimates it to be a four sigma (4σ) event, or it is 99.9936% *likely* that something supernatural was associated with its creation. It is not proof (which to this author is 5σ and above), but it's the next best thing, and there's nothing else that gives comparable objective credibility to a person's faith.

Each NT writer had pieces of a jigsaw puzzle of a picture that could only be seen if all the pieces are put together – <u>without</u> writing within a common frame and employing a harmonizing editor.

This does not happen with any other correlative anthology. A common frame such as specifications, standards, style guide, author instructions, and team lead is always used by authors tasked to write different portions of a correlative anthology. A common editor is always needed to harmonize deliverables from different authors to create a unified message. And yet, the NT didn't have a common frame and common editor.

How then is it possible for their collective writings to generate a single cosmology?

14 A LATTER-DAY SAINT ODE TO JESUS

THE GOSPEL'S COSMOLOGY

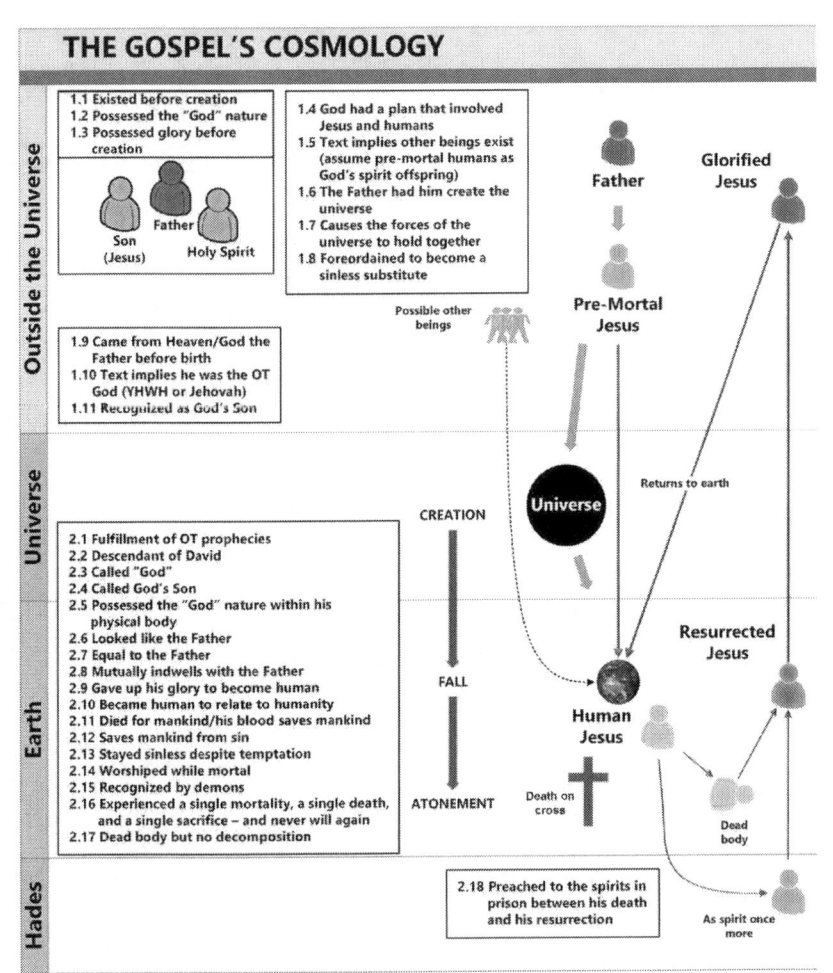

Outside the Universe

1.1 Existed before creation
1.2 Possessed the "God" nature
1.3 Possessed glory before creation

Son (Jesus)   Father   Holy Spirit

1.4 God had a plan that involved Jesus and humans
1.5 Text implies other beings exist (assume pre-mortal humans as God's spirit offspring)
1.6 The Father had him create the universe
1.7 Causes the forces of the universe to hold together
1.8 Foreordained to become a sinless substitute

1.9 Came from Heaven/God the Father before birth
1.10 Text implies he was the OT God (YHWH or Jehovah)
1.11 Recognized as God's Son

Father → Pre-Mortal Jesus

Glorified Jesus

Possible other beings

Universe

CREATION

Universe

Returns to earth

Earth

2.1 Fulfillment of OT prophecies
2.2 Descendant of David
2.3 Called "God"
2.4 Called God's Son
2.5 Possessed the "God" nature within his physical body
2.6 Looked like the Father
2.7 Equal to the Father
2.8 Mutually indwells with the Father
2.9 Gave up his glory to become human
2.10 Became human to relate to humanity
2.11 Died for mankind/his blood saves mankind
2.12 Saves mankind from sin
2.13 Stayed sinless despite temptation
2.14 Worshiped while mortal
2.15 Recognized by demons
2.16 Experienced a single mortality, a single death, and a single sacrifice – and never will again
2.17 Dead body but no decomposition

FALL

ATONEMENT

Human Jesus

Death on cross

Resurrected Jesus

Dead body

Hades

2.18 Preached to the spirits in prison between his death and his resurrection

As spirit once more

The Core Message of the Bible: A Single Coherent Cosmology (see The God Who Washes Feet sections for scripture references)

Diagram

God the Father
- 4.1 Glorified as both God and Man
- 4.2 At God the Father's right hand side
- 4.3 Worshiped in heaven
- 4.4 Given the universe for an inheritance
- 4.5 Will return to earth
- 4.6 Resurrects all mankind/changes the physical mortal bodies of humans into ideal immortal bodies
- 4.7 Replaces heaven and earth
- 4.12 He enables his true followers to be adopted by God
- 4.13 His true followers become the "Children of God" and "heirs"
- 4.14 He shares "oneness" and the "God" nature with the Children of God by his grace
- 4.15 He shares glory with the Children of God
- 4.16 He shares rule and all he has with the Children of God

The "God" nature: Son, Father, Holy Spirit

The adoption of the "Children of God" / "Heirs" (the "Elect") by Grace

The "Children of God" / "Heirs" (the "Elect")

Father — Gives all judgment to Jesus

Son (Jesus)
- 4.8 Destroys death and Hades (the human afterlife)
- 4.9 Will be acknowledged by all to be the greatest of all
- 4.10 Rules over all beneath the Father
- 4.11 Judges mankind and gives rewards or punishments

- 3.1 Rose from the dead (spirit and body rejoined as glorified immortal, material body)
- 3.2 Saved all of mankind from death/Will make us immortal
- 3.3 Became perfect, just like the Father
- 3.4 Reconciles man with God
- 3.5 Intercedes/mediates on behalf of man to God
- 3.6 He is the only way to heaven/He is the only way to God the Father
- 3.7 Belief in him brings eternal life
- 3.8 Obedience to him is a requirement
- 3.9 Addressed in prayer after resurrection
- 3.10 Worshiped after resurrection

The "Saved"

Different levels of splendor after judgment to locations collectively called "heaven"

Final Judgment

The condemned

Those whose names are not written in the "Book of Life" are thrown into the "Lake of Fire" together with Satan, the demons, the Beast, and other truly evil individuals

Human dead bodies → Resurrected humans

The human dead as spirits in the afterlife

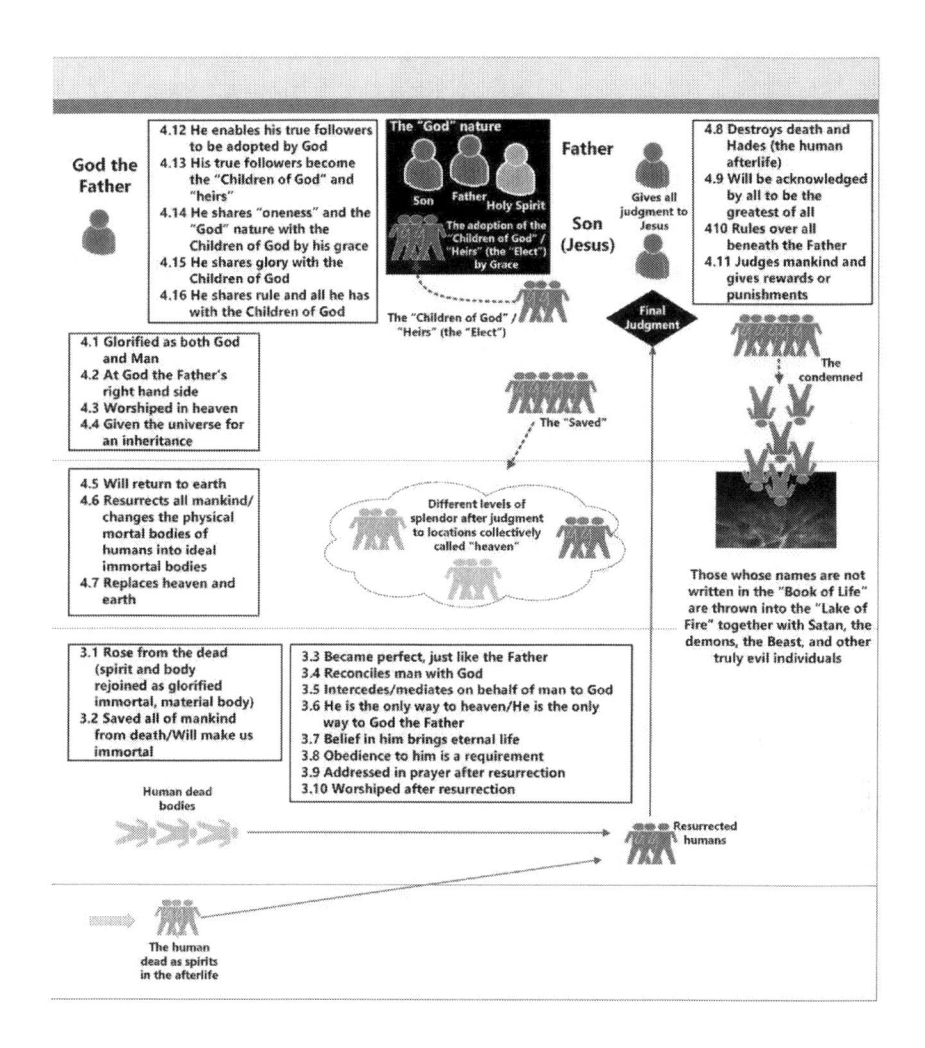

This coherent cosmology should not exist – but it does! It is an impossibility since people cannot read each other's minds to produce harmonious deliverables of abstract ideas – but there it is! Somehow, the New Testament writers, and only the New Testament writers, produced a *correlative* anthology without using a common frame and without employing a harmonizing editor.

> It is a stunning piece of evidence that something supernatural was involved in the creation of the New Testament. It challenges skeptics to explain how it's possible for nine people to magically

combine their deliverables to create a single coherent picture or cosmology given that it is demonstrably impossible to do so.

When I saw this cosmology, I instantly lost my atheism and regained my faith in Jesus Christ because I know from experience that I was seeing something that is impossible to exist.

Christians have had the objective evidence that Jesus is the Son of God all along in their hands! It's as easy to demonstrate as tearing a sheet of paper into nine irregular sections and asking nine people to draw <u>parts</u> of a face on their piece without knowing what the others draw. After ten minutes, collect the pieces and see if they make a perfect face.

They won't. This is because it isn't possible for multiple people to create perfectly harmonious pieces of a whole without operating within a common frame or using a common editor who will harmonize the deliverables to make a single whole.[1] Some will write part of a house, others will write part of a tree, or a face, or something else.

This is empirical and should give great comfort to every Christian and pause to those who dismiss Christianity. What this means is **objective evidence exists that validate Christianity as the true religion**. This is something no other religion has.

But while this aspect of the NT provides intellectual validation to the faith of the Christian, it should never override the subjective witness from the Holy Spirit since that communication from God is the most important evidence one can receive to truly appreciate the Holy Bible and its message. It is more important than any miracle or even seeing an angel because one receives a direct contact with God that results in an indelible stamp on their heart.

When the Holy Spirit reveals the truth about Jesus and his gospel to the person; that message overrides everything and the Christian's faith becomes unshakable. They then *know* Jesus is truly the Son of God and the only way we can be saved.

---

[1] Refer to *The God Who Washes Feet* (https://edwardkwatson.com/) for a detailed examination of why frameless, unharmonized, correlative anthologies are demonstrable impossibilities.

How Can You Know the Book of Mormon is True and Credible?

1. Subjective Evidence: The Holy Spirit Tells You

The best way to know the truth concerning the Book of Mormon is identical to the Holy Bible: Rely on the Holy Spirit—on God—to know the truth. He knows more than anyone else.

When one reads the Book of Mormon, one feels the Holy Spirit witness to the truthfulness of its contents. However, this does not necessarily mean the book itself is genuine scripture because the Holy Spirit may only be witnessing of the truth of the message and doctrines just like he will witness to anyone that the statement, *"Jesus Christ is the Only Begotten Son of God and only way for us to be saved"* is true regardless of which book that phrase is located. The witness is the same because the message and doctrines are the same.

To resolve this, the Book of Mormon specifically instructs the reader to ask God whether the Book of Mormon *itself* is true:

> *"Behold, I would exhort you that when ye shall read these things, if it be wisdom in God that ye should read them, that ye would remember how merciful the Lord hath been unto the children of men, from the creation of Adam even down until the time that ye shall receive these things, and ponder it in your hearts.*
>
> *4 And when ye shall receive these things, I would exhort you that ye would ask God, the Eternal Father, in the name of Christ, if these things are not true; and if ye shall ask with a sincere heart, with real intent, having faith in Christ, he will manifest the truth of it unto you, by the power of the Holy Ghost.*
>
> *5 And by the power of the Holy Ghost ye may know the truth of all things." (Moroni 10:3-5)*

This narrows down the parameters for the Holy Spirit's witness to the truthfulness of the Book of Mormon itself instead of its doctrines that align with the Holy Bible's.

The beauty of this promise is it encourages the reader to take charge and actively pursue receiving a witness of "Truth" from the Holy Spirit.

Moroni 10:3-5 is identical to the Holy Bible's repeated promise that those who sincerely ask God will receive answers:

> *"If anyone lacks wisdom, he must ask God – who gives to all generously and without rebuke – and it will be given him.*
>
> *6 When he asks, he must have faith and not doubt, for he who doubts is like an ocean wave that is driven and tossed by the wind." (James 1:5-6)*
>
> *"Ask and it shall be given to you. Seek and you shall find. Knock, and the door shall be opened to you." (Matthew 7:7)*
>
> *"If you abide in me and my words abide in you, ask for whatever you want, and it will be granted." (John 15:7)*
>
> *"I write these things to you who believe in the name of the Son of God, so that you may know that you have eternal life. 14 This is our confidence when approaching God: If anything we ask complies with his will, then he hears us. 15 And if we know that he hears us in whatever we ask, we know that our request is granted." (1 John 5:13-15)*

All who have genuine faith will receive an answer and those who are already Christians who abide in Christ[1] are promised an even greater answer.

> *There is nothing that can interfere with God's response to genuine prayer. Satan will never be able to intercept these prayers and give a false response that deceives the sincere seeker of truth. Anyone who claims otherwise is making Satan more powerful than God.*

Actively seeking an answer from God as to whether the Book of Mormon is true is significantly different from the passive receipt of a spiritual witness when reading the Holy Bible. This is because people rarely read the Bible with the intention of asking God to tell

---

[1] To "abide" means to "remain" or "stay." Those who abide in Christ "stay forever" in him. Those who have Christ's words abide in them have his words "stay forever" in them. The genuineness of the condition is manifested by how the person behaves – by how they live their life. They become replicas of Jesus Christ's behavior and attitude – they have genuine love and charity, are truly humble and empty of pride. They forgive all, tolerate trials and sufferings with grace, and keep the Father's commandments no matter what.

Christ's true followers abide in him and his words abide in them. They then *know* his words and will recognize it in the Book of Mormon when they read it and ask God to reveal its truth to them. And the reason why is because the word and Spirit within both the Holy Bible and the Book of Mormon are the same. They have the same source: God.

them whether the book itself is true.[1] Rather, they read it due to a desire to learn what it says, learn the truth concerning its doctrines, or yearn to experience the Holy Spirit touching their souls.

The absolutely beautiful thing about obtaining a positive response to a sincere prayer concerning the Book of Mormon is that single answer tells the seeker many truths because if the book itself is true then its contents are automatically true:

- If the Book of Mormon is true; then Jesus is the Son of God.[2]

- If the Book of Mormon is true; then Jesus is God made flesh and is _our_ God.[3]

- If the Book of Mormon is true; then Jesus suffered and died for all humanity.[4]

- If the Book of Mormon is true; then Jesus is the only way for humans to be saved.[5]

- If the Book of Mormon is true; then the Father, Son, and Holy Spirit are One God.[6]

---

[1] However, there's nothing stopping someone from asking God in sincerity whether the Holy Bible is true and genuine Scripture. It's a noble pursuit and should be encouraged.

[2] 2 Nephi 25:12-19; Mosiah 3:8; Alma 6:8; Alma 7:9-13; Alma 34:2; Alma 36:17-18; Helaman 3:28; Helaman 5:12; Helaman 14:12; 3 Nephi 9:15; Mormon 7:5; Mormon 9:22; Ether 4:7.

[3] 2 Nephi 6:9; Mosiah 3:5-12; Mosiah 7:27; Mosiah 13:34-35; Mosiah 15:1-14; Mormon 3:21; 2 Nephi 1:10; 2 Nephi 9:20-21; 2 Nephi 10:3-4; Mosiah 26:23-26; 3 Nephi 19:18; Moroni 8:8.

[4] 2 Nephi 2:6-9; 2 Nephi 9:4-7; Alma 22:14; Alma 33:22; Alma 34:8-12; 3 Nephi 11:14; 3 Nephi 27:13-14.

[5] 1 Nephi 13:40; 2 Nephi 9:41; 2 Nephi 30:2; Mosiah 3:12,17; Mosiah 4:8; Mosiah 5:8; Alma 38:9; Helaman 3:28-30; Helaman 5:9.

[6] 2 Nephi 31:21; Alma 11:44; 3 Nephi 11:27,36; 3 Nephi 20:35; Mormon 7:7.

- If the Book of Mormon is true; then the Holy Bible is true.[1]

Also, additional truths exist that are logical corollaries of the Book of Mormon being true:

- If the Book of Mormon is true; then Joseph Smith was a true prophet of God.
- If the Book of Mormon is true; then the True Church is restored to the earth.[2]
- If the Book of Mormon is true; then the Doctrine and Covenants and the Pearl of Great Price are also true.

One does not need a specific answered prayer to the last three provided one has an answered prayer to the truthfulness of the Book of Mormon. They logically follow the Book of Mormon being true. Alternatively, if one receives a positive answer from the Holy Spirit that one of the last three is true; then one does not need to still obtain a spiritual witness of the Book of Mormon due to it being redundant. It becomes a "nice to have" but is not necessary to have unshakable faith.

As with the Holy Spirit confirming the truth of the Holy Bible, the "testimony" from an answered prayer concerning the Book of Mormon is purely subjective and cannot be tested by outsiders. The credibility of the event can only be determined indirectly – by how the person changes his or her life for the better, by how the person joins and stays in the Church regardless of opposition or trial, and by how the person strives to obey Christ until the end of their lives.

---

[1] 1 Nephi 13:38-40; Mormon 7:9.

[2] Given the existence of other churches who believe the Book of Mormon to be scripture, knowing the book to be true does not automatically mean any specific church within the Latter-day Saint branch of Christianity is true. However, since over 98% of all believers in the Book of Mormon are members of the Church of Jesus Christ of Latter-Day Saints, it is the overwhelming likely "true" denomination. One still needs to "know" if the denomination is true – and this is done by seeking confirmation from the Holy Spirit as to whether the current Prophet is his true representative. The positive answer changes the confidence level from 98% to 100%.

This subjective witness of truth from God himself is the most important evidence one can have concerning the Book of Mormon. Nothing outweighs the Holy Spirit's witness.

2. Objective Evidence: The Book of Mormon Contains the Only Known "Dictated From Imagination" Coherent Argumentative Essays

Critics claim one does not need to pray about the Book of Mormon because it is objectively false, but this is demonstrably not so.

To the contrary, the Book of Mormon contains several objective evidence that it is genuine scripture and inspired by God. This book will examine just one due to most educated people have firsthand experience with them:

> *Argumentative essays.*

For nearly 200 years, the production of the Book of Mormon has only had one credible narrative: Joseph Smith <u>*dictated*</u> nearly the entire the book to Oliver Cowdery (between April 7 and June 30, 1829).

The story is Joseph used "interpreters"[1] – two stones that were fastened to a breastplate (Joseph Smith-History 1:35) – while looking at the engraving on the gold plates. He then dictated to his scribe what the words said. At some point, he stopped using the very powerful interpreters and switched to his "seer stone" which he placed inside a hat.[2] He then put his face into the hat to cut off

---

[1] The term "Urim and Thummim" was only used to refer to the interpreters years after the Church's establishment and was used to refer to both the interpreters and the seer stone (each of which was *a* "Urim and Thummim" not *the* "Urim and Thummim"). The term eventually became synonymous for the interpreters that came with the Book of Mormon.

[2] It appears that as Joseph grew comfortable with the revelatory process, he no longer felt he needed the interpreters and realized he could get the same result with the less powerful seer stone without exposing himself or those around him to the dangers the interpreters posed.

What is often overlooked is the interpreters that came with the gold plates were *terrifyingly* dangerous. They were a perfect example of a stunning temptation – the means to see whatever one wants whether it was in the past, present, or future (compare to D&C 130:7-8). One can ask to see next week's winning lottery numbers or what really happened on Easter Sunday. One can

outside light to see the writing that appeared on the seer stone which he then dictated to Oliver Cowdery.

> *In this manner, over 99% of the approximately 268,000-word Book of Mormon was dictated in just 65 working days at a blistering pace of 4000 words per day.[1]*

Since Joseph didn't read from a book written in English (the only language he knew) while dictating, his process is a "dictation from imagination" since there wasn't anything tangible that outsiders could examine to see the English words that he was dictating from.[2]

---

find the precise underground locations of buried treasure or valuable ore or even glimpse God himself. In Joseph's case, the temptation to use it to find valuable objects to help alleviate his family's poverty would've been overwhelming. It was this power that causes anyone who looks in them without being commanded by God to die (Mosiah 8:13). As revelation windows or portals, this feature is why Martin Harris was so scared of them because he desired to see God – and he believed he would instantly die if he looked into them.

However, Joseph Smith's seer stone could be safely wielded because it was nowhere near as powerful as the interpreters. By removing the temptation posed by the interpreters – and the associated penalty for misuse, Joseph could just focus on the translation task.

What is important to keep in mind is the gold plates, interpreters, and seer stone were just tools to help train Joseph Smith into becoming God's Prophet, Seer, and Revelator. They were no longer needed when he could give revelation from God without the aid of these tools. The gold plates and interpreters were returned to the angel after the Book of Mormon was dictated and the seer stone became a memorabilia that is currently in the possession of the Church of Jesus Christ of Latter-day Saints.

[1] 4000 words per day is a phenomenal pace and far beyond the daily word counts of virtually all famous writers (e.g., twice that of Stephen King and Mark Twain). When one takes into consideration the absence of layout changes and phrasing rewrites of a "dictated from imagination" work; Joseph Smith's "first draft is final draft" Book of Mormon's 4000 words per day output is an achievement without comparison in English literature.

[2] A textual analysis of the Original Manuscript shows Joseph Smith was reading out loud English text that appeared on the stones instead of trying to determine what the engravings meant and expressing the thoughts in his own language. And the amount of text that he could read was around 20 words at a time (see Skousen, Royal [1997] "How Joseph Smith Translated the Book of

The problem is around 20% of the Book of Mormon is comprised of argumentative or persuasive essays – a form of literature that <u>cannot</u> be dictated from imagination.

Charles Dickens, Mark Twain, Leo Tolstoy, Fyodor Dostoyevsky, and John Steinbeck are great examples of genius novelists. They were fantastic writers who brought their books alive and the reader is transported to the world they crafted. Their imaginations would've been so vivid and well-developed that one can see them successfully dictate small novels from imagination.

But this doesn't mean they can write coherent argumentative essays by dictation off the top of their heads.

Unlike a story, argumentative essays strive to convince the listener of the speaker's position using a logical structure, be internally consistent, and not make unsupportable assumptions. This type of essay relies on facts for persuasion, and these facts could be book facts, historical facts, experimental facts, or life experience facts.

Argumentative essays are a common tool in every college or university. The student is asked to argue a position, such as pro or con on a subject. The methodology takes several forms, but the structure is as follows:

Mormon," Journal of Book of Mormon Studies: Vol. 7: No. 1, Article 4. Retrieved from https://scholarsarchive.byu.edu/jbms/vol7/iss1/4). When he confirmed that Oliver wrote the block of text correctly, a new batch of text would appear. This explains why whenever resuming the translation after a break or the next day, Joseph never needed to ask his scribe to read the last line back to him to know where to start the process once more. He would just start where he left off (which is just astonishing, when one thinks about it).

> **Argumentative Essay Structure**
>
> 1. Thesis Claim: Position one wants the listener to accept as true.
> 2. The Frame of the Argument: Arguments and evidence that support the thesis claim. This form can be a rebuttal, where an opposing position is refuted (more effective), or a one-sided form, where no opposing position is refuted (less effective).
> 3. Conclusion: Summary of position and possible restatement of thesis.

Most people have no idea how hard it is to create argumentative or persuasive essays, papers, thesis, or legal briefs until they are made to write one in college.

Since most educated people have firsthand experience creating argumentative essays, they then have the ability to credibly evaluate the likelihood that an uneducated, inexperienced 23-year old farmer in 1829 could *dictate from imagination* dozens of argumentative and persuasive essays[1] from his imagination at a pace of 4000 words per day—without making any major revisions or layout changes.[2]

The Book of Mormon's argumentative essays, range in size from Nephi's 7400-word First Essay to his 427-word Third Essay. They are comprised of five different types:

  A. <u>Parental Essay</u> – Written from the perspective of a wise parent giving "truth" to his children.

---

[1] Some essays are comprised of multiple argumentative or persuasive essays (e.g., Alma 32 is structurally different than Alma 33 just as Alma 36's refined "Conversion Story" public speech is different from Alma 37's unprepared commandment). For convenience, they are treated as one when adjacent to each another if having a common author.

[2] We know this because we have the entire Printer's Manuscript (https://www.josephsmithpapers.org/articles/revelations-volume-3-printers-manuscript-of-the-book-of-mormon) and around 28% of the Original Manuscript of the Book of Mormon – they show there were no layout or major changes done to the text after Joseph Smith dictated it.

B. <u>Authoritative Essay</u> – Written from the perspective of a wise and righteous leader sharing the secret of happiness to his subjects.

C. <u>Missionary Essay</u> – Written from the perspective of a missionary trying to convince his listeners of his message so that they will come or return to faith in Jesus Christ.

D. <u>Contemporary Prophetic Essay</u> – Written from the perspective of a prophet speaking to those who can see him and hear his voice.

E. <u>Future Prophetic Essay</u> – Written from the perspective of a prophet speaking to those in the distant future.

The Book of Mormon's Argumentative Essays

1. Lehi's Essay (2 Nephi 1:6-3:25) [Type: Parental | 3953 words]
2. Nephi's First Essay (2 Nephi 25-30) [Type: Authoritative | 6422 words, excluding the 974 words from Isaiah quotations | 7396 total]
3. Nephi's Second Essay (2 Nephi 31) [Type: Authoritative | 988 words]
4. Nephi's Third Essay (2 Nephi 32) [Type: Authoritative | 427 words]
5. Jacob's First Essay (2 Nephi 6-10) [Type: Authoritative | 4142 words, excluding the 1319 words from the Isaiah quotation | 5461 total]
6. Jacob's Second Essay (Jacobs 2-3:11) [Type: Authoritative |1881 words]
7. King Benjamin's Essay (Mosiah 2:9-5:15) [Type: Authoritative | 4707 words]

8. Abinadi's Speech (Mosiah 12:25-16:15) [Type: Contemporary Prophetic | 2870 words, excluding the 548 words from Isaiah quotations | 3418 total]
9. Alma's First Essay (Alma 5) [Type: Missionary | 2786 words]
10. Alma's Second Essay (Alma 7) [Type: Missionary | 1439 words]
11. Alma's Third Essay (Alma 9-13) [Type: Missionary | 3950 words]
12. Alma's Fourth Essay (Alma 32-33) [Type: Missionary | 2279 words]
13. Alma's Fifth Essay [to Helaman] (Alma 36-37) [Type: Parental | 3255 words]
14. Alma's Sixth Essay [to Shiblon] (Alma 38) [Type: Parental | 649 words]
15. Alma's Seventh Essay [to Corianton] (Alma 39-42) [Type: Parental | 3875 words]
16. Amulek's Essay (Alma 34) [Type: Missionary | 1545 words]
17. Samuel the Lamanite's Speech (Helaman 13-15) [Type: Contemporary Prophetic | 3920 words]
18. Mormon's First Essay (Moroni 7) [Type: Future Prophetic | 1881 words]
19. Mormon's Second Essay [to Moroni] (Moroni 8) [Type: Parental | 887 words]
20. Moroni's First Essay (Mormon 9) [Type: Future Prophetic | 1561 words]
21. Moroni's Second Essay (Ether 12:6-41) [Type: Future Prophetic | 1352 words]

22. Moroni's Third Essay (Moroni 10) [Type: Future Prophetic | 1149 words]

Lehi's deathbed blessings to his children, King Benjamin's speech, Amulek's second preaching, and Alma's commandments to his sons are examples of highly complex and well-developed argumentative or persuasive essays, where ideas are built upon ideas and life experience, premises are transformed to dogma, concepts are argued and expanded, and the argument's structure of beginning, core, and end are fixed—all to one goal: to persuade the listener that the speaker's position is correct.

While an expert novelist can write a short story in a few days, an expert argumentative writer will need many days to weeks to properly research a subject to develop a convincing argumentative essay of comparable word count.[1] The novelist only needs to use his or her imagination while the argumentative writer will need to conduct an enormous amount of research on both sides of the position, test the ideas with others to determine their credibility and effectiveness, and do constant re-writes and refinements to improve the argumentative success of the essay.

> And yet, Joseph Smith, an uneducated 23-year old farmer living far from major urban centers 200 years ago, just dictated each of these argumentative essays to Oliver Cowdery in just a few hours?[2]

Anyone who has written an argumentative essay in a university knows this is impossible. It is so absurd that there has to be another explanation for their creation. Joseph Smith could not have dictated them—no one could dictate them today in an identical circumstance, methodology, and time duration.

> If Joseph Smith didn't dictate these portions of the Book of Mormon, then where did they come from?

---

[1] The actual writing could be a short as a day if the outline is properly developed and the writer is good.

[2] See Appendix: Proof the Book of Mormon Contains Argumentative and Persuasive Essays for proof that this literary form exists in the Book of Mormon.

We have a dozen eyewitnesses[1] who observed Joseph Smith dictate the Book of Mormon. Not one of them ever claimed he read from any other source material during the dictation process.

As one with over 70,000 hours of experience analyzing documents and creating complex, organized documentation, I consider the Book of Mormon's argumentative essays to be impossibilities. It does not matter how good of a novelist someone is; argumentative essays need time, an organized structure,[2] constant correction and revision, knowledge, and wisdom to

---

[1] These were: Emma Smith, Martin Harris, Oliver Cowdery, Elizabeth Ann Whitmer Cowdery, David Whitmer, William Smith, Lucy Mack Smith, Michael Morse, Sarah Hellor Conrad, Isaac Hale, Reuben Hale, and Joseph Knight Sr. (Neal A. Maxwell, *By the Gift and Power of God*, [Ensign, January 1997].)

[2] For example, Alma 36's complex chiasmus – its inverted parallelism – of 16 conceptual ribs definitely exists and contains the ethos, pathos, and logos persuasion strategies. It is a refined public speech of Alma's conversation story that was personalized for Helaman. Given the pace of 4000 word per day, its size of 1229 words means it would've taken Joseph Smith no more than three hours to dictate the entire chapter to Oliver Cowdery.

The only way for Alma 36's chiasmus to exist would be for the author to outline the inverted parallel thoughts first (the "ribs"), starting with the central thought (Jesus is a/the Son of God [vv. 17-18]), then build the parallel points from the inside-out (harrowed up by the memory of sins [vv. 17,19], pain [vv. 16,20], presence of God [vv. 15,22], limbs [vv. 10,23], ...), and then flesh out the speech's contents around each rib.

This is a three-step process and takes time. *It cannot be created off the top of one's head by dictation from front to back by someone like Joseph Smith.*

This is empirical and can be proven. What then explains Alma 36's structure and contents given that Joseph Smith "dictated from imagination" the entire chapter in less than three hours? Who today, can replicate such a feat in the same circumstances (no computers, no internet, no formal education, and no textbooks on how to create a complex chiasmus)?

> *I challenge anyone to sit on a stage for three hours, put his face in a hat and dictate with no revision a 1200-word conversion story centered on Jesus Christ using a chiasmus structure comprised of a coherent narrative containing the ethos, pathos, and logos persuasion strategies in 16 parallel conceptual ribs.*

create – none of which existed with the 23-year old Joseph Smith 200 years ago.[1]

> *It is not an issue of imagination or intelligence – but of life skills, training, experience, and <u>conscious</u> knowledge of how to create a coherent argumentative essay.*

I cannot conceive of how anyone can unconsciously *dictate* a coherent argumentative essay – much less an uneducated young man 200 years ago. Just the amount of information that needs to be fixed in a three-dimensional lattice in the person's mind and dictated in sequence to make a complete essay is an ability that I, a subject matter expert, cannot fathom.

> *This is comparable to a particle physicist observing a shaman transmute steel into gold by merely reciting an incantation and tapping the metal with a stick.*

The subject matter expert's first reaction is disbelief and desire to find an alternative explanation. This has to be a trick because the expert knows such a process is impossible. But when the same objective "impossibility" is repeated again and again within a controlled environment, the expert is left with the conclusion that something "supernatural" is likely involved in the transmutation process.

The easiest scientific explanation is to pretend the eyewitness accounts of the translation process and of the Three and Eight Witnesses do not exist and Joseph Smith did not dictate those argumentative essays. He stole someone else's work and read them out loud to Oliver Cowdery.

But this doesn't explain how these essays were integrated so completely into their surrounding text—someone needed to harmonize them into their locations where their voice and tone matched the surrounding verbiage. As one who analyzes complex documents for a living, it is obvious to me that the same writing style exists inside and outside these 22 argumentative essays, which means they were written by the same person.

---

[1] Furthermore, how could a young, inexperienced farmer come up with perspectives vastly different than what one would expect out of any young, inexperienced farmer? Which of the five argumentative narrative types could Joseph Smith relate to so that he can craft them properly?

Neither does it explain how *five* different types of argumentative essays found their way into the Book of Mormon. It takes someone with decades of experience or clear instructions to deliberately perform the mental gymnastics needed to write from perspectives not native to their own.[1] This means it is more likely that there were *five* different people who wrote those 22 essays, and one of them had to be a long-time absolute ruler over a community to explain the six authoritative essays.[2]

So improbable is the presence of argumentative essays in the Book of Mormon that this author estimates it to be a four sigma (4σ) event, or it is 99.9936% *likely* that something supernatural was associated with the book's creation. It is not proof (which to this author is 5σ and above), but it's the next best thing, and there's nothing else that gives comparable objective credibility to a person's trust in the book.

The presence of argumentative essays in the Book of Mormon is an objective fact that empirically validates the much more important subjective witness from the Holy Spirit of its authenticity.

> *What is the most reasonable explanation for the presence of these argumentative essays within a book that strives to convince us that Jesus is the Christ, the Eternal God and that the Holy Bible is true?*

3. Eyewitness Accounts

Testimonials or eyewitness accounts of an event or product are the greatest influencer for why others believe an event or purchase a product. Our entire court system is built on it. This is so well known that companies rely on testimonials to market their goods. This is especially so when the eyewitness is famous, which

---

[1] For example, I, as a "Western white man," cannot easily write arguments that are only relevant to the life experience of a "grandmother in 19th century rural China."

[2] The presence of these argumentative essays is why all the alleged reliance of the Book of Mormon on earlier books such as the Views of the Hebrews (Ethan Smith), Manuscript Found (Solomon Spalding), and The Wonders of Nature (Josiah Priest) is irrelevant because none of them have argumentative essays, much less essays that show duplication in the Book of Mormon.

explains why celebrities are paid millions to endorse products and services.

> *"Every matter must be confirmed by the testimony of two or three witnesses." (2 Corinthians 13:1).*

The principle that multiple eyewitnesses are needed for major claims has a long history (Numbers 35:30; Deuteronomy 17:6; Deuteronomy 19:15; John 8:16-18; 1 Timothy 5:19). Jesus himself advocated the importance of having eyewitnesses (Matthew 18:16). And the more eyewitnesses, the better.

In fact, the entire story of Jesus and his earthly ministry is founded upon the eyewitness accounts of Matthew, Mark, Luke, and John. Just four men's testimonies changed the world.

In this light, the lifelong claims of the eleven eyewitnesses of the Book of Mormon are facts that cannot be ignored.

The Testimony of the Three Witnesses

Every Book of Mormon contains the Testimony of the Three Witnesses. In it, Oliver Cowdery, David Whitmer, and Martin Harris testify of something incredible:

> Be it known unto all nations, kindreds, tongues, and people, unto whom this work shall come: That *we*, through the grace of God the Father, and our Lord Jesus Christ, *have seen the plates* which contain this record, which is a record of the people of Nephi, and also of the Lamanites, their brethren, and also of the people of Jared, who came from the tower of which hath been spoken. *And we also know that they have been translated by the gift and power of God, for his voice hath declared it unto us; wherefore we know of a surety that the work is true.* And we also testify that we have seen the engravings which are upon the plates; and they have been shown unto us by the power of God, and not of man. And *we declare with words of soberness, that an angel of God came down from heaven, and he brought and laid before our eyes, that we beheld and saw the plates, and the engravings thereon;* and we know that it is by the grace of God the Father, and

our Lord Jesus Christ, that we beheld and bear record that these things are true. And it is marvelous in our eyes. Nevertheless, *the voice of the Lord commanded us that we should bear record of it; wherefore, to be obedient unto the commandments of God, we bear testimony of these things*. And we know that if we are faithful in Christ, we shall rid our garments of the blood of all men, and be found spotless before the judgment-seat of Christ, and shall dwell with him eternally in the heavens. And the honor be to the Father, and to the Son, and to the Holy Ghost, which is one God. Amen.

These three men provided a firsthand account that they had a supernatural encounter with an angel who "came down from heaven" and showed them the gold plates that is the Book of Mormon. They also claimed they heard God's voice instruct them to witness unto all of the event.

All three were excommunicated from the Church some years later. Two eventually sought rebaptism but one, David Whitmer, never returned and lived for 50 years outside the Church.[1] Despite his hostility to the Church, he repeatedly affirmed his testimony until the end of his life.[2] As an example, when David Whitmer heard

---

[1] David Whitmer was excommunicated in 1838 for several reasons, but mainly because his pride caused him to reject the later revelations of Joseph Smith. David was a "theorist purist" in the sense that he believed whatever revelation that was given in the first years of the Church is all that is needed and his views on what was "right" overrode the formulations of the designated leaders of the Church. His idea of the church excluded the organizational infrastructure needed for self-perpetuation and efficient operation which is why despite becoming the leader of the Church of Christ (Whitmerite) – a church that believed in both the Holy Bible and the Book of Mormon, he never "got his hands dirty" with running the faith and it dissolved soon thereafter.

[2] The year before his death, David Whitmer wrote *An Address to All Believers in Christ* (1887). In it he stated:

"It is recorded in the American Cyclopaedia and the Encyclopaedia Britannica, that I, David Whitmer, have denied my testimony as one of the three witnesses to the divinity of the Book of Mormon; and that the other two witnesses, Oliver Cowdery and Martin Harris, denied their testimony to that Book. *I will say once more to all mankind, that I have never at any time denied that testimony or any*

that a Mr. "John Murphy" claimed he denied his testimony to him, David took out a newspaper ad where he reiterated the truthfulness of his testimony and had many leading figures of the state who've known him for decades attest to his credibility and honesty. He even had part of the Testimony of the Three Witnesses engraved on his tombstone.

These three men, each of whom went his own way in life, fearlessly bore witness that they saw the gold plates in a supernatural event. They could've become wealthy and famous for denying it on the religious lecture circuit but they never did. Any one of them could've put a dagger into the heart of the Church's credibility by claiming the whole thing was made up – but they never did. Instead, they told only one message despite constant ridicule:

> An angel of God showed them the gold plates and they heard God's voice command them to witness of the event to the world.

Three eyewitnesses of a supernatural event that validates the credibility of the Book of Mormon. Other religions have been started on much less.

The Testimony of the Eight Witnesses

In addition to the three eyewitnesses, the Book of Mormon contains the Testimony of the Eight Witnesses which states:

> Be it known unto all nations, kindreds, tongues, and people, unto whom this work shall come: That _Joseph Smith, Jun., the translator of this work, has shown unto us the plates of which hath been spoken, which have the appearance of gold_; and as many of the leaves as the said

---

part thereof. I also testify to the world, that neither Oliver Cowdery or Martin Harris ever at an time denied their testimony. They both died reaffirming the truth of the divine authenticity of the Book of Mormon. I was present at the death bed of Oliver Cowdery, and his last words were, 'Brother David, be true to your testimony to the Book of Mormon.' He died here in Richmond, Mo., on March 3d, 1850. Many witnesses yet live in Richmond, who will testify to the truth of these facts, as well as to the good character of Oliver Cowdery. The very powers of darkness have combined against the Book of Mormon, to prove that it is not the word of God, and this should go to prove to men of spiritual understanding, that the Book is true."

> *Smith has translated we did handle with our hands; and we also saw the engravings thereon,* all of which has the appearance of ancient work, and of curious workmanship. And this we bear record with words of soberness, that *the said Smith has shown unto us, for <u>we have seen and hefted, and know of a surety that the said Smith has got the plates of which we have spoken</u>*. And we give our names unto the world, to witness unto the world that which we have seen. And we lie not, God bearing witness of it.

These eight men, to the very end of their lives, testified that they saw with their own eyes the gold plates and handled it with their own hands. Even after Hiram Page and Jacob and John Whitmer were excommunicated and did not return to the Church, they never denied seeing the gold plates. Jacob Whitmer also testified to his son just prior to his death that he truly saw the gold plates and had no reason to lie just before dying. Like his brother David, he too referred to his testimony on his gravestone.

The only difference between the two groups is the Three Witnesses experienced a supernatural event when seeing the gold plates while the Eight Witnesses only saw the plates.

Twelve Witnesses

Joseph Smith, the Three Witnesses, and the Eight Witnesses saw the gold plates and they repeated and confirmed their testimony despite all ridicule, persecution, and opposition throughout the remainder of their lives. It did not matter whether they stayed faithful members or were excommunicated, or whether they died inside or outside the Church; not one denied what they testified until their last breath. And this during a period where they would've received wealth, fame, and praise from the masses of Christian churches who were vehement in their opposition to the Restored Church.

> *There has never been a religious book with more eyewitnesses to its credibility than the Book of Mormon. The fact that <u>all</u> twelve men maintained their testimonies concerning the Book of Mormon throughout their lives regardless of what happened to them is an objective fact that cannot be ignored.*

Yes, One Can Know That the Book of Mormon is True and Credible

The Book of Mormon exists and demands an explanation. The testimonies of the twelve eyewitnesses and especially the witness from the Holy Spirit cannot easily be dismissed. Since it is demonstrable that no one can produce its structured contents by dictation; those who ridicule or dismiss it without thought do themselves a serious disservice that has eternal consequences.

> *And now, my beloved brethren, and also Jew, and all ye ends of the earth, hearken unto these words and believe in Christ; and if ye believe not in these words believe in Christ. And if ye shall believe in Christ ye will believe in these words, for they are the words of Christ, and he hath given them unto me; and they teach all men that they should do good.*
>
> *11 And if they are not the words of Christ, judge ye—for Christ will show unto you, with power and great glory, that they are his words, at the last day; and you and I shall stand face to face before his bar; and ye shall know that I have been commanded of him to write these things, notwithstanding my weakness. (2 Nephi 33:10-11)*

The Book of Mormon is the only *external* empirical evidence that the Holy Bible is genuine scripture. It is the second witness to the New Testament's *internal* witness that Jesus is truly God's Son and the only way for us to be saved.

Those who have Christ's words abiding in them will recognize the Book of Mormon as genuine scripture because the words and spirit within it are Christ's. Those who fearlessly follow Christ no matter what will find him within its pages.

The "predestined" or those whose character is such that they will become the exalted Children of God that the Father adopts into his divine nature, will recognize the Book of Mormon for what it is:

> *Evidence for God that one can hold in their hands.*

Latter-day Saint Theology is Christian and Basic Trinitarian

This book contains references to the modern scriptures[1] of the Church of Jesus Christ of Latter-day Saints to show they say the same thing the Bible does on the subjects. This edition also quotes specific modern scripture in the Stanza Clarifications.

Common Beliefs With Other Christians

The Holy Bible states very clearly that liars cannot be saved (Revelation 21:8; Revelation 22:15). In this light, it is dishonest to claim the Church of Jesus Christ of Latter-day Saints is not Christian when its modern scriptures teach utterly "Christian" doctrines:[2]

- Jesus Christ is "God" by Nature[3]
- Jesus Christ is *Our* God[4]

---

[1] More accurately, the "Latter-day Scriptures," comprised of the Book of Mormon, the Doctrine and Covenants, and the Pearl of Great Price.

[2] This recognition does not mean one is obligated to accept the Latter-day Saints as the "True Church." It is just a simple acceptance of objective truth that devout Latter-day Saints are not just "Christian" in behavior but "Christian" in theology as well.

[3] There are no less than 75 places in the Latter-day Scriptures that state Jesus Christ is "God." Some of these are: 1 Nephi 19:7-10; 2 Nephi 6:9; 2 Nephi 9:5,20-21; Mosiah 3:5-12; Mosiah 7:27; Mosiah 13:28,34-35; Mosiah 17:8; Mosiah 26:23-26; Alma 11:38-40; Alma 42:15; 3 Nephi 11:14; Ether 3:6-18; D&C 19:1-4,16-19,24; D&C 39:1; D&C 93:3-9; Abraham 3:22-24.

[4] How many times does the Latter-day Scriptures need to state Jesus is *our* "God" before our critics recognize that we are Christians?: 2 Nephi 1:10; 2 Nephi 9:20-21; 2 Nephi 10:3-4; Mosiah 26:23-26; 3 Nephi 19:18; Moroni 8:8; D&C 10:70; D&C 17:9; D&C 18:33,47; D&C 27:1; D&C 33:1,17-18; D&C 35:1-2; D&C 43:27,34; D&C 51:1,20; D&C 53:1-2; D&C 62:1; D&C 66:13; D&C 72:8; D&C 78:1,20; D&C 81:1,6-7; D&C 98:8,18,38; D&C 103:4-5; D&C 132:2,11-12; D&C 133:1-2,74.

We pray to the Father because Jesus told us to, but we recognize Jesus to be our God because he said he was our God just like he said the Father is our God.

- Jesus Christ is the Son of God[1]
- Jesus Christ is the Only Way for Us to Be Saved[2]
- The Father, Son, and Holy Spirit are One God[3]
- The Father and Son Mutually Indwell Within One Another[4]

For example, the Holy Bible *and* the Book of Mormon *and* the Doctrine and Covenants all teach Jesus is "one" with the Father and he is within the Father and the Father is within Jesus *even when* he was on earth and the Father was up in heaven. However, what they do *not* say is whether this oneness and mutual indwelling exist as a functional result of divine will (they share a common space because they *want* to,[5] or whether it is an ontologically innate state (they share a common space without will or effort on their part).[6]

---

[1] Jesus is the "Only Begotten Son" of God from before the creation of the universe: 1 Nephi 13:40; 2 Nephi 25:12-13; Jacob 4:5,11; Alma 5:48; Alma 9:26; Alma 12:33-34; Alma 13:5; Helaman 3:28; 3 Nephi 11:1-17; Mormon 9:29; D&C 6:21; D&C 10:57; D&C 11:28; D&C 20:21; D&C 29:42; D&C 45:51-53; D&C 49:5; D&C 76:13-14,20,23,25,35,57; D&C 138:14,57; Moses 1:32; Moses 5:57; Moses 6:52; Moses 7:50.

[2] Jesus is the Father's Gatekeeper. No one can approach the Father without going through his Son. No one can be saved without having the Son's blood wash them clean: 1 Nephi 13:40; 2 Nephi 9:41; 2 Nephi 25:20,26,28-29; 2 Nephi 30:2; 2 Nephi 31:19-21; Mosiah 3:12,17; Mosiah 4:8; Mosiah 5:8; Mosiah 16:13; Alma 21:9; Alma 34:9,15; Alma 38:9; Helaman 3:28-30; Helaman 5:9; Helaman 8:15; Helaman 14:8; D&C 18:23; D&C 109:4; D&C 132:12; Moses 6:52.

[3] Only the Latter-day Scriptures explicitly state this most Christian of doctrines outside the Johannine Comma interpolation of 1 John 5:7: 2 Nephi 31:21; Alma 11:44; 3 Nephi 11:27,36; 3 Nephi 20:35; Mormon 7:7; D&C 20:28; D&C 50:43.

[4] Disagreements exist on what this mutual indwelling looks like, but the statements are explicit and cannot be questioned – somehow, the Father is in the Son and the Son is in the Father: 3 Nephi 9:15; 3 Nephi 11:27; 3 Nephi 19:23,29; D&C 50:43; D&C 76:13,25,39; D&C 93:3-4,17,20.

[5] This aligns with the New Testament's Basic Trinitarianism where Jesus performed the Atonement utterly alone without the presence of the Father – Matthew 27:46; Mark 15:34.

[6] Also known as Expanded Trinitarianism or the Trinity.

The problem for all parties is we are unable to picture what this oneness and mutual indwelling looks like since our everyday experience tells us material bodies cannot inhabit the same three-dimensional space. But since God dwells outside this universe[1] while also straddling this universe at the same time; what we perceive to be reality likely does not apply to entities that simultaneously exist inside this universe and in a realm outside it. A literal mutual indwelling may make perfect sense when one "steps back" and sees the entirety of reality.

Latter-day Saints assume the physical separation into distinct forms that Stephen (Acts 7:55-56) and Joseph Smith (Joseph Smith—History 1:17) saw is the default ontological state of God's oneness while other Christians assume the mutual indwelling passages describe the default state.

The fact is, we don't know the default state because the Lord has never told us. However, the divine oneness and mutual indwelling[2] is a critical concept[3] because the oneness and mutual indwelling that the Father and Son enjoy is *extended* to those who become the exalted "Children of God" after Judgment Day.[4]

The advantages are obvious: The bestowal of the same divine oneness and mutual indwelling prevents those who are exalted from creating disasters while they're learning (the "Clumsy God" problem) or reverting to evil (the "Evil God" problem). It is a self-correcting condition that protects all the Children of God (as well as those who would be negatively affected by their actions).

The exalted Children of God dwell with Heavenly Father "in the Celestial Kingdom" while at the same time they will be heirs of this universe and fellow-heirs with Jesus in ruling it. Just as God can be anywhere in the universe; so will they, due to sharing the same oneness and mutual indwelling.

---

[1] The Father had his Son create this universe, so their dwelling is external to it.

[2] Some Latter-day Saints like to describe it as an "interpenetration."

[3] And goes far beyond the "Divine Investiture of Authority," which is limited to just one aspect of this oneness and mutual-indwelling.

[4] John 15:1-11; John 17:11,21-23; Romans 8:16-17; 1 Corinthians 6:17; Galatians 3:26-29; John 6:56; John 14:20,23; 1 John 5:20; Romans 8:9-11; 1 Corinthians 3:16-17; Galatians 2:20; Ephesians 1:4; Colossians 1:27; 3 Nephi 19:23,29; D&C 35:2,18; D&C 50:43; D&C 88:49-50.

Because of the explicitness of "the Father, Son, and Holy Spirit are one God" passages in the Latter-day Scriptures as well as the over 70 passages that describe Jesus to be "God" (including the 24 passages that say he is "our God") and the half-dozen mutual indwelling passages; Latter-day Saint theology is definitely Trinitarian despite it rejects the 4th century Greek philosophy foundations of the Traditional Trinity. This shows it is possible to create two types of Trinitarianism: the Basic and the Expanded.

Basic Trinitarianism Versus Expanded Trinitarianism

Basic Trinitarianism is a statement of what the New Testament *says* about the Father, Son, and Holy Spirit collectively when one does not attempt to explain why. It accepts the fact that some things aren't clarified and that's ok. It takes what the Holy Bible says as fact without getting hung up on what they *mean* (that is, interpretation is ultimately irrelevant). When asked to explain how the Father, Son, and Holy Spirit are One God, adherents can merely shrug their shoulders and point to what the NT text says while conceding that they cannot explain the how or what of the reality of the triadic God's nature and oneness since it is outside our reality.[1] Neither do we have the ability to comprehend the fundamental nature of an entity who simultaneously straddles this universe and the external realm where he dwells.[2]

Basic Trinitarianism is the Holy Bible's Trinitarianism because its components are the only ones that have genuine *prima facie* biblical support.[3] There's no need to argue the passages don't say what they are saying or interpret them using a theological filter.

---

[1] That is, whatever God's nature and oneness is, it already existed before the universe was created.

[2] This isn't hard to understand. The Holy Bible describes God as existing *before* Jesus created this universe. God then existed somewhere before the Big Bang. Since we cannot see past this universe's membrane to know what reality is like outside this universe; it is impossible for us to say with any authority what God's default ontological nature is or isn't.

[3] Matthew 3:16-17; Matthew 28:19; Luke 3:22; John 20:21-22; 1 Corinthians 12:3 cf. Acts 5:3-4; John 10:30,38; John 12:45; John 13:31-32; John 14:7-12,20; John 17:21-23; 2 Corinthians 4:4-6; 2 Corinthians 5:19; Colossians 1:15; Colossians 1:19; Colossians 2:9; Hebrews 1:2-3; John 1:1; Philippians 2:5-7; John 5:17-18; John 10:33; John 5:23; John 14:16; John 16:26; John 17:9,15,20.

The Latter-day Saint conception of God is definitely a Basic Trinitarian theology.

Expanded Trinitarianism is what is called the "Trinity." It blends the New Testament's Basic Trinitarianism with ideas from Greek philosophy. Its extra-biblical components are derived from Greek philosophical ideas (mostly Neoplatonic) that were merged with the biblical ideas in the fourth century by four brilliant figures: Athanasius of Alexandria (296/298–373) and the Three Cappadocians – Basil the Great (330–379), Gregory of Nyssa (335–395), and Gregory of Nazianzus (329–389) to create the fusion that is the "Trinity."[1]

Expanded Trinitarianism attempts to explain the "how" of the oneness and mutual indwelling of God as well as the composition of the nature of God. In short, Athanasius and the Three Cappadocians attempted to frame the orthodox definition of the three-in-one God using philosophical concepts that dominated their fourth-century intellectual environment. They succeeded spectacularly, and their core Expanded Trinitarian version has remained unchallenged for over 1600 years,[2] even after the *same* philosophical foundations were obsoleted by modern science and has been extinct for centuries in our civilization's milieu outside Christian theology.

Expanded Trinitarianism is the standard Trinitarian definition of nearly all Christian denominations[3] outside the Protestant Nontrinitarian family and the Latter-day Saint Christian branch).

---

[1] While the word "Trinity" was first used by Theophilus of Antioch in the late second century to describe the Basic Trinitarian concept of deity, it is now solely used in reference to the Expanded Trinitarian understanding.

[2] I believe Athanasius and the Three Cappadocians are the most impactful Christian figures after Paul, even exceeding the effects of Augustine of Hippo and Thomas Aquinas, because their formulation of the Trinity is still accepted without question by the vast majority of Christian thinkers. I cannot think of any other small group of thinkers that has had comparable impact on more people that these four men. Even now, thousands will argue to the death that their formulation is the only possible interpretation of the triadic NT God. I am in awe at what they achieved.

[3] An important clarification needs to be made. The Eastern Christian branch of Christianity has families that follow different Expanded Trinitarian models, but the core concept remains.

Christian Theology

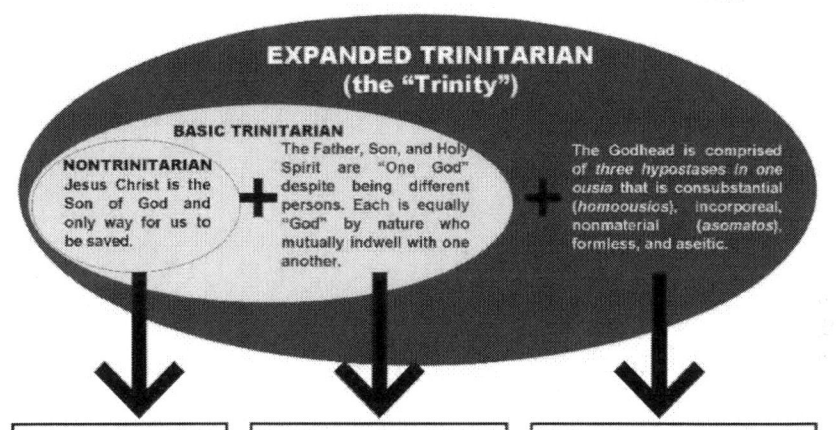

EXPANDED TRINITARIAN (the "Trinity")

BASIC TRINITARIAN

NONTRINITARIAN: Jesus Christ is the Son of God and only way for us to be saved.

+

The Father, Son, and Holy Spirit are "One God" despite being different persons. Each is equally "God" by nature who mutually indwell with one another.

+

The Godhead is comprised of three *hypostases* in one *ousia* that is consubstantial (*homoousios*), incorporeal, nonmaterial (*asomatos*), formless, and aseitic.

BIBLICAL	BIBLICAL	NONBIBLICAL
Matt 3:17; Matt 17:5; Heb 1:5; 2 Pet 1:17; John 1:14; John 3:16,18,35; 1 John 4:9-10; John 14:6; Rev 7:17; 1 Tim 2:5; Acts 4:10-12	Matt 3:16-17; Matt 28:19; Luke 3:22; John 20:21-22; 1 Cor 12:3 cf. Acts 5:3-4; John 10:30,38; John 12:45; John 13:31-32; John 14:7-12,20; John 17:21-23; 2 Cor 4:4-6; 2 Cor 5:19; Col 1:15; Col 1:19; Col 2:9; Heb 1:2-3; John 1:1; Phil 2:5-7; John 5:17-18; John 10:33; John 5:23; John 14:16; John 16:26; John 17:9,15,20	Athanasius of Alexandria (296/298–373); Basil the Great (330–379), Gregory of Nyssa (335–395), and Gregory of Nazianzus (329–389) used concepts derived from Greek philosophy (mostly Neoplatonic) to explain the "how" of the oneness and mutual indwelling of God. This fusion of biblical and nonbiblical ideas is what is now called the "Trinity."

If a person needs to understand concepts derived from Greek philosophy to correctly describe the Christian God without falling into "heresy"; then that depiction is an Expanded Trinitarian view that uses elements that did not originate from the Holy Bible.

Expanded Trinitarianism's use of Greek philosophical foundations is why, to this day, to "correctly" understand the Trinity (without falling into heresy), one first needs to understand the Greek philosophical concepts of The One, hypostases, ousia, and asomatos to justify a wholly incorporeal, formless deity despite the resurrected Jesus – he who can never again experience death[1] – was a physical body that could be felt in a discernable form.[2]

Given that any separation of the spirit from the body is death (James 2:26), then the resurrected Jesus Christ exists and will exist forevermore as a physically immortal entity.

Trinity advocates assume the mutual indwelling is innate while Latter-day Saints presume it is by will – but the Bible never says which view is correct. All it says is they mutually indwell within each other.

Unique Beliefs of the Latter-day Saints

The Church of Jesus Christ of Latter-day Saints is definitely Christian while at the same time is completely unique among the rest of the Christian denominations by virtue of having:

- Additional scripture of equal weight to the Holy Bible
- Joseph Smith and modern prophets and apostles
- Doctrines that when combined solve the logical problem of theodicy (God and the problem of evil)[3]
- Doctrines that all humans are part of a divine family that needs to be linked with one another (pre-existence as God's literal spirit offspring, eternal families, temple sealings, "We are Saved individually but Exalted as a family")[4]

---

[1] Romans 6:9-10; Romans 8:34; 2 Corinthians 5:15.

[2] Matthew 28:9; Luke 24:36-51; Acts 1:1-11; John 20:19-20; John 20:25-29; 1 Corinthians 15:5-8 cf. 1 John 4:2-3 and 2 John 1:7.

[3] The problem of evil is atheism's only positive argument: *"If God is all-good, all-knowing, and all-powerful, why does evil exist?"* No theistic theodicy has been able to refute it despite centuries of effort. However, when one puts together Joseph Smith's teachings on the pre-existence, uncreated intelligence (the "grit" or monad that God himself cannot create or destroy but can manipulate to become spirits), and beginningless dynamic multiverse with infinite regress; it then becomes possible to create a coherent explanation that refutes atheism's argument.

[4] This explains why God would send his only Begotten Son to perform the infinite Atonement and why the Son would willingly experience infinite pain

- Doctrines of active instruction and conversion in the temporary afterlife for eventual reward in a multi-destination, multi-tiered heaven.[1]

The Fifth Branch of Christianity

The common "Christian" beliefs of the Latter-day Saints means the Church of Jesus Christ of Latter-day Saints is definitely a Christian denomination.

However, its unique differentials mean it is not a Protestant faith (does not believe in Sola Scriptura or Sola Fide). Neither is it Catholic, Eastern Christian, nor Anglican/Independent Catholic.

---

and terror for the sake of humanity. Their willingness was due to *familial* love instead of concern for created objects (we were the Father's spirit children and Jesus was our eldest "spirit" brother despite he was also the only one of us who was "God" by nature).

By way of comparison, no one in their right mind would sacrifice their child for the sake of some videogame characters. If we were created entities, the Atonement does not make sense.

[1] Every human will have an opportunity to accept the Gospel of Jesus Christ, either in this life or in the temporary afterlife as disembodied spirits. Every human will be baptized with water and the spirit, either personally or vicariously, now or during the Millennium. Every human will be sealed to their parents and to one another going all the way back to Adam and Eve.

Personalities and moral characteristics do not change when we die (Alma 34:34). Those who would've accepted the fulness of the Gospel on Earth if only they had a chance would accept it after death (D&C 137:1-10) while those who wouldn't accept it in its entirety would refuse the work done for them (D&C 76:76-77).

As a result, it is a separate branch of Christianity. In fact, it is the first new branch since the formation of Protestantism and Anglicanism/Independent Catholicism in the 16th century.

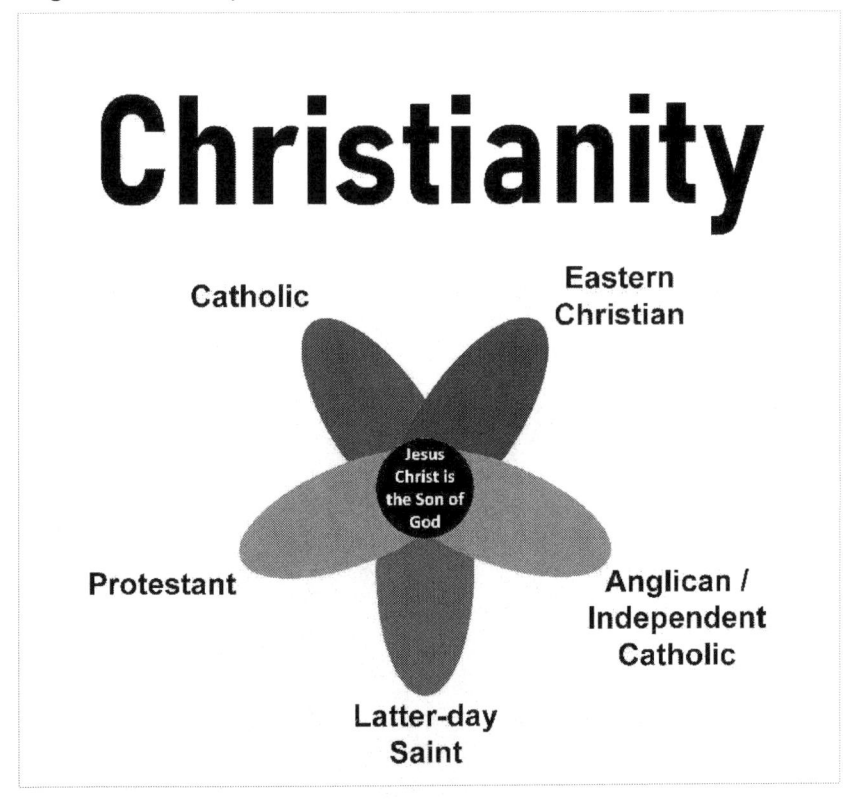

Christianity

Catholic

Eastern Christian

Jesus Christ is the Son of God

Protestant

Anglican / Independent Catholic

Latter-day Saint

As the largest denomination in the fifth branch of Christianity,[1] the Church of Jesus Christ of Latter-day Saints believes everything the Bible teaches. And just like each of the other four branches of Christianity, it has its own perspective on how biblical passages are to be interpreted or understood.

---

[1] There's no doubt the Latter-day Saints group is an outlier within Christianity, making it a distinct branch, since its difference is not merely due to alternative interpretations or authority claims, but due to the existence of additional Scripture of equal weight to the Bible.

My Witness

As a member of the Church of Jesus Christ of Latter-day Saints, I know Jesus is God's Only Begotten Son[1] who died for our sins and is the only way we can be saved. I *strive* to follow him until the end of my days. **Jesus Christ is *my* God just as the Father is my God.**

I also know Joseph Smith is a true prophet of God. – I know this not just because my over 70,000 hours of experience analyzing complex documentation allows me to see the evidence for God in the Book of Mormon, but more importantly, because I received an answered prayer concerning the Book of Mormon's authenticity. It was that communication from the Holy Spirit – from *God*, that stamped my heart with an inerasable confirmation.

I make a habit of regularly reading the hymns within this book or whenever I feel down or face problems. I find that saying them out loud and pondering them helps me feel better and I feel the Holy Spirit within me, where he gives peace and certitude that all is in accordance with God's plan.

I wasn't always this way. Despite being a follower for a long time, I fell away into disbelief and was an atheist for many years. While writing what became *The God Who Washes Feet* in early 2016 and seeing the New Testament's core message fall into place, my faith suddenly reappeared because I know firsthand that it is impossible for different people to have the same perspective about anything, especially if not sharing a common frame to put constraints on their views, and not using a common editor to harmonize their perspectives.

The evidence for the authenticity of the New Testament, and by extension, Jesus Christ as the Son of God, was staring us in the face all along! But we've never noticed it before because we're so used to assuming the NT is a single book instead of an anthology or collection of books from many authors combined into one.

---

[1] I do not add, "in the flesh" to the statement. The clarification is undoubtedly true, but Jesus Christ's status as the Father's "Only Begotten Son" is vastly greater than his incarnation. He was already the Father's "Only Begotten Son" before he became human and even before he created the universe.

The Exalted Children of God

Christians of every denomination can take great comfort in knowing our faith in Jesus Christ does have empirical support even though it doesn't need it. Christians can also be pleased to know that our faith has resulted in more tangible good to mankind than any other belief system—and everyone living today owes a great debt to it.

Latter-day Saints have an additional reason to rejoice:

> *The Book of Mormon exists and provides evidence—both subjective and objective—that shows the world the True Church of Jesus Christ is once again on the Earth.*

No other Christian group has a comparable credible claim that provides such a high likelihood of being Christ's True Church.

Christ's resurrection has sealed our fate and that of the universe. There's nothing anyone can do to impede his will and dominion over all. Everyone will eventually stand before him to be judged, and all will acknowledge Jesus is our Lord and our God and deserves his glory and honor.

A select few will be exalted and transformed into the "Children of God" – those who strive to follow Christ wherever he leads them. These are those who have genuine love and charity in their hearts and do the best they can to obey him, regardless of impediments and opposition.

No other religion has a concept of the afterlife that can even come close to the ultimate fate of the New Testament's "Children of God." Their destiny is so enormous, so overwhelming, that our minds have difficulty comprehending God's adumbrated promise:

- They will be "adopted" by God and share in the divine nature—the very essence of what makes God "God"
- They will enjoy oneness and mutual indwelling with God
- They will become God's heirs and fellow-heirs with Jesus
- They will share in God's glory
- They will share in Jesus Christ's rule and dominion over the universe (all things)

The Christian branches primarily differ on perceived authority to act in God's name. However, only the Latter-day Saint branch can provide objective evidence that can be tested to determine the credibility of its claim to be the True Church: **The Book of Mormon**. If it is true, then the True Church is limited to those that accept the book as scripture.

If you've fallen away or want to experience the transforming joy one receives when following Christ; listen! He's knocking on your door at this very moment – open it and let him in. His Church is here and willing to help.

But if you prefer another church, here's a handy guide to know the difference between the Christian branches:

48 A LATTER-DAY SAINT ODE TO JESUS

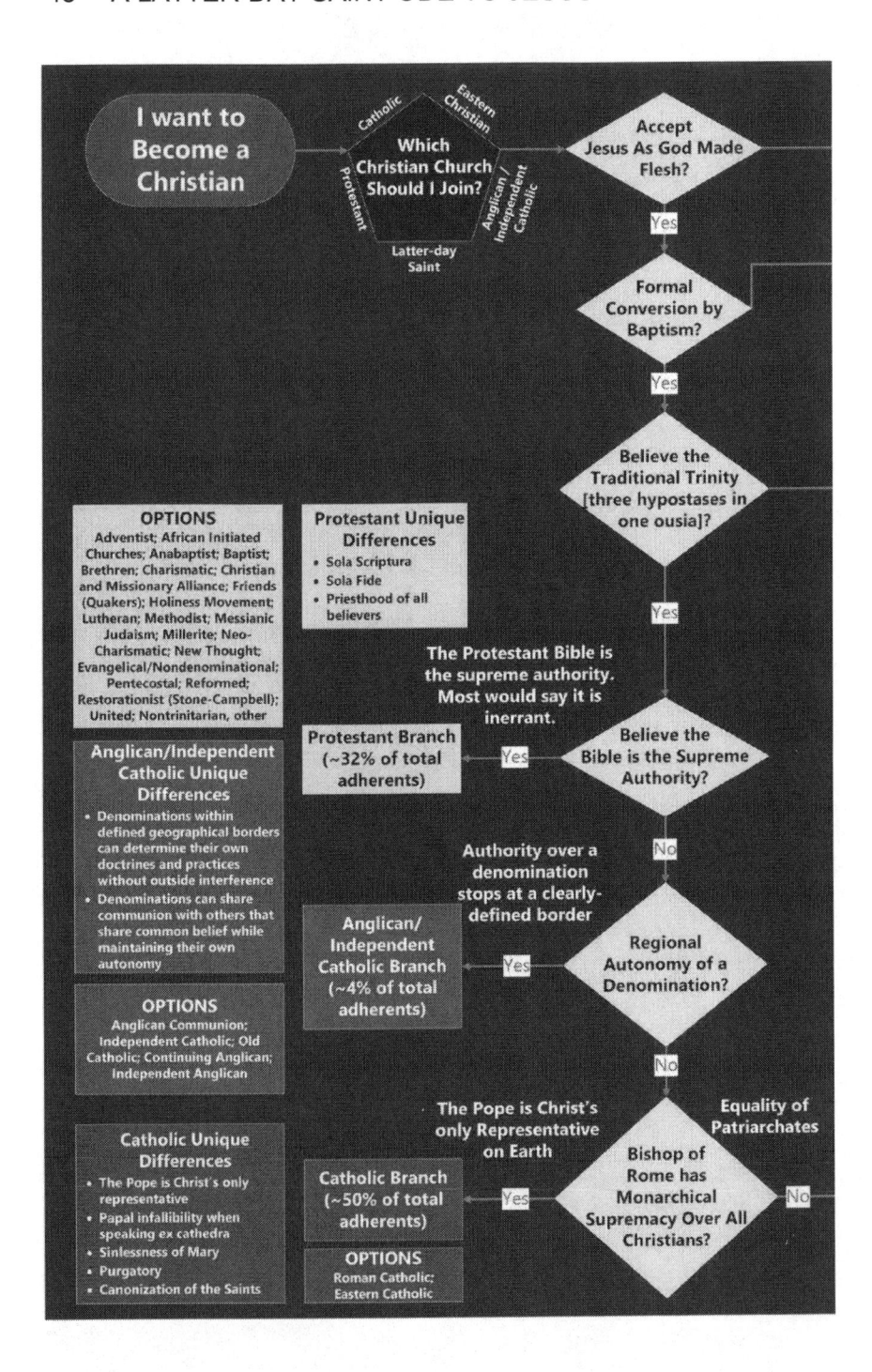

I want to Become a Christian

Which Christian Church Should I Join?
- Catholic
- Eastern Christian
- Protestant
- Anglican/Independent Catholic
- Latter-day Saint

Accept Jesus As God Made Flesh? → Yes

Formal Conversion by Baptism? → Yes

Believe the Traditional Trinity [three hypostases in one ousia]? → Yes

Believe the Bible is the Supreme Authority? → No

Regional Autonomy of a Denomination? → No

Bishop of Rome has Monarchical Supremacy Over All Christians? → No

OPTIONS
Adventist; African Initiated Churches; Anabaptist; Baptist; Brethren; Charismatic; Christian and Missionary Alliance; Friends (Quakers); Holiness Movement; Lutheran; Methodist; Messianic Judaism; Millerite; Neo-Charismatic; New Thought; Evangelical/Nondenominational; Pentecostal; Reformed; Restorationist (Stone-Campbell); United; Nontrinitarian, other

Protestant Unique Differences
- Sola Scriptura
- Sola Fide
- Priesthood of all believers

The Protestant Bible is the supreme authority. Most would say it is inerrant.

Protestant Branch (~32% of total adherents) ← Yes

Anglican/Independent Catholic Unique Differences
- Denominations within defined geographical borders can determine their own doctrines and practices without outside interference
- Denominations can share communion with others that share common belief while maintaining their own autonomy

Authority over a denomination stops at a clearly-defined border

Anglican/Independent Catholic Branch (~4% of total adherents) ← Yes

OPTIONS
Anglican Communion; Independent Catholic; Old Catholic; Continuing Anglican; Independent Anglican

Catholic Unique Differences
- The Pope is Christ's only representative
- Papal infallibility when speaking ex cathedra
- Sinlessness of Mary
- Purgatory
- Canonization of the Saints

The Pope is Christ's only Representative on Earth

Catholic Branch (~50% of total adherents) ← Yes

OPTIONS
Roman Catholic; Eastern Catholic

Equality of Patriarchates

INTRODUCTION 49

Jesus is inferior in nature to God the Father
No →

Protestant Branch / Nontrinitarian Family (<1.0% of total adherents)

OPTIONS
Unitarian; Unitarian/Universalist; Jehovah's Witnesses; Oneness Pentecostal; Iglesia Ni Cristo; etc.

Baptism is not essential for membership or salvation
No →

Protestant Branch / Quaker or Nondenominational (<1.0% to 15% of total adherents, depending on interpretation)

OPTIONS
Friends (Quakers); Salvation Army; Grace Gospel Fellowship; Some Protestant families and some nondenominational/unaffiliated

The Father, Son, and Holy Ghost are "One God" by will instead of innate
No →

Latter-day Saint Branch (<1.0% of total adherents)

OPTIONS
Church of Jesus Christ of Latter-day Saints (>98% of total); Community of Christ; Church of Jesus Christ (Bickertonite), Church of Christ With the Elijah Message, Church of Christ (Temple Lot); Fundamentalist Mormons

Latter-day Saint Unique Differences
- Probable logical solution to theodicy (God and the problem of evil)
- The Father, Son, and Holy Ghost are "One God" by will instead of innate
- God is a spirit entity with a physical body, just like the glorified Jesus and currently-mortal humans
- God is functionally omnipresent, not ontologically omnipresent
- Beginningless reality (multiversal cosmology)
- Heavenly family – humans are spirit offspring of God
- Marriages and families can be together forever
- The glorified exalted "Children of God" share the divine oneness and mutual-indwelling by Christ's Grace and can become "gods"
- Baptism for the dead
- Hades is called "Spirit World" and comprises Paradise/Hell
- Three-tiered heavens + outer darkness
- Modern scripture that supplement the Bible including the Book of Mormon, with its empirical evidence for God (numerous argumentative essays by "dictation from imagination")
- Continuous revelation
- Modern prophets and apostles lead the Church

Eastern Christian Unique Differences
- The leaders of the different denominations have equal authority with one another (no one is greater than any other)
- Rejection of some Ecumenical and General Councils
- Rejection of the "Filioque" addition to the Nicene Creed
- The ontological gap between God and Man was bridged by Jesus and it's possible for man to mystically share the divine nature

Common Catholic – Eastern Christian – Anglican/Independent Catholic – Protestant Beliefs
- Nonmaterial God
- Unmoved Mover God
- God is "Mind"
- Ontologically omnipresent God
- Aseitical God
- Traditional Trinity of three hypostases in one ousia
- No new revelation
- No new Scripture beyond the Bible
- All reality contingent upon God
- Ex nihilo creation
- Unbridgeable ontological separation between God and man

Eastern Christian Branch (~12% of total adherents)

OPTIONS
Eastern Orthodox; Oriental Orthodox; Dyophysite/Nestorian; Old Believers; Independent Orthodox; Independent Oriental Orthodox

Common Catholic – Eastern Christian – Anglican/Independent Catholic Beliefs
- Apocrypha is part of the Bible
- Devotional paraphernalia
- Bodily assumption of Mary
- Mary's perpetual virginity
- Prayer for the dead
- Veneration of saints, icons, and relics
- Clerical celibacy (Catholic/Eastern Christian only)

Despite the differences, virtually all Christian denominations can share common declarations:

The 14 Declarations of a Christian

1. The Father, Son, and Holy Spirit are "One God."
2. The Bible is the word of God.
3. God created the universe through his Son, Jesus Christ.
4. Jesus Christ is God's only begotten Son and the only way to be saved. *No one can go to God except through him.*
5. Jesus Christ is 100% God and 100% human. All that makes God "God" and all that makes humans "human" were in his body. God *became* flesh.
6. Jesus Christ suffered and died on the cross for our sins.
7. Jesus Christ rose from the dead.
8. Jesus Christ experienced a single mortality, a single death, a single resurrection, and a single sacrifice for all time.
9. Jesus Christ intercedes and mediates on our behalf to God.
10. Jesus Christ will come again, and when he does, he will raise the dead and make all humans immortal.
11. Jesus Christ judges mankind and imposes rewards/punishments.
12. Those who believe and strive to obey Jesus Christ are forgiven of their sins and will be rewarded with eternal life in his kingdom.
13. Jesus Christ rules over all beneath the Father and will be acknowledged by all, to be the greatest of all.
14. *I am not ashamed or frightened to admit Jesus Christ is my Lord and Savior. I pledge my life to follow him and show it by my words and actions.*

So, have your faith in Jesus as the center of your life and <u>live in a manner where the Holy Spirit within you is constantly refining and purifying you</u>. This is done by sincere repentance and receiving the Holy Spirit by the laying on of hands by those possessing the authority to give him. It is continued by sincere repentance, genuine effort to keep God's commandments, and regular partaking of the Sacrament (the consumption of the body and blood of Christ that the Holy Spirit uses to reset our soteriological status back to "sinless" on our path to perfection).

I want to be a true disciple of Jesus Christ

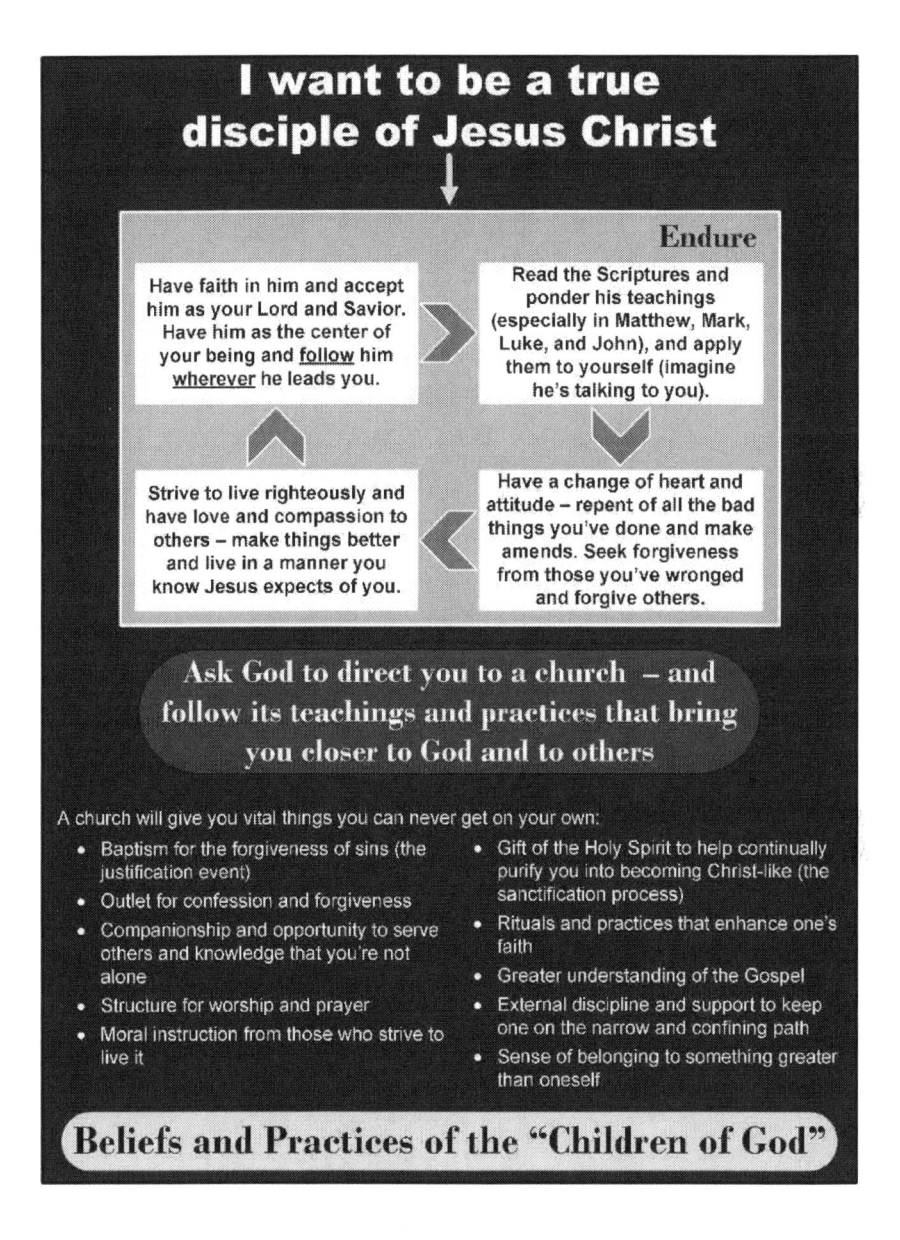

Endure

- Have faith in him and accept him as your Lord and Savior. Have him as the center of your being and <u>follow</u> him <u>wherever</u> he leads you.

- Read the Scriptures and ponder his teachings (especially in Matthew, Mark, Luke, and John), and apply them to yourself (imagine he's talking to you).

- Strive to live righteously and have love and compassion to others – make things better and live in a manner you know Jesus expects of you.

- Have a change of heart and attitude – repent of all the bad things you've done and make amends. Seek forgiveness from those you've wronged and forgive others.

Ask God to direct you to a church – and follow its teachings and practices that bring you closer to God and to others

A church will give you vital things you can never get on your own:

- Baptism for the forgiveness of sins (the justification event)
- Outlet for confession and forgiveness
- Companionship and opportunity to serve others and knowledge that you're not alone
- Structure for worship and prayer
- Moral instruction from those who strive to live it
- Gift of the Holy Spirit to help continually purify you into becoming Christ-like (the sanctification process)
- Rituals and practices that enhance one's faith
- Greater understanding of the Gospel
- External discipline and support to keep one on the narrow and confining path
- Sense of belonging to something greater than oneself

Beliefs and Practices of the "Children of God"

Become Christ's true disciple in word and deed. Show love to God and others. Forgive those who've wronged you. Be humble and don't let your pride destroy your glorious future. Do good. Be honest. Make the world better and show kindness to all. Show genuine charity and compassion towards others – after all, Jesus

Christ saves you because of his charity (you do not *deserve* to be saved); at least be genuinely charitable towards others.

You will know when you're on the right path by paying attention to the Holy Spirit dwelling within you and following his promptings. If you feel him leave or feel the joy that he gives disappear, you'll immediately know you've strayed and need to repent and go back to a state where it returns.

And when, not if, but when the world doesn't appreciate your contribution for good and tries to crush you or attempts to make you ashamed or afraid to be Jesus Christ's true follower: *Endure*.

So, come, and raise your voice to heaven. Let us sing together. Praise our Lord and Savior. Praise our God who took upon himself our sins and paid our debt!

ODE TO JESUS HYMNS

Prologue
Meter 87.87

---

(1) There are many things we don't know.
Seekers seek explanation.
Four big questions without answer.
All to do with creation.

(2) How did the cosmos come to be?
Fine-tuned for life's emergence!
What or who caused the universe?
Science and faith's convergence!

(3) How did living things come to be?
Living cell's complexity!
How did complex come from simple?
Impossible chemistry!

(4) How did modern man come to be?
With stunning ability!
What's with our superiority?
Reason and morality?

(5) The New Testament has one voice.
It shouldn't have, but it has!
Many authors, but one message.
Removed by time and distance!
No common editor nor frame.
Correlative components!
Impossible accomplishment.
Great joy to its proponents!

(6) The world owes a great debt to Christ.
Mankind's life is much better!
Tangible benefits to all –
All thanks to his followers!
Foundation of all our science.
Annulment of slavery!
Innate value of all humans.
Real freedom from tyranny!

(7) *So, come, and meet the real Jesus –*
The one who improved your life!
Discover who he truly is.
Why not have eternal life?

1. The Pre-Existence of Jesus
Meter 86.86

(a)   In the beginning was the Word.
And the Word was with God!
He existed before the world.
And ere the universe!

(b)   The Son has the Father's nature.
By nature, he is God!
The Son radiates God's glory.
Exact image of God!

(c)   He had glory ere creation.
He shared God's glory!
He gave up his equality.
He emptied his glory!

(d)   He was foreordained to atone –
Before the world was made!
He was ordained to save mankind.
Before the earth was laid!

(e)   He came from heaven before birth.
The Son came from heaven!
He gave up heaven to come here.
God's only Son left heaven!

(f)   Jesus came from God the Father.
Thank you, God, for your Son!
Jesus was sent by his Father.
Thank you, O holy one!

(g)   Jesus is the Lord of Israel.
He is the Great I AM!
God's only Son is the Lord of lords.
He is the King of kings!

(h) God gave his only Son for us.
His great work had begun!
God's Son obeyed his Father's will.
Thank you, Lord, for your Son!

(a) **HE EXISTED BEFORE CREATION**: John 1:1-3,10,14; 1 John 1:1-2; 1 John 2:13; Colossians 1:15-17; 1 Peter 1:19-20; 2 Timothy 1:9-10 | *3 Nephi 9:15; 3 Nephi 26:5; D&C 93:7,21; D&C 128:22; D&C 132:28; Moses 2:26; Moses 5:9; Moses 5:57; Abraham 3:23-25*

(b) **HE WAS "GOD" BY NATURE**: John 1:1; Philippians 2:5-7; Hebrews 1:2-3 | *Mosiah 3:5-8; Mosiah 7:27; Mosiah 13:34-35; Ether 3:6-18; D&C 39:1; Abraham 3:22-24*

(c) **HE POSSESSED GLORY**: John 17:5,22,24; Philippians 2:6-8 | *Alma 5:50; Alma 9:26; D&C 93:3-9*

(d) **HE WAS FOREORDAINED TO BE THE SINLESS SUBSTITUTE**: Acts 3:20; 1 Peter 1:20 | *Mosiah 4:6-7; Alma 12:25-35; Alma 18:39; Alma 22:13; Alma 42:26; Ether 3:14*

(e) **HE CAME FROM HEAVEN**: John 3:13,31-32; John 6:33,38,41-42,50-51,58,62; John 8:23; 1 Corinthians 15:47; Ephesians 4:9-10 | *Mosiah 3:5-8; Abraham 3:22-27*

(f) **HE CAME FROM THE FATHER**: John 3:16-17; John 6:32,38-40,44,46,57; John 7:33-34; John 8:18,42; John 10:36; John 12:41-50; John 13:3; John 16:5; John 16:28; John 17:3,8,21,23,25; 1 John 4:9-10,14; Romans 8:3; Galatians 4:4 | *3 Nephi 27:13-14; Ether 4:12; Abraham 3:22-27*

(g) **HE WAS THE OLD TESTAMENT GOD**: (John 8:24,28,58; John 13:19; John 18:5-8 cf. Exodus 3:14; Deuteronomy 32:39; Isaiah 41:4; Isaiah 43:10; Isaiah 46:4) / (Acts 4:10-12; 1 John 4:14 cf. Isaiah 43:11; Hosea 13:4); Revelation 17:14; Revelation 19:13-16 | *1 Nephi 19:7-10,13; 2 Nephi 6:9,14-18; 2 Nephi 10:3-4; 3 Nephi 15:1-5*

(h) **HE IS GOD'S ONLY BEGOTTEN SON**: Matthew 3:17; Matthew 17:5; Hebrews 1:5; 2 Peter 1:17; John 1:14; John 3:16,18,35; 1 John 4:9-10 | *1 Nephi 13:40; 2 Nephi 25:12-13; Jacob 4:11; Alma 5:48; Alma 9:26; Helaman 3:28; 3 Nephi 11:1-17; Mormon 9:29; D&C 6:21; D&C 10:57; D&C 11:28; D&C 20:21; D&C 29:42; D&C 45:51-53; D&C 76:13-14,20,23,25,35; Moses 6:52; Moses 7:50; Joseph Smith-History 1:17*

2. Jesus Mutually Indwells With the Father

Meter 86.86

(a) Father, Son, and Holy Spirit—
They dwell in each other!
Whether by will or innately,
Within one another!

(b) Christ is in the image of God,
God's glory on his face!
He is an exact duplicate –
Of God's very essence!

(c) The Son is in God the Father.
The Father's in the Son!
They indwell in one another.
Always within each one!

(d) The Son is one with the Father.
Father and Son are one!
Jesus said God was one with him.
A oneness with the Son!

(e) The Father glorifies the Son.
Christ gives glory to God!
God honors Christ within himself.
Son's glorified by God!

(f) The Son's equal to the Father.
Eternal equality!
Equal praise to Father and Son.
Equal eternally!

(g)   God's fulness dwelt in Christ's body.
God's fulness in his flesh!
God's fulness was in his body.
God's fulness in Christ's flesh!

(h)   To see one, one sees the other.
Jesus, show me your face!
To see him, one sees the Father.
Father, give us your grace!

(a) **THE FATHER, SON, AND HOLY SPIRIT SHARE A COMMON SPACE**: John 10:38; John 14:10-11,20; John 17:21,23; 2 Corinthians 5:19 | *3 Nephi 9:15; 3 Nephi 11:27; 3 Nephi 19:23,29; D&C 50:43; D&C 76:13,25,39; D&C 93:3-4,17,20*

(b) **HE IS IN THE IMAGE OF GOD**: 2 Corinthians 4:4-6; Colossians 1:15; Hebrews 1:2-3 | *Abraham 3:24*

(c) **HE IS IN THE FATHER; THE FATHER IS IN HIM**: John 10:38; John 14:10-11,20; John 17:21,23; John 13:31-32; 2 Corinthians 5:19 | *3 Nephi 9:15; 3 Nephi 11:27; 3 Nephi 19:23,29; D&C 50:43; D&C 76:13,25,39; D&C 93:3-4,17,20*

(d) **HE IS ONE WITH THE FATHER**: John 10:30; John 17:11,21-22 | *3 Nephi 19:23,29; 3 Nephi 20:35; 3 Nephi 28:10; D&C 93:3*

(e) **THE FATHER IS GLORIFIED IN JESUS**: John 13:31-32; 2 Corinthians 5:19 | *3 Nephi 9:15; 3 Nephi 11:7,11; 3 Nephi 23:9; Ether 12:7-8; D&C 45:4; D&C 76:40-43*

(f) **HE IS EQUAL TO THE FATHER**: John 5:17-18; John 10:33; John 5:23; John 14:16; John 16:26; John 17:9,15,20 | *3 Nephi 28:10; Abraham 3:24*

(g) **THE FULNESS OF GOD WAS WITHIN HIS BODY**: Colossians 1:19; Colossians 2:9 | *D&C 93:4-6,16*

(h) **ONE SEES THE FATHER WHEN LOOKING AT JESUS**: John 12:45; John 14:7-12

3. Jesus is the Creator
Meter 86.86

(a) God made the universe through Christ.
Sire ordered; Son obeyed!
This reality came to be –
Father designed; Son made!

(b) God's only Son made the cosmos.
Every planet and star!
He made the big bang's time and space.
And all things near and far!

(c) Nothing exists without Christ's word.
There's naught he didn't make!
Everything in heaven and earth –
All things he did create!

(d) Jesus sustains the universe.
He keeps it together!
By the power of our Lord's word –
He holds it together!

(e) The Son of God formed this great world.
He created this earth!
Although man did not know he did.
Made long before his birth!

(f) He breathed life into matter.
Structured life formed from clay!
He brought complexity from base.
In all of life's array!

(g) Most of all, he created man.
The pinnacle of life!
Capable of moral reason,
Can discern wrong from right!

(h) He gave us genuine freedom.
We are free to obey him!
He does not force us to be good.
We must freely heed him!

(a) **THE FATHER CREATED THE UNIVERSE THROUGH HIM**: 1 Corinthians 8:6; Hebrews 1:2-3; Revelation 3:14 | *Moses 1:3-8,27-38*
(b) **HE CREATED THE UNIVERSE**: John 1:3,10,14; Colossians 1:13-17; Hebrews 1:8-10; Hebrews 2:10 | *Mosiah 3:8; Mosiah 4:2; Mosiah 5:15; Mosiah 26:23; Mosiah 27:30; Helaman 14:12; 3 Nephi 9:15; Ether 3:14-15; D&C 14:9; D&C 38:1-3; D&C 45:1-3; D&C 76:23-24; D&C 93:7-11; D&C 117:6; Moses 1:3-8,27-38; Moses 7:30; Abraham 3:11-13*
(c) **NOTHING EXISTS THAT WASN'T CREATED BY HIM**: John 1:3; Colossians 1:13-17 | *Mosiah 3:8; Mosiah 4:2*
(d) **HE SUSTAINS THE UNIVERSE**: Colossians 1:17; Hebrews 1:3
(e) **HE CREATED THIS EARTH**: John 1:10; Colossians 1:16; Hebrews 1:8-10 | *3 Nephi 9:15; D&C 38:1-3; D&C 93:7-11; D&C 117:6*
(f) **HE CREATED LIFE**: Colossians 1:16 | *D&C 45:1-4*
(g) **HE CREATED MAN**: 1 Corinthians 8:6; Colossians 1:16 | *Mosiah 26:23; Ether 3:14-16; D&C 93:7-11*
(h) **WE HAVE FREE WILL**: Mark 8:34; John 1:12-13; Romans 10:9-10; 2 Corinthians 9:7; Galatians 5:1,13; Revelation 3:20 | *2 Nephi 2:26-27; 2 Nephi 10:23; Helaman 14:30-31; Alma 30:7-12*

4. Jesus Became Human Flesh

Meter 86.86

(a) The Creator became human.
Jesus Christ became flesh!
He did not enter a body.
He transmuted to flesh!

(b) He transformed from spirit to flesh.
He changed his state to mine!
Without this metamorphosis,
He couldn't save mankind!

(c) He needed to relate to man.
He had to become man!
Jesus condemned sin in the flesh.
By becoming human!

(d) Jesus bridged divine and human.
He was both God and man!
He wasn't half-God and half-man –
He was full God and man!

(e) He humbled himself to be born.
The great God became man!
He emptied himself of glory,
From divine to mere man!

(f) He was tempted but never sinned.
Jesus never sinned!
He resisted all temptation.
Our Lord stayed free from sin!

(g) He only becomes mortal once.
Just one mortality!
Death cannot again embrace him.
He rules death and Hades!

JESUS BECAME HUMAN FLESH 63

(h)   The devils recognized Jesus.
They knew he was God's Son!
They begged him to let them be.
They feared God's only Son!

(a) **HE BECAME FLESH**: John 1:14; 1 John 4:2-3; 2 John 1:7; Romans 8:3 | *2 Nephi 2:4; 2 Nephi 6:9; 2 Nephi 9:5; 2 Nephi 32:6; Jacob 4:11; Enos 1:8; Mosiah 7:27; Ether 3:16,21; Moses 7:54*
(b) **HE BECAME FLESH TO BECOME A REAL HUMAN**: John 1:14; 1 John 4:2-3; 2 John 1:7; Romans 8:3 | *2 Nephi 2:4; 2 Nephi 6:9; 2 Nephi 9:5; 2 Nephi 32:6; Jacob 4:11; Enos 1:8; Mosiah 7:27; Ether 3:16,21; Moses 7:54*
(c) **HE BECAME HUMAN TO RELATE TO HUMANITY**: John 3:16; 1 John 1:1-2; Romans 1:3; 1 Corinthians 15:21; Galatians 4:4; Philippians 2:7-8; Hebrews 2:14-18; Revelation 5:5,9,12 | *Alma 7:12-13*
(d) **HE BRIDGED THE GOD AND HUMAN NATURES**: John 1:1; Hebrews 1:2-3 cf. John 3:16; 1 John 1:1-2; Romans 1:3; 1 Corinthians 15:21; Galatians 4:4; Philippians 2:7-8; Hebrews 2:14-18; Colossians 1:20-22; Revelation 5:5,9,12 | *2 Nephi 6:9; 2 Nephi 9:5; 2 Nephi 25:12-13; Mosiah 7:27*
(e) **HE HUMBLED HIMSELF TO BECOME HUMAN**: Philippians 2:7-8 | *1 Nephi 19:9-10; 2 Nephi 31:7; Mosiah 15:5; D&C 88:6; D&C 122:8*
(f) **HE WAS TEMPTED BUT NEVER SINNED**: 2 Corinthians 5:21; Hebrews 4:15; Hebrews 7:26; Hebrews 9:14; 1 Peter 2:22; 1 John 3:5; Hebrews 2:18; Matthew 4:1,7 | *Mosiah 15:5; D&C 20:22; D&C 45:4*
(g) **HE CAN ONLY HAVE A SINGLE INCARNATION**: Romans 6:9-10; Romans 8:34; 2 Corinthians 5:15; John 10:15; Romans 6:10; Hebrews 7:27; Hebrews 9:12,25-28; Hebrews 10:10-14; 1 Peter 3:18
(h) **HE WAS RECOGNIZED BY DEMONS**: Mark 1:34; Mark 3:11-12; Luke 4:41

5. The Atonement of Jesus

Meter 86.86

(a)   Jesus suffered for mankind's sins.
He took our punishments!
God placed upon himself our sins.
To save us from torments!

(b)   Christ's Atonement was infinite.
Pain, inconceivable!
It was infinite hurt and fear.
Unimaginable!

(c)   He was a sinless substitute.
He was the Lamb of God!
He was a stain-free sacrifice.
An offering to God!

(d)   Jesus ransomed himself for us.
Because of him, we're free!
Christ's holy blood paid the ransom.
We slaves can now be free!

(e)   Jesus died for humanity.
He died for you and me!
God's only Son died for our sins.
Despite we're not worthy!

(f)   He reconciles us to our God.
His blood justifies us!
His sacrifice reconciles us.
His blood sanctifies us!

(g)   We're redeemed through his holy blood.
We're washed clean in his blood!
His shed blood removes mankind's sins.
Made sinless through his blood!

THE ATONEMENT OF JESUS

(h)   We are nailed to the cross with him.
We're crucified with Christ!
We share his death; we share his rise.
We live to God in Christ!

(a) **HE SUFFERED**: Matthew 20:28; Romans 3:23-25; Romans 8:32; Galatians 1:4; 1 Timothy 2:6; Titus 2:14; Hebrews 10:10-20; 1 Peter 1:11,18-20; 1 Peter 2:21-24; 1 John 4:9-10,14; Luke 22:42-44; Acts 26:23; Hebrews 5:7-9 | *2 Nephi 9:7,20-22; Mosiah 3:5-8; Alma 7:11-13; Alma 16:19; Alma 21:9; Alma 22:14, Alma 33:22; D&C 18:11; D&C 19:16-19,24*

(b) **HE EXPERIENCED AN INFINITE ATONEMENT**: 1 Timothy 2:6; Hebrews 10:10-20; 1 Peter 1:11,18-20; Hebrews 2:9-10; Colossians 1:20-22; Hebrews 7:25-28; Hebrews 9:11-28; 1 Peter 3:18; Revelation 5:9 | *2 Nephi 2:6-10; 2 Nephi 9:7,20-21; 2 Nephi 25:16; Alma 13:8-14; D&C 18:11; D&C 19:16-19,24; D&C 133:53*

(c) **HE WAS A SINLESS SUBSTITUTE**: Matthew 20:28; Romans 3:23-25; Romans 8:32; Galatians 1:4; 1 Timothy 2:6; Titus 2:14; Hebrews 10:10-20; 1 Peter 1:11,18-20; 1 Peter 2:21-24; 1 John 4:9-10,14 | *Mosiah 26:23; Alma 7:9-14; Alma 34:8; 3 Nephi 11:14*

(d) **HE PAID OUR RANSOM AND FREED US**: Galatians 1:4; Galatians 3:13; 1 Timothy 2:6; Titus 2:14; 1 Peter 1:18-20; Revelation 1:5 | *Mosiah 5:7-9; D&C 98:8*

(e) **HE DIED FOR MANKIND**: John 10:15,17-18; John 17:19; Romans 5:6-8; 2 Corinthians 5:14-15; Galatians 2:20-21; 1 Thessalonians 5:9-10; Hebrews 2:9-10; Hebrews 9:15,26-28 | *1 Nephi 11:32-33; 2 Nephi 10:3; Mosiah 15:5-7; Mosiah 13:28; Alma 21:9; Alma 22:14; Alma 33:22; Helaman 14:14-16; D&C 18:11; D&C 21:9; D&C 54:1; D&C 76:41*

(f) **HIS SACRIFICE/BLOOD RECONCILES US TO GOD**: Romans 5:9-11; Ephesians 2:13-16; Colossians 1:20-22; Hebrews 7:25-28; Hebrews 9:11-28; 1 Peter 3:18; Revelation 1:5; Revelation 5:9 | *2 Nephi 10:24; Jacob 4:11; Alma 42:23; Helaman 14:17; Mormon 9:12-13; Ether 3:13*

(g) **HIS BLOOD FORGIVES SINS**: Matthew 26:28; Luke 22:15-16,19-20,42-44; Ephesians 1:7; Hebrews 9:11-14; 1 John 1:7 | *1 Nephi 12:10-11; Mosiah 3:11,16; Alma 34:36; Mormon 9:6; Ether 13:10-11; Moroni 10:23; D&C 27:2; Moses 6:59*

(h) **WE PARTICIPATE WITH HIM**: Romans 6:3-11; Romans 7:4; Romans 8:17; 2 Corinthians 4:14; Galatians 2:20-21; Ephesians 2:5-6; Philippians 3:10; Colossians 2:14; 2 Timothy 2:11; 1 Peter 2:24

6. The Resurrection of Jesus
Meter 86.86

(a) Meeting the spirits in prison,
Jesus preached to the dead!
The Son of God fulfilled his task –
The Atonement ended!

(b) Angels proclaimed glorious news:
Jesus came back from death!
He is not here; he is risen.
He once again has breath!

(c) Jesus Christ was resurrected.
Jesus conquered the grave!
Returning from the realm of death,
Never again death's slave!

(d) He spent time with his disciples.
His body could be felt!
Forty days they walked together,
Then rising up to dwelt!

(e) He's first to be resurrected.
The first immortal flesh!
Our Lord's the firstborn from the dead.
Praise him who conquered death!

(f) Christ will forever destroy death.
I no longer fear death!
Christ holds the keys of death and Hades.
Jesus will annul death!

(g) Jesus can never die again.
Just one mortality!
Death can never again have him.
He lives eternally!

THE RESURRECTION OF JESUS

(h)   Christ makes everyone immortal –
Both righteous and flawed!
This free gift he gives to us all.
In my flesh, I'll see God!

(a) **HE PREACHED TO THE SPIRITS IN PRISON**: 1 Peter 3:18-20 | *D&C 76:73-74; D&C 138:6-52*

(b) **ANGELS ANNOUNCED HIS RESURRECTION**: Matthew 28:5-7; Luke 24:3-8

(c) **HE ROSE FROM THE DEAD**: Mark 16:9; Acts 13:37; Acts 17:31; Romans 6:9-10; 1 Corinthians 15:4,12-26; 2 Corinthians 5:15; Ephesians 1:20; 1 Thessalonians 4:14; 2 Timothy 2:8; 1 Peter 3:21 | *1 Nephi 10:11; 2 Nephi 2:8; 2 Nephi 25:13-14; Mosiah 3:10; Mosiah 18:2; Alma 33:22; 3 Nephi 11:8-17; Mormon 7:5; D&C 18:11-12; D&C 110:4; D&C 138:51; Moses 7:62*

(d) **MANY EYEWITNESSES SAW, INTERACTED WITH, AND FELT THE RESURRECTED JESUS**: Matthew 28:9; Luke 24:36-51; Acts 1:1-11; John 20:19-20; John 20:25-29; 1 Corinthians 15:5-8

(e) **HE WAS FIRST TO RESURRECT FROM THE DEAD WITH AN IMMORTAL BODY**: Acts 26:23; 1 Corinthians 15:20,23; Colossians 1:18; Revelation 1:5 | *2 Nephi 2:8*

(f) **HE WILL DESTROY DEATH AND HADES**: 1 Corinthians 15:26; 2 Timothy 1:10; Revelation 20:13-14; Revelation 1:18 | *2 Nephi 9:10-12,26; Mosiah 15:8,23; Mosiah 16:7-8; Alma 22:14; Mormon 7:5*

(g) **HE CAN NEVER DIE AGAIN**: Romans 6:9-10; Romans 8:34; 2 Corinthians 5:15 | *2 Nephi 9:10-12,26; Mosiah 15:8,23; Mosiah 16:7-8; Alma 22:14; Mormon 7:5*

(h) **HE MAKES EVERYONE IMMORTAL**: Acts 24:15; John 5:28-29; Romans 5:15-18; 1 Corinthians 15:12-30; 1 Corinthians 15:35,40-57 | *2 Nephi 9:7-13,22; Mosiah 16:7-11; Alma 11:41-45; Helaman 14:15-16; 3 Nephi 26:4-5; Mormon 6:21; D&C 88:97-102; D&C 138:17; Moses 7:62*

7. The Glorification of Jesus

Meter 86.86

(a)   The Father glorifies his Son.
He has God's own glory!
Christ is exalted above all.
Because he was worthy!

(b)   His name is above all names.
Jesus is over all!
All will concede Jesus is Lord.
Jesus is Lord of all!

(c)   Exalted to the Father's right.
Our Lord's at God's right hand!
Seat of honor, might, and glory –
Before of which we'll stand!

(d)   Jesus is the only way to God.
He stands before God's throne!
No one can receive salvation –
Lest going through God's Son!

(e)   God gave his Son the universe.
Dominion over all!
An eternal inheritance.
Beneath his feet are all!

(f)   Jesus Christ will return to earth.
He will come suddenly!
With angels and the righteous dead.
With great might and glory!

(g)   Jesus will resurrect us all –
Both the good and the bad!
He will judge all men and women –
To be saved or condemned!

(h) He will replace heaven and earth.
A new heaven and earth!
The old versions obsoleted,
The new: No sin, no death!

(a) **HE IS GLORIFIED AND EXALTED ABOVE ALL**: Acts 2:32-33; John 13:31-32; John 17:1-2,5,24; Revelation 5:5,9,12-13; Hebrews 2:9; Hebrews 7:26; 2 Peter 1:17; Philippians 2:9-11; 1 Peter 3:22; Ephesians 1:21 | *Alma 5:50; Moroni 9:26; D&C 19:2; D&C 58:22; D&C 63:59; D&C 76:106-109*

(b) **HIS NAME IS ABOVE ALL NAMES/HE IS LORD**: Philippians 2:9-11; Revelation 5:13-14 | *Mosiah 3:12,17; D&C 10:70; D&C 17:9; D&C 35:1; D&C 95:17; D&C 138:60*

(c) **HE IS EXALTED TO GOD'S RIGHT-HAND SIDE**: Matthew 26:64; Mark 14:62; Mark 16:19; Luke 22:69; Acts 2:32-33; Acts 7:55-56; Romans 8:34; Ephesians 1:20; Colossians 3:1; Hebrews 1:13; Hebrews 8:1; Hebrews 10:12; Hebrews 12:2; 1 Peter 3:22 | *Moroni 7:27; Moroni 9:26; D&C 20:24; D&C 49:6; D&C 76:20,23,106-109; Joseph Smith-Matthew 1:1*

(d) **HE IS THE ONLY WAY TO GOD/HE IS THE ONLY WAY FOR US TO BE SAVED**: John 14:6; Revelation 7:17; 1 Timothy 2:5; Acts 4:10-12 | *1 Nephi 13:40; 2 Nephi 9:41; 2 Nephi 25:20,26,28-29; 2 Nephi 30:2; 2 Nephi 31:19-21; Mosiah 3:12,17; Mosiah 4:8; Mosiah 5:8; Mosiah 16:13; Alma 21:9; Alma 34:9,15; Alma 38:9; Helaman 3:28-30; Helaman 5:9; Helaman 8:15; Helaman 14:8; D&C 18:23; D&C 109:4; D&C 132:12; Moses 6:52*

(e) **HE IS GIVEN THE UNIVERSE AS AN INHERITANCE AND REIGNS OVER IT**: Matthew 11:27; John 3:35; Hebrews 1:2; Hebrews 2:10; Matthew 28:18; John 13:3; Romans 9:5; Colossians 1:16-20; John 16:15; John 17:10; Matthew 19:28; Acts 10:36; 1 Corinthians 15:25-28; Ephesians 1:10,20-23 | *1 Nephi 22:24; D&C 58:22; D&C 63:59; D&C 76:61,106*

(f) **HE WILL RETURN TO EARTH WITH GREAT POWER AND GLORY**: Matthew 26:64; Colossians 3:4; 1 Thessalonians 5:9-10; 2 Thessalonians 1:7-10; 2 Thessalonians 2:8; 1 Timothy 6:14; 2 Timothy 4:1,8; Titus 2:13; Hebrews 9:28; 1 Peter 5:4; Revelation 22:12; Luke 12:40; Matt 16:27; Matt 25:31; 1 Corinthians 15:23; 1 Thessalonians 3:13; 1 Thessalonians 4:14-17; Jude 1:14; Mark 14:62; Matthew 24:30; Acts 1:9-11 | *2 Nephi 6:14-15; 2 Nephi 30:10; Jacob 6:2-3; 3 Nephi 28:7-8; Mormon 9:2; Ether 4:9; D&C 5:19; D&C 29:11-26; D&C 34:7-9; D&C 38:8; D&C 45:44-55; D&C 51:20; D&C 61:38-39; D&C 88:91-98; D&C 101:23-25*

- (g) **HE WILL RESURRECT AND JUDGE MANKIND**: Revelation 1:18; Acts 24:15; 1 Corinthians 15:12-30; Matthew 16:27; Matthew 25:31-34,41,46; John 5:22-30; Revelation 20:10-15; Revelation 22:12; Acts 10:42; Acts 17:31; 2 Corinthians 5:10; 2 Timothy 4:1; 1 Peter 4:5-6 | *2 Nephi 9:10-15,22; Mosiah 16:7-11; Alma 11:41-45; Alma 21:9; Alma 33:22; Alma 40:2-25; 3 Nephi 27:14; Mormon 6:21; Mormon 7:5-7; Mormon 9:13-14; D&C 29:26-28*
- (h) **HE WILL REPLACE HEAVEN AND EARTH**: Matthew 19:28; Hebrews 1:10-12; 2 Peter 3:10-13; Revelation 21:1,5; Revelation 20:11; Romans 8:19-21 | *Ether 13:9; D&C 29:23-27; D&C 43:32; D&C 101:25*

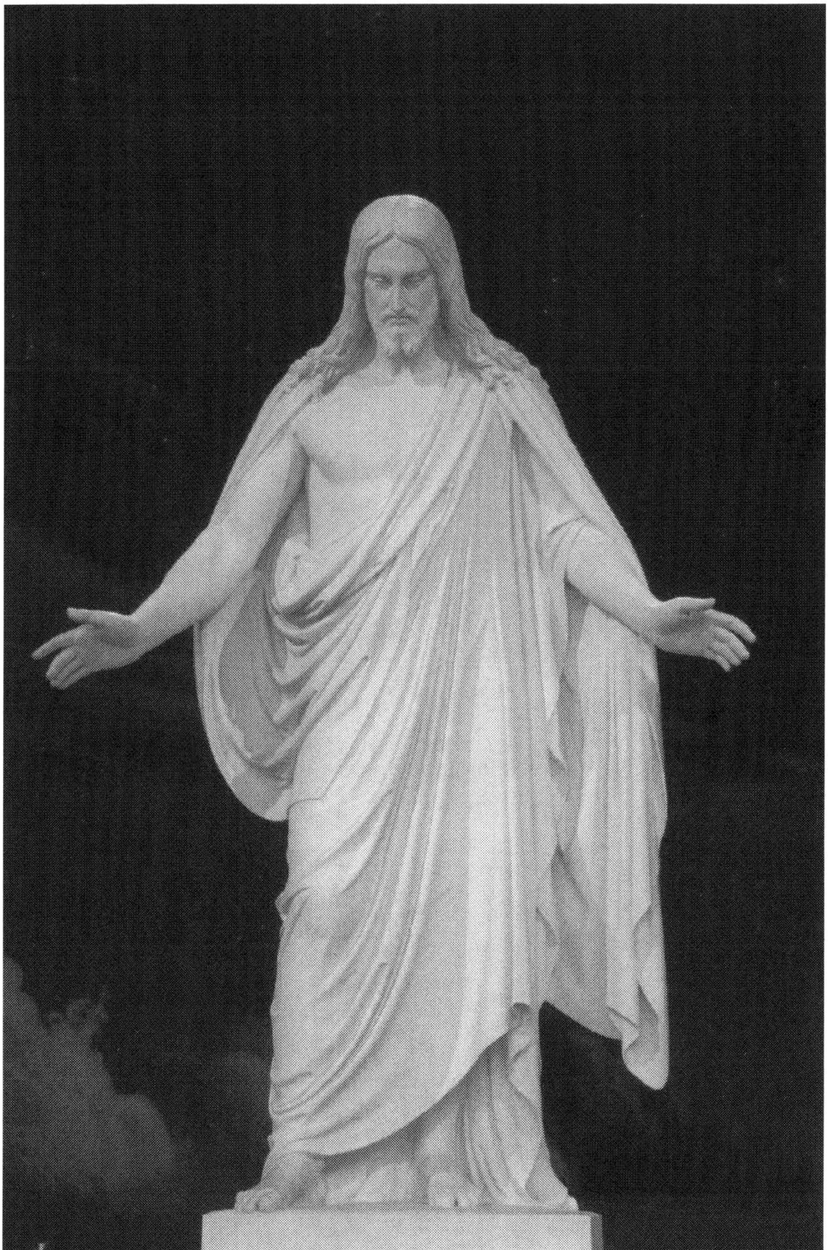

8. Jesus Creates the Children of God
Meter 86.86

(a) Follow Christ for eternal life.
Believe him and be saved!
He's the living bread from heaven.
Have faith, repent, be kind!

(b) We are to keep his commandments.
Believe him and obey!
Do good and show love and mercy.
Love all, and always pray!

(c) God adopts us because of Christ.
We can be born of God!
The Lord's foster sons and daughters.
By grace, Children of God!

(d) The Children of God are his heirs.
By grace, we are his heirs!
No longer specks, but now his heirs –
With Jesus, fellow-heirs!

(e) God's children share oneness with him.
Dwelling in each other!
We live in them; they live in us.
None without the other!

(f) Sharing in the divine nature.
God shares himself with us!
Transforming to Christ's same image,
Awaits his followers!

(g) Christ shares glory with God's children.
God's heirs share in glory!
Christ gives us his glory from God.
His heirs receive glory!

(h)   Jesus shares all he has with us –
       For those who stay faithful!
       Those who endure will rule with him–
       A gift so wonderful!

(a) **BELIEF IN HIM BRINGS SALVATION**: Matthew 19:27-29; John 3:15-16,36; John 6:40,47, 51,54-58; John 10:28; John 17:2-3; 1 John 1:2; 1 John 2:25; 1 John 5:9-13,20; Romans 5:21; Romans 6:23; Titus 3:7; Hebrews 5:9; 1 Peter 5:10; Jude 1:21 | *Mosiah 26:21-23; Alma 11:40; Alma 34:15; Helaman 14:13; 3 Nephi 11:32-38; Mormon 7:5-7; D&C 11:30; D&C 20:29; D&C 45:8; Moses 5:15*
(b) **WE MUST OBEY HIM**: Romans 1:5; Romans 6:16; Romans 16:26; Hebrews 5:9; 1 Peter 1:2; 1 Peter 1:13-14,22-23; John 15:10; 1 John 5:3; 2 John 1:4,6 | *Mosiah 5:8; D&C 56:3; D&C 59:21; D&C 82:8-10; D&C 93:1,20-22; D&C 98:22; D&C 130:20-21; D&C 138:4*
(c) **HE ENABLES HIS FOLLOWERS TO BE ADOPTED BY GOD**: Romans 8:15,22-23; Galatians 3:26-4:7; Ephesians 1:4-5
(d) **HIS TRUE FOLLOWERS BECOME THE CHILDREN OF GOD AND GOD'S HEIRS**: John 1:12-13; 1 John 2:29-3:3; 1 John 3:9; 1 John 5:1-5; Revelation 21:7; Romans 8:14-21; Galatians 3:26-4:7; Hebrews 2:10-17; Acts 20:32; Acts 26:18; Ephesians 1:11-18; Colossians 1:12-13; Colossians 3:24; Titus 3:7; Hebrews 1:14; Hebrews 9:15; James 2:5; 1 Peter 1:3-5 | *Mosiah 4:2; Mosiah 5:7; Mosiah 15:10-13; Mosiah 18:22; Mosiah 27:25-26; 3 Nephi 9:15-17; 3 Nephi 12:44-45; 4 Nephi 1:17; Mormon 9:26; Ether 3:14; Moroni 7:19,26,48; D&C 11:30; D&C 25:1; D&C 34:3; D&C 35:2; D&C 39:1-4; D&C 42:52; D&C 45:8; D&C 70:8; D&C 76:23-24,58; D&C 88:107; D&C 93:20-22; Moses 1:10-13; Moses 6:68; Moses 7:1; Moses 8:13*
(e) **THE CHILDREN OF GOD SHARE ONENESS AND MUTUAL INDWELLING WITH GOD**: John 15:1-11; John 17:11,21-23; Romans 8:16-17; 1 Corinthians 6:17; Galatians 3:26-29; John 6:56; John 14:20,23; 1 John 5:20; Romans 8:9-11; 1 Corinthians 3:16-17; Galatians 2:20; Ephesians 1:4; Colossians 1:27 | *3 Nephi 19:23,29; D&C 35:2,18; D&C 50:43; D&C 88:49-50*
(f) **THE CHILDREN OF GOD SHARE THE DIVINE NATURE**: Romans 8:28-30; 1 Corinthians 1:9; 1 Corinthians 15:48-49; 2 Corinthians 3:18; 2 Corinthians 8:9; Ephesians 3:19; Ephesians 4:13,15,24; Colossians 2:9-10; Colossians 3:10; Hebrews 3:14; Hebrews 12:9-10; 2 Peter 1:3-4; 1 John 1:3-7; 1 John 2:29-3:3 | *3 Nephi 28:10; Moroni 7:48; D&C 76:58-59; D&C 93:19-20; D&C 88:107*

- (g) **THE CHILDREN OF GOD SHARE GLORY**: John 17:22; Romans 5:2; Colossians 3:4; 2 Timothy 2:10; 2 Peter 1:3-4; Romans 8:17-21,28-30; Romans 9:23-24; 2 Corinthians 4:17; Ephesians 1:11-18; Colossians 1:27; 1 Thessalonians 2:12; 2 Thessalonians 2:13-14; Hebrews 2:10 | *D&C 58:4; D&C 63:66; D&C 66:2; D&C 76:5-6; D&C 76:55-59; D&C 88:17-20; D&C 93:20-22; D&C 133:57; Abraham 3:26*
- (h) **THE CHILDREN OF GOD SHARE RULE AND EVERYTHING HE HAS**: Revelation 3:21; Revelation 20:4; 2 Timothy 2:12; Luke 12:44; Romans 8:32; 1 Corinthians 3:21-23; 2 Corinthians 6:10; Hebrews 3:14; 2 Timothy 4:7-8; James 1:12; Luke 12:32; Luke 22:29-30; Ephesians 2:5-7; James 2:5; Revelation 1:6; Revelation 5:10; Revelation 22:5; Revelation 21:7; Mark 13:13 | *D&C 50:26-28; D&C 52:13; D&C 59:2; D&C 66:12; D&C 76:55-59,94-95; D&C 78:5-6,22; D&C 84:36-38; D&C 88:107; D&C 104:7; D&C 121:29,46; D&C 132:19-23,37,49,57; Moses 7:59; Joseph Smith-Matthew 1:49-50*

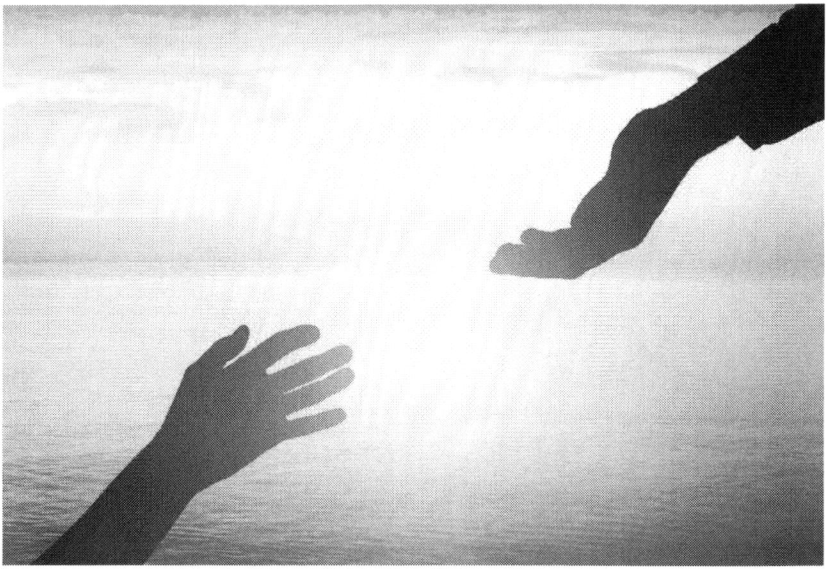

Epilogue
Meter 86.86

(1) Jesus was, before time and space.
With the Father was he!
Before the universe became,
The Son of God was he!

(2) Father, Son, and Holy Spirit –
They dwell in each other!
To see the Son, one sees his sire,
The Son's like the Father!

(3) He made the universe and earth –
Billions of years ago!
He made life from sterile matter,
He formed us long ago!

(4) Jesus Christ humbly became man.
He became human flesh!
He did not enter a body –
God transformed into flesh!

(5) He placed upon himself our sins.
He took our hurt and sins!
An infinite substitution –
For those who accept him!

(6) Christ died in ghastly pain and fear.
The Lord disrespected!
And yet our Lord came back to life.
Jesus resurrected!

(7) He triumphed over sin and death.
His name's above all names!
He will judge all men and women.
To eternal acclaims!

(8) Jesus calls us to follow him.
He saves those who obey!
He makes us the Children of God.
Please Lord, show us the way!

78   A LATTER-DAY SAINT ODE TO JESUS

STANZA CLARIFICATIONS

Most stanza references for hymns 1 through 8 quote at least one scripture passage that validates the stanza. These quotations are <u>paraphrased</u> text based on Nestle-Aland 28, which is considered by many biblical scholars to be the most accurate New Testament of modern times.

These conceptual (not linguistic) paraphrases are written by this author and derived from his *THE GOD WHO WASHES FEET*, where the following methodology was done to each NT verse that resulted in a paraphrased output:

Colossians 1:16-17

Colossians 1:16	
https://www.biblegateway.com/verse/en/col%201:16	
Nestle-Aland 28	ὅτι ἐν αὐτῷ ἐκτίσθη τὰ πάντα ἐν τοῖς οὐρανοῖς καὶ ἐπὶ τῆς γῆς, τὰ ὁρατὰ καὶ τὰ ἀόρατα, εἴτε θρόνοι εἴτε κυριότητες εἴτε ἀρχαὶ εἴτε ἐξουσίαι· τὰ πάντα δι' αὐτοῦ καὶ εἰς αὐτὸν ἔκτισται·
Transliteration	hoti en autō ektisthē ta panta en tois ouranois kai epi tēs gēs, ta horata kai ta aorata, eite thronoi eite kyriotētes eite archai eite exousiai; ta panta di' autou kai eis auton ektistai;
Literal	Because by him were created all things in the heavens and upon the earth, the visible and the invisible, whether thrones or lordships or rulers or authorities, all things by him and for him have been created.
Paraphrase	*He created the universe. Everything in heaven and earth, everything we see and haven't seen, including thrones, powers, rulers, or authorities; he created them all, and they are for him.*

Colossians 1:17	
https://www.biblegateway.com/verse/en/col%201:17	
Nestle-Aland 28	καὶ αὐτός ἐστιν πρὸ πάντων καὶ τὰ πάντα ἐν αὐτῷ συνέστηκεν,
Transliteration	kai autos estin pro pantōn kai ta panta en autō synestēken,
Literal	And he is before all things and all things in him hold together.
Paraphrase	He existed before the universe and causes it to hold together.

Colossians 1:16-17 *He created the universe. Everything in heaven and earth, everything we see and haven't seen, including thrones, powers, rulers, or authorities; he created them all, and they are for him. 17 He existed before the universe and causes it to hold together.*

The Prologue hymn doesn't contain any scripture references since it is focused on science and logic. Neither is a similar methodology done for the Epilogue hymn since it merely summarizes each of the core eight hymns into a corresponding stanza of its own.

Clarification of the "Prologue" Stanzas

1. Wisdom is knowing one does not know everything. For centuries, atheism has made dogmatic assertions "proving" God isn't real that later generations realized were wrong—and this trend has continued to this day.

Modern atheism has four empirical (testable) issues it needs to resolve, that currently give a much higher probability of having "God" as cause.

2. The first empirical question is, "*What caused the universe to come into existence?*"

Atheism mostly claims "quantum fluctuation" – a characteristic of this universe's spacetime, somehow traversed the infinite singularity to trigger the big bang.

Remarkably, the same people who cannot merge quantum field theory with general relativity, who cannot explain what comprises 95% of the universe's mass and energy by simply calling them "dark matter" and "dark energy"; somehow, confidently claim to know what happened before this universe's time and space existed?

What this actually means is they're just guessing what caused the universe. They have no idea except the belief that God wasn't involved.

3. The second empirical question is, "*What caused life to come into existence?*"

Biologists and atheists blithely proclaim life naturally evolved on a prebiotic earth (*abiogenesis*). Mix some chemicals together, throw in some lightning, heat, UV rays, and let it simmer for millions of years—and life inevitably emerges.

However, the real experts on the development of complex molecules from simpler ones, the synthetic chemists, know this is an impossible process. There are no known pathways to create the components that make up a living cell. They have no idea how saccharides, lipids, proteins, and nucleotides can be formed naturally in a prebiotic Earth, especially before the advent of enzymes to catalyze chemical reactions.

Life arising naturally out of nonliving materials not only cannot be proven; it actually contradicts synthetic chemistry's practices—

which comprise of very strict purity and environmental controls as well as experimental and sequential methodology. These are the exact *opposite* of what happens in nature, because contamination, water, sunlight, oxygen, heat, and impurities all degrade complex molecules or prevent them from forming.

The artificial creation of the precursors of RNA, amino acids, or lipids is more comparable to the creation of rivets whereas the complexity of a living cell is more comparable to an airplane. Just because rivets may be used in creating an airplane does not mean rivets are airplanes.

> *Anyone who knows how life can be created out of nonliving materials will become the richest person who ever lived – because he or she would've created the foundation for feeding the planet using industrial means, without the need for farming or raising food.*

4. The third empirical question is, "*What caused anatomically modern humans to come into existence?*"

Modern humans (*Homo sapiens sapiens*) are not just incrementally superior to every other hominid or animal; we're qualitatively different. We possess over forty (40) traits and characteristics that are completely absent in every other animal, and somehow acquired them within a span of just 50,000 to 300,000 years, a "blink of an eye," evolutionarily speaking.

As an example, we are the only species with our posture; who can throw a rock or baseball accurately; who can create and use fire; speak and use language via different modes; create complex, multi-part and multi-step tools like a spear or bow and arrow; read and write; wear and produce clothing; and have dozens of other unique traits and characteristics.

We have evolutionary evidence going back billions of years with millions of species, and we've never seen just one of these traits and behaviors replicated in any other species outside the archaic human Homo sapiens by evolutionary change. Not one. And yet, they all appeared in just one genus, within a time span too short for these major evolutionary changes to occur.

It is as if someone or something did some germline genetic modifications to one or more hominids at some point or points in the past hundred thousand years that drastically altered Homo sapiens to create the anatomically modern human *Homo sapiens sapiens*.

One or two genetic mutations are certainly possible, but what kind of mutations can explain all of modern human's unique characteristics, especially when there are no precedents in other species despite over 650 million years of animal evolution?

We have no models to show how it can be done and the more we learn about genetics; the harder it is to justify the absence of deliberate design in explaining why we're so different and so superior to every other animal.

> *We share the same DNA with every other form of life and are, without a doubt, genetic descendants of hominid ancestors; but notwithstanding the common heritage, we're so totally and completely different from everyone else that we might as well be from another planet.*

5. The New Testament is the only known frameless, unharmonized, correlative anthology. Somehow, at least nine different authors, separated by decades and distance, wrote harmonious and correlative deliverables that perfectly blend together into one voice.

That does *not* happen without *external* constraints.

It is human nature for each person to have unique perspectives and views—and these cannot be blended with other views without writing within a common frame (style guide, instructions) or employing the help of a harmonizing editor.

And yet, Matthew, Mark, Luke, John, Paul, Peter, the Hebraist, James, and Jude didn't have a common frame or set of instructions to follow to ensure their writings were "orthodox." It's as if each writer had unique pieces of a puzzle that when put together created a complete picture. Also, the New Testament books weren't edited by a common editor to harmonize their contents.

As an example, if one were to ask nine people to draw parts of a "human-designed structure" on pieces of paper and give them no further details, the pieces will not perfectly fit together to create a seamless whole. Some will draw part of a house, another a car, another an airplane, and so forth.

And yet, the New Testament has a single core cosmology. Somehow, multiple authors produced a correlative anthology without using a common frame or editor.

So unlikely is this accomplishment that this author, as an expert on correlative anthologies like major project execution plans and proposals, estimates the New Testament to be a four sigma (4σ) event, or it is 99.9936% *likely* that something supernatural was associated with its creation. It isn't proof of God—but it's the next best thing.

6. As mentioned in the Introduction, belief in Jesus was the glue that resulted in the creation of the modern nations of Europe and America. All "civilized" nations share common ethics and laws that can be traced to Christians. All inventions and technology that make our lives better owe a debt to the Christians who established the foundations of modern science hundreds of years ago. Even those who have never been Christian owe so much to Christianity because Christians were the ones who influenced their nations into creating universities and hospitals, educational degrees, libraries, book publishing, mass production, and so forth.

Without Christianity, there wouldn't be any freedom of speech, freedom of and from religion, freedom of travel, freedom of assembly, property rights, and so forth. The world didn't get them from Islam, Buddhism, Sikhism, Shintoism, Taoism, the Bahá'í, or Hinduism—they came from Christianity and those whose moral compass was guided by it. It is why someone can leave and ridicule the dominant religion without fear in Salt Lake City or Rome – but get killed if done in Mecca.

> *If Jesus Christ never existed, there never would've been an England, or France, or Spain, or Germany, or the United States of America. We wouldn't have the scientific method, universal health care, general literacy, social services, or recognition of our natural rights.*

The world we know would be a very different, uglier, bleaker, and miserable place. Half of our children would still be dying before reaching their fifth year; we would have an average life expectancy of less than 40; and, at least, a quarter of us will die violent deaths. Most of us would be enslaved farmers ruled by superstition, and only a minority of us will even know how to read.

STANZA CLARIFICATIONS 85

There's no doubt Jesus has and is continuing to have, the greatest positive impact on the world and everyone, regardless of country, race, religion, or culture, has directly benefitted from his influence.

Clarification of the "1. The Pre-Existence Of Jesus" Stanzas

a) He existed before creation

Our cosmology is vastly different than those of the biblical writers. For the first time in history, we can finally understand enigmatic biblical passages that describe Jesus existing before "creation" (i.e., big bang) in a location outside the universe, in another universe or realm. (It is possible this reality is a designed world like an advanced video game or simulation while God lives in the "real" world outside it.)

> "He is the image of the God who's never been seen and existed before the universe was created. 16 He created the universe. Everything in heaven and earth, everything we see and haven't seen, including thrones, powers, rulers, or authorities; he created them all, and they are for him. 17 He existed before the universe and causes it to hold together." (Holy Bible: Colossians 1:15-17)

> "Behold, I am Jesus Christ the Son of God. I created the heavens and the earth, and all things that in them are. I was with the Father from the beginning. I am in the Father, and the Father in me; and in me hath the Father glorified his name." (Book of Mormon: 3 Nephi 9:15)

b) He was "God" by nature

Our movement away from deductive inference philosophy to empirical science has allowed us to view "nature" as comparable to science's "species." Jesus is God by nature (belongs to the "God" species) just as he is also a man by nature (belongs to the *Homo sapiens sapiens* species).

Summary Table: Jesus is God[1]

Passage	Paraphrase Based on Nestle-Aland 28	+50 Parallel Bible Versions
JESUS IS GOD		
John 1:1	In the beginning was the Word; the Word existed with God; and the Word was God.	https://www.biblegateway.com/verse/en/John%201:1

---

[1] Table taken from *The God Who Washes Feet*, Chapter 7, Re: Section 2.3 Jesus Was Called "God."

JESUS IS GOD

Passage	Paraphrase Based on Nestle-Aland 28	+50 Parallel Bible Versions
John 1:3,10,14	He created the universe—nothing exists that wasn't created by him ... 10 He went and lived on Earth and even though he created it, the Earth's inhabitants didn't know who he was ... 14 The Word became flesh and lived among us. We have seen his glory—the glory of the only Son of the Father, full of grace and truth.	https://www.biblegateway.com/verse/en/John%201:3 https://www.biblegateway.com/verse/en/John%201:10 https://www.biblegateway.com/verse/en/John%201:14
Hebrews 1:8-10	But to the Son he said: "Your throne, O God, will last forever. You rule your kingdom with a scepter of righteousness. 9 You have loved righteousness and hated wickedness. Therefore, O God, your God, has anointed you with the oil of joy above anyone else. . . 10 And in the beginning, you, Lord, laid the foundation of the earth. Your hands created the heavens."	https://www.biblegateway.com/verse/en/hebrews%201:8 https://www.biblegateway.com/verse/en/hebrews%201:9 https://www.biblegateway.com/verse/en/hebrews%201:10
Philippians 2:5-11	Be as humble as Jesus Christ: 6 Although having the same nature of God, he didn't think to forcefully cling to his equality with God, 7 but emptied himself of it and took upon himself the nature of a slave and became human. 8 As a mortal man, he humbled himself and was so obedient to the Father's will, that he stooped to die the utterly degrading death on the cross. 9 This is why God elevated him higher than anything possible and made his name	https://www.biblegateway.com/verse/en/Philippians%202:5 https://www.biblegateway.com/verse/en/Philippians%202:6 https://www.biblegateway.com/verse/en/Philippians%202:7 https://www.biblegateway.com/verse/en/Philippians%202:8 https://www.biblegateway.com/verse/en/Philippians%202:9 https://www.biblegateway.com/verse/en/Philippians%202:10 https://www.biblegateway.com/verse/en/Philippians%202:11

	JESUS IS GOD	
Passage	Paraphrase Based on Nestle-Aland 28	+50 Parallel Bible Versions
	more exalted than any other name. 10 And at the mention of Jesus' name, every knee in heaven, on earth, and in the underworld shall bend, 11 and everyone will concede that Jesus Christ is Lord, to the glory of God the Father."	
Colossians 1:12-22	Giving thanks to the Father, the one who certified us to share the inheritance in the light of Christ's true followers. 13 He has rescued us from the subjugation of darkness and resettled us to the kingdom of his beloved Son, 14 in whom we have been redeemed and had our sins forgiven. 15 He is the image of the God who's never been seen, and existed before the universe was created. 16 He created the universe. Everything in heaven and earth, everything we see and haven't seen, including thrones, powers, rulers, or authorities; he created them all and they are for him. 17 He existed before the universe and causes it to hold together. 18 And he is the head of the body, which is the church. He is the beginning and the firstborn from the dead so that he might have supremacy over the universe. 19 God was pleased that all of his fulness dwelt in Jesus. 20 And through Jesus, God reconciled the universe to himself, whether things on earth or in the heavens—by making peace through Jesus' blood on the cross.	https://www.biblegateway.com/verse/en/Colossians%201:12 https://www.biblegateway.com/verse/en/Colossians%201:13 https://www.biblegateway.com/verse/en/Colossians%201:14 https://www.biblegateway.com/verse/en/Colossians%201:15 https://www.biblegateway.com/verse/en/Colossians%201:16 https://www.biblegateway.com/verse/en/Colossians%201:17 https://www.biblegateway.com/verse/en/Colossians%201:18 https://www.biblegateway.com/verse/en/Colossians%201:19 https://www.biblegateway.com/verse/en/Colossians%201:20 https://www.biblegateway.com/verse/en/Colossians%201:21 https://www.biblegateway.com/verse/en/Colossians%201:22

JESUS IS GOD

Passage	Paraphrase Based on Nestle-Aland 28	+50 Parallel Bible Versions
	21 You were once alienated from God, with a hostile mind because of your evil actions, 22 but now, Jesus has reconciled you in his flesh through his death, to present you to God, holy, unblemished, and beyond reproach.	
Hebrews 1:2-3	And now, God has spoken to us through his Son in these last days. God has given the universe to him as an inheritance, and created it through him. 3 The Son radiates God's glory and is the exact copy of the very essence of God. He sustains the universe by the power of his word. After he had cleansed us from our sins; he sat down at the right-hand side of the majestic God in heaven!	https://www.biblegateway.com/verse/en/Hebrews%201:2
		https://www.biblegateway.com/verse/en/Hebrews%201:3
Hebrews 2:14-18	Since God's children are humans with flesh and blood, he too shared in that same nature so that by his death, he may annul the devil, who holds the power of death, 15 and liberate those who were in slavery and terrified of death. 16 He did not come to help the angels; he came to help Abraham's descendants. 17 This is why he needed to fully have the same human nature as his siblings, so that he may be a merciful and empathetic high priest before God, and offer an authentic sacrifice for the sins of mankind. 18 Because he knows what it's like to suffer when	https://www.biblegateway.com/verse/en/Hebrews%202:14
		https://www.biblegateway.com/verse/en/Hebrews%202:15
		https://www.biblegateway.com/verse/en/Hebrews%202:16
		https://www.biblegateway.com/verse/en/Hebrews%202:17
		https://www.biblegateway.com/verse/en/Hebrews%202:18

Passage	Paraphrase Based on Nestle-Aland 28	+50 Parallel Bible Versions
	tempted; he is able to help those who are being tempted.	
2 Corinthians 8:9	You know the grace of our Lord Jesus Christ: though he were rich, he became poor for your sakes so that through his poverty, you may become rich.	https://www.biblegateway.com/verse/en/2Corinthians%208:9
John 17:5,22,24	Now Father, please give me back the glory that I shared with you before the world's creation ... 22 I gave them the glory you gave me so that they may be one just as we are one ... 24 Father, I want those you gave me to be with me where I am. I want them to see the glory you gave me because you already loved me before the world was even created.	https://www.biblegateway.com/verse/en/John%2017:5 https://www.biblegateway.com/verse/en/John%2017:22 https://www.biblegateway.com/verse/en/John%2017:24
1 Corinthians 8:6	To us, there's only one God, the Father, the originator of the universe and for whom we live; and there's one Lord Jesus Christ, the Creator of the universe and Creator of mankind.	https://www.biblegateway.com/verse/en/1corinthians%208:6
John 1:18	No one has ever seen God; he has been revealed by the only God who is at the Father's side.	https://www.biblegateway.com/verse/en/john%201:18
John 20:28	Thomas exclaimed to him, "My Lord and my God!"	https://www.biblegateway.com/verse/en/john%2020:28
Acts 20:28	Guard yourselves and the flock that the Holy Spirit entrusted to you. Feed the church of God, which he paid for with his own blood.	https://www.biblegateway.com/verse/en/acts%2020:28
Romans 9:5	Theirs are the patriarchs (Abraham, Isaac, and Jacob) and of whose lineage Christ became flesh. Christ, who is God and rules over the universe, is blessed forever. Amen.	https://www.biblegateway.com/verse/en/romans%209:5

JESUS IS GOD

Passage	Paraphrase Based on Nestle-Aland 28	+50 Parallel Bible Versions
2 Thessalonians 1:12	So that the name of our Lord Jesus may be glorified in you and you in him, according to the grace of our God and Lord Jesus Christ.	https://www.biblegateway.com/verse/en/2thessalonians%201:12
Titus 2:13	Looking for the blessed hope and manifestation of the glory of the great God and Savior Jesus Christ.	https://www.biblegateway.com/verse/en/titus%202:13
2 Peter 1:1	Simon Peter, a servant and apostle of Jesus Christ, writing to those who share the same precious faith through the righteousness of Jesus Christ, our God and Savior.	https://www.biblegateway.com/verse/en/2peter%201:1
1 Jn 5:20	We know the Son of God came and gave us understanding so that we may know him who is true. We are in him who is true—in his Son, Jesus Christ. He is the true God and is life eternal.	https://www.biblegateway.com/verse/en/1john%205:20
Revelation 22:6,16	And he said unto me, "Everything you've heard is reliable and true. The Lord God of the prophets sent his angel to show his servants the things that are about to occur." . . . 16 I, Jesus, have sent my angel to witness to you of these things for the churches. I am the root and descendant of David, the bright morning star.	https://www.biblegateway.com/verse/en/revelation%2022:6 https://www.biblegateway.com/verse/en/revelation%2022:16
Isaiah 9:6	For a child will be born to us—a son will be given. He will rule the government and will be called the Wonderful Counselor, the Mighty God, the Father of Eternity, and the Prince of Peace!	https://www.biblegateway.com/verse/en/isaiah%209:6
Micah 5:2	But you, Bethlehem Ephratah, even though you are tiny among the people of Judah, out of you shall come the one who is destined to	https://www.biblegateway.com/verse/en/micah%205:2

JESUS IS GOD		
Passage	Paraphrase Based on Nestle-Aland 28	+50 Parallel Bible Versions
	rule over Israel – and whose origins are from the beginning, from the days of eternity.	

> "For behold, the time cometh, and is not far distant, that with power, the Lord Omnipotent who reigneth, who was, and is from all eternity to all eternity, shall come down from heaven among the children of men, and shall dwell in a tabernacle of clay, and shall go forth amongst men, working mighty miracles, such as healing the sick, raising the dead, causing the lame to walk, the blind to receive their sight, and the deaf to hear, and curing all manner of diseases. 6 And he shall cast out devils, or the evil spirits which dwell in the hearts of the children of men. 7 And lo, he shall suffer temptations, and pain of body, hunger, thirst, and fatigue, even more than man can suffer, except it be unto death; for behold, blood cometh from every pore, so great shall be his anguish for the wickedness and the abominations of his people.
>
> 8 And he shall be called Jesus Christ, the Son of God, the Father of heaven and earth, the Creator of all things from the beginning; and his mother shall be called Mary." (Book of Mormon: Mosiah 3:5-8)

c) He possessed glory

Jesus was honored as the Son of God and as one who is "God" by nature before this universe came into existence. He gave up that glory and honor when he decided to become a lowly human.

> "Now Father, please give me back the glory that I shared with you before the world's creation. . . 22 I gave them the glory you gave me so that they may be one just as we are one. . . 24 Father, I want those you gave me to be with me where I am. I want them to see the glory you gave me because you already loved me before the world was even created." (Holy Bible: John 17:5,22,24)

> "Yea, thus saith the Spirit: Repent, all ye ends of the earth, for the kingdom of heaven is soon at hand; yea, the Son of God cometh in his glory, in his might, majesty, power, and dominion. Yea, my beloved brethren, I say unto you, that the Spirit saith: Behold the glory of the King of all the earth; and also the King of heaven shall very soon shine forth among all the children of men." (Book of Mormon: Alma 5:50)

d) He was foreordained to be the sinless substitute

Jesus was foreordained to perform the Atonement – the annulment of the Fall before this Earth was even made. This means if he was foreordained to atone, then Adam had to be foreordained to Fall for the Atonement to make sense. Thus, Adam's Fall (the introduction of death, sin, moral weakness, and trials) wasn't a cosmic accident that an all-knowing God didn't anticipate. The Fall, although planned, had to be <u>freely</u> done by man for the Atonement to be valid.

> "So that the times of refreshment will come from the presence of the Lord, and he shall send Jesus Christ, who was foreordained for you." (Holy Bible: Acts 3:20)

> "Who was chosen before the world was created, and for your sakes, was revealed to you in these last days." (Holy Bible: 1 Peter 1:20)

> "Behold, I am he who was prepared from the foundation of the world to redeem my people. Behold, I am Jesus Christ. I am the Father[1] and the Son. In me shall all mankind have life, and that eternally, even they who shall believe on my name; and they shall become my sons and my daughters." (Book of Mormon: Ether 3:14)

e) He came from heaven

The pre-mortal Jesus lived in heaven before he was born on this earth and returned to it after his resurrection. This "heaven" already existed before this universe was made, which means it's a realm that exists external to this universe (either another universe or something else we can't even conceive).

> "For the bread of God is the bread who comes down from heaven and gives life to the world. . . 38 God sent me down from heaven to do what he wants, not what I want." (Holy Bible: John 6:33,38)

---

[1] The Book of Mormon calls Jesus the "Father" as well as the "Son" but this does not mean he was whom we consider to be "Heavenly Father" or the Father of Jesus. Jesus is our Father in three senses:

1. He created the universe, so is the Father of creation.
2. He adopts us at our conversion, so is our adopted Father.
3. He is the Father of our salvation.

> "Now the Lord had shown unto me, Abraham, the intelligences that were organized before the world was; and among all these there were many of the noble and great ones; 23 And God saw these souls that they were good, and he stood in the midst of them, and he said: These I will make my rulers; for he stood among those that were spirits, and he saw that they were good; and he said unto me: Abraham, thou art one of them; thou wast chosen before thou wast born.
>
> 24 And there stood one among them that was like unto God, and he said unto those who were with him: We will go down, for there is space there, and we will take of these materials, and we will make an earth whereon these may dwell; 25 And we will prove them herewith, to see if they will do all things whatsoever the Lord their God shall command them; 26 And they who keep their first estate shall be added upon; and they who keep not their first estate shall not have glory in the same kingdom with those who keep their first estate; and they who keep their second estate shall have glory added upon their heads for ever and ever.
>
> 27 And the Lord said: Whom shall I send? And one answered like unto the Son of Man: Here am I, send me. And another answered and said: Here am I, send me. And the Lord said: I will send the first." (Pearl of Great Price: Abraham 3:22-27)

f) He came from the Father

The pre-mortal Jesus came from the Father (who dwells in "heaven") when he became human. Jesus wasn't a thought but had a real existence as the only "Son of God" who was also "God" by nature prior to becoming human.

> "Jesus then told them, 'I'm only going to be with you for a little while longer and then I'm going to the one who sent me to earth. 34 You will look for me but will not find me, and cannot go to where I'm going.' " (Holy Bible: John 7:33-34)

> "Jesus said to them, 'If God were your Father, you would love me because I came from God. I am not here on my own accord—he sent me.' " (Holy Bible: John 8:42)

> "Behold I have given unto you my gospel, and this is the gospel which I have given unto you—that I came into the world to do the will of my Father, because my Father sent me.
>
> 14 And my Father sent me that I might be lifted up upon the cross; and after that I had been lifted up upon the cross, that I might draw all men unto me, that as I have been lifted up by men even so should men be lifted up by the Father, to stand before

me, to be judged of their works, whether they be good or whether they be evil." (Book of Mormon: 3 Nephi 27:13-14)

g) He was the Old Testament God[1]

The dominant figure of the Old Testament was the Hebrew God, YHWH (pronounced "Jehovah" or "Yahweh"). The dominant figure of the New Testament was Jesus Christ.

Jesus was frequently identified as the "Son of God" which was understood by his contemporary Jews to mean he was the "Son of Jehovah" since they viewed "God" to be "Jehovah." To this day, many think that the Bible describes Jesus to be the Son of the Old Testament God, Jehovah.

But there's a problem with this understanding because the New Testament writers repeatedly and consistently referred to Jesus using words and descriptions that were solely used to refer to Jehovah in the Hebrew Scriptures instead of using language that treated him as the Son of Jehovah.

This is not just a few instances where one can dismiss as coincidence. Eight of the nine New Testament writers (James excepted) did this around 90 times paralleling 80 Old Testament locations.

The word selection was intentional – they were alluding to Jesus being Jehovah without saying "Jesus is Jehovah" explicitly.

Why didn't they just say it out loud? Because if they did so, Christianity could've never been established due to the cultural practice of the Jews of that era. They violently reacted to anything that they perceived demeaned Jehovah such as by uttering his name or bringing down his glory to the human level. It would've been impossible for Jesus to get any followers (who were all Jews) and he would've been killed a lot sooner. His self-reference as the "I AM" (John 8:58-59) was sufficient for the Jews to try to kill him, how much more if he blatantly went around saying he was Jehovah made flesh?

---

[1] This subsection is copied from this author's *The God Who Washes Feet*, Chapter 7, Re: Section 1:10 Jesus Was Implied to be the Old Testament God (YHWH or Jehovah).

Given the first century milieu, it is a miracle that the New Testament contains the passages it does concerning the deity of Jesus Christ.

Nontrinitarians may not like it, but the parallels are clear and indisputable:

Summary Table: Jesus is Jehovah

\multicolumn{3}{c}{JESUS IS JEHOVAH}
Description	Old Testament (Jehovah)	New Testament (Jesus Christ)
1. I AM	Ex 3:14; Deut 32:39; Isa 41:4; Isa 43:10; Isa 46:4	John 8:58; John 8:24, 28; John 13:19; John 18:5-8
2. SAVIOR	Hos 13:4; Isa 43:11	Luke 2:11; Acts 4:10-12; 1 Jn 4:14-15
3. REDEEMER	Isa 43:14; Isa 44:24; Isa 49:26; Isa 54:5	Gal 3:13; Eph 1:7; Col 1:13-14; Tit 2:13-14
4. PIERCED	Zech 12:10	John 19:34-37; Rev 1:7
5. FIRST/LAST	Isa 44:6; Isa 48:12	Rev 1:8,17-18; Rev 22:12-16
6. CREATOR	Gen 2:4; Job 38:1-4; Ps 8:1-3; Ps 102:25; Isa 44:24; Isa 45:11-12; Isa 66:2	John 1:1,3,10,14; Col 1:13-17; Heb 1:10
7. HUSBAND / GROOM	Isa 54:5; Isa 62:5; Jer 3:1-2; Hos 2:16	Luke 5:34-35; Rev 19:7-8; Rev 21:9
8. SENDS PROPHETS	2 Kg 17:13; 2 Chr 36:15-16	Matt 23:34
9. SAVES FROM DEATH	Hos 13:14	1 Cor 15:20-22
10. JUDGE	1 Chr 16:33; Ps 9:7; Ps 50:6; Ps 96:13	Matt 16:27; John 5:22; 2 Cor 5:10
11. SHEPHERD	Ps 23:1; Ezek 34:11-16	John 10:14-16; 1 Pet 2:25; 1 Pet 5:4
12. LORD OF LORDS	Deut 10:17; Ps 136:3	1 Tim 6:14-15; Rev 17:14; Rev 19:13-16
13. EVERY KNEE SHALL BOW UNTO HIM	Isa 45:23	Phil 2:10-11
14. SEEN BY ISAIAH	Isa 6:1-10	John 12:39-41; John 1:18
15. PRECEDED BY VOICE IN THE DESERT	Isa 40:3-9; Mal 3:1	Matt 3:3,11-12; Matt 11:10; Luke 1:76; Luke 3:4-6; Luke 7:27; John 1:6-8,15-36
16. CALL UPON HIS NAME	Ps 99:6; Ps 116:13,17; Isa 12:4; Joel 2:32; Zeph 3:9; Zech 13:8-9	Acts 7:59; Acts 9:5,13-14,17,21; Rom 10:9,13; 1 Cor 1:2; Rev 22:20

STANZA CLARIFICATIONS

Description	Old Testament (Jehovah)	New Testament (Jesus Christ)
17. ROCK	Ex 13:21-22; Deut 32:3-4; Ps 62:6-7; Ps 118:22; Isa 8:13-14	Acts 4:10-12; Rom 9:33; 1 Cor 10:1-4; 1 Pet 2:4-8
18. HOLY ONE	Isa 43:14-15; Hos 11:9; Hab 1:12	Mark 1:24; Acts 3:14; 1 Jn 2:20
19. OUR RIGHTEOUSNESS	Jer 23:5-6	1 Cor 1:30
20. GATHERS LIKE A HEN GATHERS HER CHICKS	Ps 31:20; Ps 32:7; Ps 57:1; Ps 91:1-10; Isa 31:5	Matt 23:37-38; Luke 13:34-35
21. HIS BREATH SLAYS THE WICKED	Job 4:9; Isa 11:4	2 Thes 2:8
22. WILL RETURN WITH HIS HOLY ONES	Zech 14:5; Deut 33:2	Jude 1:14; 1 Tim 6:14; 2 Tim 4:1; Tit 2:13; 1 Thes 3:13
23. PRESERVES ALL THINGS	Neh 9:6; Ps 148:5-6	Col 1:17; Heb 1:3
24. GONE UP/COME DOWN WITH A SHOUT, WITH TRUMPETS BLARING	Ps 47:5	1 Thes 4:16
25. THOU SHALT NOT TEMPT THE LORD THY GOD	Deut 6:16	Matt 4:7; 1 Cor 10:9
26. WALKS ON THE SEA	Job 9:8	Matt 14:25-33; Mark 6:48-51; John 6:19-21
27. CALMS WIND AND WAVES	Ps 65:5-8	Matt 8:23-27
28. DAY OF THE LORD	Isa 2:12; Jer 46:10; Ezek 30:3; Joel 1:15; Obad 1:15; Zeph 1:7,14; Mal 4:5	Acts 2:20; 1 Cor 1:7-8; 1 Cor 5:5; 2 Cor 1:14; 1 Thes 5:2; 2 Pet 3:10
29. HIS THRONE IS FOREVER	Ps 45:6-7	Heb 1:8-9
30. LAID EARTH'S FOUNDATION	Ps 102:24-27	Heb 1:10-12
31. RECEIVES OUR SPIRITS	Ps 31:5	Acts 7:59
32. ANGELS WORSHIP HIM	Deut 32:43 LXX; Ps 97:7 LXX	Heb 1:6

"And the God of our fathers, who were led out of Egypt, out of bondage, and also were preserved in the wilderness by him, yea, the God of Abraham, and of Isaac, and the God of Jacob,

> yieldeth himself, according to the words of the angel, as a man, into the hands of wicked men, to be lifted up, according to the words of Zenock, and to be crucified, according to the words of Neum, and to be buried in a sepulchre, according to the words of Zenos, which he spake concerning the three days of darkness, which should be a sign given of his death unto those who should inhabit the isles of the sea, more especially given unto those who are of the house of Israel." (Book of Mormon: 1 Nephi 19:10)
>
> "Nevertheless, the Lord has shown unto me that they should return again. And he also has shown unto me that the Lord God, the Holy One of Israel, should manifest himself unto them in the flesh; and after he should manifest himself they should scourge him and crucify him, according to the words of the angel who spake it unto me." (Book of Mormon: 2 Nephi 6:9)
>
> "And now it came to pass that when Jesus had ended these sayings he cast his eyes round about on the multitude, and said unto them: Behold, ye have heard the things which I taught before I ascended to my Father; therefore, whoso remembereth these sayings of mine and doeth them, him will I raise up at the last day.
>
> 2 And it came to pass that when Jesus had said these words he perceived that there were some among them who marveled, and wondered what he would concerning the law of Moses; for they understood not the saying that old things had passed away, and that all things had become new. 3 And he said unto them: Marvel not that I said unto you that old things had passed away, and that all things had become new. 4 Behold, I say unto you that the law is fulfilled that was given unto Moses.
>
> 5 Behold, I am he that gave the law, and I am he who covenanted with my people Israel; therefore, the law in me is fulfilled, for I have come to fulfil the law; therefore it hath an end." (Book of Mormon: 3 Nephi 15:1-5)

There's no doubt that the Old Testament Jehovah and the New Testament Jesus are the same person.

> If Jesus never told us about the Father, then the New Testament would've been describing Jesus as Jehovah becoming human flesh instead of God becoming flesh.

h) He is God's Only Begotten Son

Jesus is frequently described as God's "Only Begotten Son," which is not just a depiction of him being the "Son of God" but encompasses a special relationship between Father and Son that does not exist between the Father and any other entity.

> *"God loved mankind so much, that he gave up his only Son, so that whoever believes in him shall not perish but have eternal life." (Holy Bible: John 3:16)*

> *"God showed his love towards us by sending his only Son into the world so that we might live through him. 10 This is real love: Not that we loved God, but because he loved us—and sent his Son to be the substituting sacrifice for our sins!" (Holy Bible: 1 John 4:9-10)*

> *"God did what the Law of Moses was incapable of doing due to the weakness of flesh: God condemned sin in the flesh by sending his own Son to become flesh. . . 32 Since God didn't spare his own Son but gave him up for our sakes; there is then nothing that he wouldn't also give us." (Holy Bible: Romans 8:3,32)*

> *"And now it came to pass that there were a great multitude gathered together, of the people of Nephi, round about the temple which was in the land Bountiful; and they were marveling and wondering one with another, and were showing one to another the great and marvelous change which had taken place. 2 And they were also conversing about this Jesus Christ, of whom the sign had been given concerning his death.*

> *3 And it came to pass that while they were thus conversing one with another, they heard a voice as if it came out of heaven; and they cast their eyes round about, for they understood not the voice which they heard; and it was not a harsh voice, neither was it a loud voice; nevertheless, and notwithstanding it being a small voice it did pierce them that did hear to the center, insomuch that there was no part of their frame that it did not cause to quake; yea, it did pierce them to the very soul, and did cause their hearts to burn. 4 And it came to pass that again they heard the voice, and they understood it not. 5 And again the third time they did hear the voice, and did open their ears to hear it; and their eyes were towards the sound thereof; and they did look steadfastly towards heaven, from whence the sound came. 6 And behold, the third time they did understand the voice which they heard; and it said unto them:*

> *7 Behold my Beloved Son, in whom I am well pleased, in whom I have glorified my name—hear ye him.*

> *8 And it came to pass, as they understood they cast their eyes up again towards heaven; and behold, they saw a Man*

descending out of heaven; and he was clothed in a white robe; and he came down and stood in the midst of them; and the eyes of the whole multitude were turned upon him, and they durst not open their mouths, even one to another, and wist not what it meant, for they thought it was an angel that had appeared unto them.

9 And it came to pass that he stretched forth his hand and spake unto the people, saying: 10 Behold, <u>I am Jesus Christ</u>, whom the prophets testified shall come into the world. 11 And behold, I am the light and the life of the world; and I have drunk out of that bitter cup which the Father hath given me, and have glorified the Father in taking upon me the sins of the world, in the which I have suffered the will of the Father in all things from the beginning.

12 And it came to pass that when Jesus had spoken these words the whole multitude fell to the earth; for they remembered that it had been prophesied among them that Christ should show himself unto them after his ascension into heaven.

13 And it came to pass that the Lord spake unto them saying: 14 Arise and come forth unto me, that ye may thrust your hands into my side, and also that ye may feel the prints of the nails in my hands and in my feet, that ye may know that <u>I am the God of Israel, and the God of the whole earth, and have been slain for the sins of the world</u>.

15 And it came to pass that the multitude went forth, and thrust their hands into his side, and did feel the prints of the nails in his hands and in his feet; and this they did do, going forth one by one until they had all gone forth, and did see with their eyes and did feel with their hands, and did know of a surety and did bear record, that it was he, of whom it was written by the prophets, that should come. 16 And when they had all gone forth and had witnessed for themselves, they did cry out with one accord, saying: 17 <u>Hosanna! Blessed be the name of the Most High God! And they did fall down at the feet of Jesus, and did worship him</u>."
(Book of Mormon: 3 Nephi 11:1-17)

"It no sooner appeared than I found myself delivered from the enemy which held me bound. When the light rested upon me I saw two Personages, whose brightness and glory defy all description, standing above me in the air. One of them spake unto me, calling me by name and said, pointing to the other— *This is My Beloved Son. Hear Him!*" (Joseph Smith History 1:17)

Clarification of the "2. Jesus Mutually Indwells With the Father" Stanzas

a) The Father, Son, and Holy Spirit share a common space

Jesus repeatedly claimed he dwelt in the Father and his Father dwelt in him. At the same time, his words and actions showed they were not the same entity but were distinct from one another and had their own personalities.

> "But if I do the work, even though you don't believe me, at least believe the works, so that you will know that the Father is in me, and I am in him." (Holy Bible: John 10:38)

> "Don't you believe that I am in the Father, and the Father is in me? The words I say are not from me but from the Father who dwells in me. 11 Believe me when I say I am in the Father and the Father is in me or at least believe because of the work that I do... 20 On that day, you will understand that I am in my Father, and you are in me, and I am in you." (Holy Bible: John 14:10-11,20)

> "That they may be one just as you are in me and I in you. May they be in us, so that the world may believe that you sent me... 23 I in them and you in me, so that they may become perfectly united. The world will then know that you sent me and loved them just as you loved me." (Holy Bible: John 17:21,23)

> "Behold, I am Jesus Christ the Son of God. I created the heavens and the earth, and all things that in them are. I was with the Father from the beginning. I am in the Father, and the Father in me; and in me hath the Father glorified his name." (Book of Mormon: 3 Nephi 9:15)

> "And after this manner shall ye baptize in my name; for behold, verily I say unto you, that the Father, and the Son, and the Holy Ghost are one; and I am in the Father, and the Father in me, and the Father and I are one." (Book of Mormon: 3 Nephi 11:27)

> "And now Father, I pray unto thee for them, and also for all those who shall believe on their words, that they may believe in me, that I may be in them as thou, Father, art in me, that we may be one... 29 Father, I pray not for the world, but for those whom thou hast given me out of the world, because of their faith, that they may be purified in me, that I may be in them as thou, Father, art in me, that we may be one, that I may be glorified in them." (Book of Mormon: 3 Nephi 19:23,29)

> "And the Father and I are one. I am in the Father and the Father in me; and inasmuch as ye have received me, ye are in me and I in you." (Doctrine and Covenants: Section 50:43)

> "And that I am in the Father, and the Father in me, and the Father and I are one—4 The Father because he gave me of his fulness, and the Son because I was in the world and made flesh my tabernacle, and dwelt among the sons of men. . . 17 And he received all power, both in heaven and on earth, and the glory of the Father was with him, for he dwelt in him. . . 20 For if you keep my commandments you shall receive of his fulness, and be glorified in me as I am in the Father; therefore, I say unto you, you shall receive grace for grace." (Doctrine and Covenants: Section 93:3-4,17,20)

The Son is not Heavenly Father, and neither is the Father the Son, but somehow, through a process we do not understand, these beings who simultaneously straddle this universe and an external realm are, from our perspective, literally within each other's three-dimensional[1] space. This explains Jesus Christ's anguish when the Father withdrew from him when he was hanging on the cross ("*My God, my God, why have you forsaken me?*" [Mark 15:34]), when the Father withdrew from that indwelling so that Jesus could complete his sacrifice by himself.

However, the Holy Bible, Book of Mormon, and Doctrine and Covenants only describe the mutual indwelling—<u>they do *not* say if this state is the default natural state of God or if it's done by mutual consent</u>.

The fourth-century developers of the Trinity believed the mutual indwelling was innate. However, many thinkers familiar with modern scientific thought consider it more likely to be a function of divine will (i.e., "The Father and Son literally occupy the same three-dimensional space *if they want* just as the glorified Jesus can be in multiple places at the same time *if he wants*"). This latter position assumes ontological separation is the natural state of the Father, Son, and Holy Spirit, to preserve the individuality of each person and to stay true to the natural reading of numerous biblical passages (such as when Stephen saw Jesus standing *beside* God the Father just before he was martyred [Acts 7:55-56]).

---

[1] For lack of a better description.

b) He is in the image of God

Whatever the Father is, the Son is the exact duplicate. Whatever makes God "God" makes the Son "God" as well.

> "In the beginning was the Word; the Word existed with God; and was God." (Holy Bible: John 1:1)

> "He is the image of the God who's never been seen and existed before the universe was created." (Holy Bible: Colossians 1:15)

> "And now, God has spoken to us through his Son in these last days. God has given the universe to him as an inheritance, and created it through him. 3 The Son radiates God's glory and is the exact copy of the very essence of God. He sustains the universe by the power of his word. After he had purified sins; he sat down at the right-hand side of the majestic God in heaven!" (Holy Bible: Hebrews 1:2-3)

> "And there stood one among them that was like unto God, and he said unto those who were with him: We will go down, for there is space there, and we will take of these materials, and we will make an earth whereon these may dwell." (Pearl of Great Price: Abraham 3:24)

c) He is in the Father; the Father is in him

Jesus said:

> "Don't you believe that I am in the Father, and the Father is in me? The words I say are not from me but from the Father who dwells in me. 11 Believe me when I say I am in the Father and the Father is in me or at least believe because of the work that I do. . . 20 On that day, you will understand that I am in my Father, and you are in me, and I am in you." (Holy Bible: John 14:10-11,20)

> "And now Father, I pray unto thee for them, and also for all those who shall believe on their words, that they may believe in me, that I may be in them as thou, Father, art in me, that we may be one. . . 29 Father, I pray not for the world, but for those whom thou hast given me out of the world, because of their faith, that they may be purified in me, that I may be in them as thou, Father, art in me, that we may be one, that I may be glorified in them." (Book of Mormon: 3 Nephi 19:23,29)

> "And that I am in the Father, and the Father in me, and the Father and I are one." (Doctrine and Covenants: Section 93:3)

Interestingly, Jesus described this mutual indwelling as being extended to those who are his true followers.

d) He is one with the Father

Jesus said:

> *"Holy Father, I'm about to leave this world and go to you, but they are staying in this world. Protect them by the power of your name so that they may be one as we are one. . . 21 That they may be one just as you are in me and I in you. May they be one in us so that the world may believe that you sent me. 22 I gave them the glory you gave me so that they may be one just as we are one. 23 I in them and you in me, so that they may become perfectly united. The world will then know that you sent me and loved them just as you loved me." (Holy Bible: John 17:11,21-23)*

> *"And after this manner shall ye baptize in my name; for behold, verily I say unto you, that the Father, and the Son, and the Holy Ghost are one; and I am in the Father, and the Father in me, and the Father and I are one." (Book of Mormon: 3 Nephi 11:27)*

Just as with mutual indwelling, the oneness the Son enjoys with the Father is extended to his true followers.

e) The Father is glorified in Jesus

Jesus said:

> *"The time has come for the Son of Man to be glorified, and God is glorified in him. 32 [If God is glorified in him,] God will glorify the Son of Man within himself, and shall immediately glorify him." (Holy Bible: John 13:31-32)*

> *"Behold, I am Jesus Christ the Son of God. I created the heavens and the earth, and all things that in them are. I was with the Father from the beginning. I am in the Father, and the Father in me; and in me hath the Father glorified his name." (Book of Mormon: 3 Nephi 9:15)*

f) He is equal to the Father

Jesus is equal to the Father in several ways:

(i) By nature

> *"But Jesus answered, 'My Father is constantly working and so am I.' 18 When they heard this, the Jews sought all the more to have him killed because not only did he break the Sabbath by*

working, he called God his Father, making himself equal with God." (Holy Bible: John 5:17-18)

"The Son radiates God's glory and is the exact copy of the very essence of God. He sustains the universe by the power of his word. After he had purified sins; he sat down at the right-hand side of the majestic God in heaven!" (Holy Bible: Hebrews 1:3)

"And for this cause ye shall have fulness of joy; and ye shall sit down in the kingdom of my Father; yea, your joy shall be full, even as the Father hath given me fulness of joy; and ye shall be even as I am, and I am even as the Father; and the Father and I are one;" (Book of Mormon: 3 Nephi 28:10)

"And there stood one among them that was like unto God, and he said unto those who were with him: We will go down, for there is space there, and we will take of these materials, and we will make an earth whereon these may dwell." (Pearl of Great Price: Abraham 3:24)

(ii) By Honor

"So that everyone may honor the Son just as they honor the Father. Whoever does not honor the Son is not honoring the one who sent him, the Father." (John 5:23)

(iii) Self-recognition (by the use of "*erotao*" instead of "*aiteo*")

"And I will _ask_ the Father to give you another Agent like myself, to be with you forever." (Holy Bible: John 14:16)

"In that day you will ask in my name. I do not speak of _asking_ the Father for you." (Holy Bible: John 16:26)

g) The fulness of God was within his body

All of God's "fulness" dwelt within Christ. This can be understood several ways, most notably, all that makes God "God" was in the physical body of Jesus, or the Father literally dwelt within the physical body of Jesus.

"God was pleased that all of his fulness dwelt in Jesus." (Holy Bible: Colossians 1:19)

"All of God's fulness dwells in the body of Jesus." (Holy Bible: Colossians 2:9)

"The Father because he gave me of his fulness, and the Son because I was in the world and made flesh my tabernacle, and dwelt among the sons of men. 5 I was in the world and received of my Father, and the works of him were plainly manifest. 6 And

> John saw and bore record of the fulness of my glory, and the fulness of John's record is hereafter to be revealed. . . 16 And I, John, bear record that he received a fulness of the glory of the Father." (Doctrine and Covenants: Section 93:4-6,16)

h) One sees the Father when looking at Jesus

Jesus said:

> "Anyone who has seen me has seen the Father. How then can you ask me to show him to you? 10 Don't you believe that I am in the Father, and the Father is in me? The words I say are not from me but from the Father who dwells in me. 11 Believe me when I say I am in the Father and the Father is in me or at least believe because of the work that I do." (Holy Bible: John 14:9-11)

Clarification of the "3. Jesus is the Creator" Stanzas

a) The Father created the universe through him

Heavenly Father ordered his Only Begotten Son, Jesus, to create this vast, inconceivably huge universe:

> "To us, there's only one God, the Father, the originator of the universe and for whom we live; and there's one Lord Jesus Christ, the Creator of the universe and Creator of mankind." (Holy Bible: 1 Corinthians 8:6)

> "And God spake unto Moses, saying: Behold, I am the Lord God Almighty, and Endless is my name; for I am without beginning of days or end of years; and is not this endless? 4 And, behold, thou art my son; wherefore look, and I will show thee the workmanship of mine hands; but not all, for my works are without end, and also my words, for they never cease.

> 5 Wherefore, no man can behold all my works, except he behold all my glory; and no man can behold all my glory, and afterwards remain in the flesh on the earth. 6 And I have a work for thee, Moses, my son; and thou art in the similitude of mine Only Begotten; and mine Only Begotten is and shall be the Savior, for he is full of grace and truth; but there is no God beside me, and all things are present with me, for I know them all. 7 And now, behold, this one thing I show unto thee, Moses, my son, for thou art in the world, and now I show it unto thee. 8 And it came to pass that Moses looked, and beheld the world upon which he was created; and Moses beheld the world and the ends thereof, and all the children of men which are, and which were created; of the same he greatly marveled and wondered. . .

> 27 And it came to pass, as the voice was still speaking, Moses cast his eyes and beheld the earth, yea, even all of it; and there was not a particle of it which he did not behold, discerning it by the Spirit of God. 28 And he beheld also the inhabitants thereof, and there was not a soul which he beheld not; and he discerned them by the Spirit of God; and their numbers were great, even numberless as the sand upon the sea shore. 29 And he beheld many lands; and each land was called earth, and there were inhabitants on the face thereof. 30 And it came to pass that Moses called upon God, saying: Tell me, I pray thee, why these things are so, and by what thou madest them? 31 And behold, the glory of the Lord was upon Moses, so that Moses stood in the presence of God, and talked with him face to face. And the Lord God said unto Moses: For mine own purpose have I made

these things. Here is wisdom and it remaineth in me. 32 And by the word of my power, have I created them, which is mine Only Begotten Son, who is full of grace and truth.

33 And worlds without number have I created; and I also created them for mine own purpose; and by the Son I created them, which is mine Only Begotten.

34 And the first man of all men have I called Adam, which is many. 35 But only an account of this earth, and the inhabitants thereof, give I unto you. For behold, there are many worlds that have passed away by the word of my power. And there are many that now stand, and innumerable are they unto man; but all things are numbered unto me, for they are mine and I know them.

36 And it came to pass that Moses spake unto the Lord, saying: Be merciful unto thy servant, O God, and tell me concerning this earth, and the inhabitants thereof, and also the heavens, and then thy servant will be content.

37 And the Lord God spake unto Moses, saying: The heavens, they are many, and they cannot be numbered unto man; but they are numbered unto me, for they are mine. 38 And as one earth shall pass away, and the heavens thereof even so shall another come; and there is no end to my works, neither to my words." (Pearl of Great Price: Moses 1:3-8,27-38)

b) He created the universe

Modern cosmology has allowed us to conceptualize just what the Bible means when it describes all reality as being created by Jesus Christ:

"He is the image of the God who's never been seen and existed before the universe was created. 16 He created the universe. Everything in heaven and earth, everything we see and cannot see, including thrones, powers, rulers, or authorities; he created them all, and they are for him." (Holy Bible: Colossians 1:15-16)

"Behold, I am Jesus Christ the Son of God. I created the heavens and the earth, and all things that in them are. I was with the Father from the beginning. I am in the Father, and the Father in me; and in me hath the Father glorified his name." (Book of Mormon: 3 Nephi 9:15)

"And he bore record, saying: I saw his glory, that he was in the beginning, before the world was; 8 Therefore, in the beginning the Word was, for he was the Word, even the messenger of salvation— 9 The light and the Redeemer of the world; the Spirit of truth, who came into the world, because the world was made by him, and in him was the life of men and the light of men.

10 The worlds were made by him; men were made by him; all things were made by him, and through him, and of him.

11 And I, John, bear record that I beheld his glory, as the glory of the Only Begotten of the Father, full of grace and truth, even the Spirit of truth, which came and dwelt in the flesh, and dwelt among us." (Doctrine and Covenants: Section 93:7-11)

c) Nothing exists that wasn't created by him

Jesus is described as follows:

> "He created the universe—nothing exists that wasn't created by him. . . 10 He went and lived on earth and even though he created it, the earth's inhabitants didn't know who he was. . . 14 The Word became flesh and lived among us. We have seen his glory—the glory of the only Son of the Father, full of grace and truth." (Holy Bible: John 1:3,10,14)

> "And he shall be called Jesus Christ, the Son of God, the Father of heaven and earth, the Creator of all things from the beginning; and his mother shall be called Mary." (Book of Mormon: Mosiah 3:8)

d) He sustains the universe

The Bible describes Jesus to be the active source of the universe's fundamental integrity:

> "He existed before the universe and causes it to hold together." (Holy Bible: Colossians 1:17)

> "He sustains the universe by the power of his word." (Holy Bible: Hebrews 1:3)

He is the reason why the universe appears "fine-tuned" for the emergence of the complex molecules called "life." This support is a <u>continuous</u> process, which implies his will or effort is the only thing keeping the universe's integrity together.

e) He created this earth

Jesus created this world:

> "He went and lived on earth and even though he created it, the earth's inhabitants didn't know who he was." (John 1:10)

> "Behold, I am Jesus Christ the Son of God. I created the heavens and the earth, and all things that in them are. I was with the

Father from the beginning. I am in the Father, and the Father in me; and in me hath the Father glorified his name." (Book of Mormon: 3 Nephi 9:15)

"Thus saith the Lord your God, even Jesus Christ, the Great I AM, Alpha and Omega, the beginning and the end, the same which looked upon the wide expanse of eternity, and all the seraphic hosts of heaven, before the world was made; 2 The same which knoweth all things, for all things are present before mine eyes; 3 I am the same which spake, and the world was made, and all things came by me." (Doctrine and Covenants: Section 38:1-3)

f) He created life

As the Creator of all things, Jesus created life—which explains how the incredibly complex living cells can arise out of simple molecules despite abiogenesis is an impossible process within the environment of the prebiotic Earth. A moving, growing watch that gives birth to other watches can never spontaneously arise out of a vat of simple molecules, regardless of the amount and duration of chemical reactions, since most complex molecules easily break apart at the slightest temperature or environmental change.

"Hearken, O ye people of my church, to whom the kingdom has been given; hearken ye and give ear to him who laid the foundation of the earth, who made the heavens and all the hosts thereof, and by whom all things were made which live, and move, and have a being. 2 And again I say, hearken unto my voice, lest death shall overtake you; in an hour when ye think not the summer shall be past, and the harvest ended, and your souls not saved. 3 Listen to him who is the advocate with the Father, who is pleading your cause before him— 4 Saying: Father, behold the sufferings and death of him who did no sin, in whom thou wast well pleased; behold the blood of thy Son which was shed, the blood of him whom thou gavest that thyself might be glorified." (Doctrine and Covenants: Section 45:1-4)

g) He created man

As the Creator of all things, Jesus created humanity:

"To us, there's only one God, the Father, the originator of the universe and for whom we live; and there's one Lord Jesus Christ, the Creator of the universe and Creator of mankind." (Holy Bible: 1 Corinthians 8:6)

"Behold, I am he who was prepared from the foundation of the world to redeem my people. Behold, I am Jesus Christ. I am the

Father and the Son. In me shall all mankind have life, and that eternally, even they who shall believe on my name; and they shall become my sons and my daughters. 15 And never have I showed myself unto man whom I have created, for never has man believed in me as thou hast. Seest thou that ye are created after mine own image? Yea, even all men were created in the beginning after mine own image. 16 Behold, this body, which ye now behold, is the body of my spirit; and man have I created after the body of my spirit; and even as I appear unto thee to be in the spirit will I appear unto my people in the flesh." (Book of Mormon: Ether 3:14-16)

h) We have free will

God does not manipulate us or force us to be good and obey his will. We have genuine freedom. Christ knocks on our door—and we can either let him in, ignore him, or tell him to go away.

"Now there was no law against a man's belief; for it was strictly contrary to the commands of God that there should be a law which should bring men on to unequal grounds. 8 For thus saith the scripture: Choose ye this day, whom ye will serve. 9 Now if a man desired to serve God, it was his privilege; or rather, if he believed in God it was his privilege to serve him; but if he did not believe in him there was no law to punish him. 10 But if he murdered he was punished unto death; and if he robbed he was also punished; and if he stole he was also punished; and if he committed adultery he was also punished; yea, for all this wickedness they were punished. 11 For there was a law that men should be judged according to their crimes. Nevertheless, there was no law against a man's belief; therefore, a man was punished only for the crimes which he had done; therefore all men were on equal grounds." (Book of Mormon: Alma 30:7-11)

Clarification of the "4. Jesus Became Human Flesh" Stanzas

a) He became flesh

This is such an important issue that it is crucial to provide some clarity on what "became flesh" means.

The Holy Bible never describes Jesus entering and leaving his human body as a possession. Rather, it repeatedly insists that Jesus *became* flesh, and everything that makes God "God" was in the physical body of Jesus Christ.

> *"<u>The Word became flesh</u> and lived among us. We have seen his glory—the glory of the only Son of the Father, full of grace and truth." (Holy Bible: John 1:14)*

> *"This is how you will know the Spirit of God: Every spirit that acknowledges <u>Jesus Christ came in the flesh</u> is of God! 3 Those who do not acknowledge Jesus are not from God. This is the spirit of the antichrist and is already in the world." (Holy Bible: 1 John 4:2-3)*

> *"There are many deceivers in the world who do not acknowledge <u>Jesus Christ came in the flesh</u>. These are deceivers and the antichrist." (Holy Bible: 2 John 1:7)*

> *"God did what the Law of Moses was incapable of doing due to the weakness of flesh: <u>God condemned sin in the flesh by sending his own Son to become flesh</u>." (Holy Bible: Romans 8:3)*

> *"God was pleased that <u>all of his fulness dwelt in Jesus</u>." (Holy Bible: Colossians 1:19)*

> *"<u>All of God's fulness dwells in the body of Jesus</u>." (Holy Bible: Colossians 2:9)*

> *"Nevertheless, the Lord has shown unto me that they should return again. And he also has shown unto me that <u>the Lord God, the Holy One of Israel, should manifest himself unto them in the flesh</u>; and after he should manifest himself they should scourge him and crucify him, according to the words of the angel who spake it unto me." (Book of Mormon: 2 Nephi 6:9)*

The Metamorphosis of Jesus

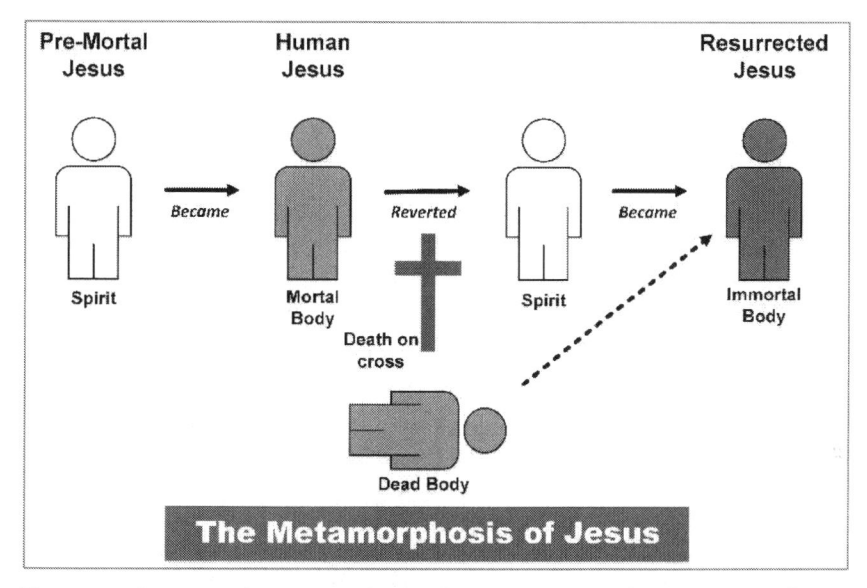

Pre-Mortal Jesus: Spirit — Became →
Human Jesus: Mortal Body — Reverted → (Death on cross, Dead Body)
Spirit — Became →
Resurrected Jesus: Immortal Body

By way of comparison, a tadpole does not enter the body of a frog. A caterpillar does not enter the body of a butterfly. Rather, a tadpole <u>becomes</u> the frog. The caterpillar <u>becomes</u> the butterfly. *The process is a transformation or metamorphosis.*

His spirit nature *transformed* into flesh instead of possessing a physical body. He reverted back to spirit form when he died, and then transformed once more into a glorified and immortal *physical* entity after his resurrection—one that could be physically felt, could eat and drink, and could be discerned and communicated with by other humans.

b) *He became flesh to become a real human*

Jesus was a spirit entity who became human flesh. It was not a possession like a hand possesses a glove, but a transformation. The glove doesn't share the same nature of the hand that possesses it. A human does not become a car whenever he or she is enclosed within it.

c) *He became human to relate to humanity*

Jesus becoming human flesh allowed him to fully share whatever we humans experience – our fear, pain, urges, and everything that makes us human – while at the same time, he kept himself free from sin. By human flesh, we sin and die; but by human flesh, we are made sinless and are resurrected.

> *"God condemned sin in the flesh by sending his own Son to become flesh." (Holy Bible: Romans 8:3)*
>
> *"Since death came because of a man; it is necessary for the resurrection of the dead to also come from a man." (Holy Bible: 1 Corinthians 15:21)*
>
> *"And he will take upon him death, that he may loose the bands of death which bind his people; and he will take upon him their infirmities, that his bowels may be filled with mercy, according to the flesh, that he may know according to the flesh how to succor his people according to their infirmities. 13 Now the Spirit knoweth all things; nevertheless the Son of God suffereth according to the flesh that he might take upon him the sins of his people, that he might blot out their transgressions according to the power of his deliverance; and now behold, this is the testimony which is in me." (Book of Mormon: Alma 7:12-13)*

d) He bridged the God and human natures

This transformation instead of possession is a tremendously important detail since it means Jesus merged or fused within himself the two ontologically separate natures of God and Man.

> *Christ becoming human flesh makes the Incarnation, Atonement, Resurrection, and transformation of the Children of God after Judgment Day real and valid.*

e) He humbled himself to become human

Jesus, the almighty Creator of the universe, is the ultimate example of humility:

> *"Be as humble as Jesus Christ:*
>
> *6 Despite having the same nature of God, he didn't think to forcefully cling to his equality with God, 7 but emptied himself of it, and took upon himself the nature of a slave and became human.*
>
> *8 As a mortal man, he humbled himself and was so obedient to the Father's will, that he stooped to die the utterly degrading death on the cross.*
>
> *9 This is why God elevated him higher than anything possible and made his name more exalted than any other name.*
>
> *10 And at the mention of Jesus' name, every knee in heaven, on earth, and in the underworld shall bend, 11 and everyone will concede that Jesus Christ is Lord, to the glory of God the Father." (Holy Bible: Philippians 2:5-11)*

> "Know ye not that he was holy? But notwithstanding he being holy, he showeth unto the children of men that, according to the flesh he humbleth himself before the Father, and witnesseth unto the Father that he would be obedient unto him in keeping his commandments." (Book of Mormon: 2 Nephi 31:7)
>
> "He that ascended up on high, as also he descended below all things, in that he comprehended all things, that he might be in all and through all things, the light of truth." (Doctrine and Covenants: Section 88:6)
>
> "The Son of Man hath descended below them all. Art thou greater than he?" (Doctrine and Covenants: Section 122:8)

f) He was tempted but never sinned

Jesus stayed sinless throughout his life while being subject to the same urges and temptations we experience as humans.

> "We do not have a high priest who is incapable of empathizing with our weaknesses. He understands—he was also tempted in the same manner we're tempted—only he didn't sin." (Holy Bible: Hebrews 4:15)

g) He can only have a single incarnation

Jesus Christ can only become a mortal human <u>once</u>. He will never again become mortal and again subject to sin and death. There is no divine Christ who entered and left the human Jesus. There is no such thing as the repetitive mortality of the divine Christ, who manifests himself in different humans throughout history.

The point of the **Incarnation** was for the divine and human to unite completely, to create a bridge and conjoining that never existed before. All that makes God "God" was in Jesus Christ's flesh.

The point of the **Atonement** was for the divine to annul the Fall (the introduction of sin, death, weakness, and trials to humanity) and allow some humans to become one with the divine. And this substitutionary sacrifice for sin was only going to occur one time:

> "It is God's will that we are purified and made spotless through the <u>one-time sacrifice</u> of the body of Jesus Christ.
>
> 11 Whereas every priest under the Law of Moses performed daily rituals and repeatedly offered the same sacrifices that could never remove sins; 12 but <u>Jesus offered one sacrifice for sins, once for all time</u>, and now sits at the right-hand side of God.

> *13 He is now just waiting for the appointed time when his enemies will be placed under his feet. 14 For <u>by one sacrifice, he has forever perfected those who are being purified and made spotless.</u>" (Holy Bible: Hebrews 10:10-14)*

The point of the **Resurrection** was to destroy death and allow all who've ever lived as humans to live again with immortal physical bodies.

What this means is, it is *impossible* for anyone to validly claim they are the returning Jesus or Christ if they have a mortal body that can die, get sick, or feel pain.

The returning Jesus or Christ will have a glorified immortal body that is incapable of feeling pain or getting killed. Punching him on the nose does nothing—he cannot feel pain, and no damage will ever occur. Stabbing him with a knife is like stabbing granite. Hitting him with a bat only breaks the bat and hurts your hand. Dunking his head under water will never cause him to drown. Poking him with a lit cigarette will never cause him to flinch or jump—and never burn his skin.

Also, the real returning Jesus or Christ will come back in a manner visible to all, descending from the sky, and accompanied by an enormous entourage—by his angels and his resurrected followers—after a global catastrophe.

> *Anyone who claims to be the returning Jesus or Christ should be willing to undergo simple tests to confirm he is who he claims to be. Bring a bat.*

h) He was recognized by demons

Recognition of who Jesus is isn't enough for salvation since even the demons recognized him:

> *"And demons also came out of many while shrieking: 'You are the Son of God!'" (Holy Bible: Luke 4:41)*

Clarification of the "5. The Atonement of Jesus" Stanzas

a) He suffered

Christ's Atonement entailed real pain and suffering:

> "Jesus said, 'Father, if you're willing, please take this cup away from me. Nonetheless, let your will be done, not mine.' 43 An angel then appeared from heaven and encouraged him to go through with it.
>
> 44 While being subjected to incomprehensible agony, he prayed to the Father even more fervently, and his sweat looked like blood and fell to the ground in clumps." (Holy Bible: Luke 22:42-44)

> "You were called for this purpose because Christ suffered for you. He is your example; follow his footsteps. 22 He never committed sin and never deceived anyone. 23 When they vilified him, he didn't retaliate; when he suffered, he didn't make threats. He just relied upon God who always judges justly. 24 He personally bore our sins in his body on the cross so that we would die to sin but then live for righteousness. You have been healed by his wounds!" (1 Peter 2:21-24)

> "For behold, I, God, have suffered these things for all, that they might not suffer if they would repent; 17 But if they would not repent they must suffer even as I; 18 Which suffering caused myself, even God, the greatest of all, to tremble because of pain, and to bleed at every pore, and to suffer both body and spirit— and would that I might not drink the bitter cup, and shrink—
>
> 19 Nevertheless, glory be to the Father, and I partook and finished my preparations unto the children of men. . . 24 I am Jesus Christ; I came by the will of the Father, and I do his will." (Doctrine and Covenants: Section 19:16-19,24)

b) He experienced an infinite Atonement

Every human who has ever and will ever live is covered by Christ's Atonement due to the infinite worth of Christ's blood as God incarnate:

> "Jesus was temporarily made lower than angels. He is now crowned with glory and honor because he subjected himself to death. By God's grace, <u>he died for everyone</u>! 10 It was appropriate that he who Inherits the universe and created it, and who brought many children to glory as the source of their

salvation, would become perfect through his suffering." (Holy Bible: Hebrews 2:9-10)

"They sought to know the time and circumstance the Spirit of Christ was alluding to, when he told them in advance that the Messiah was going to suffer, and his great glory afterward. . . 18 As you know, gold and silver were not used to pay your ransom from the futile life you received from your ancestors, 19 but with the <u>incalculably valuable</u> blood of Christ, the unblemished and spotless Lamb of God, 20 who was chosen before the world was created and recently was manifested to you." (Holy Bible: 1 Peter 1:11,18-20)

"And now, behold, I will testify unto you of myself that these things are true. Behold, I say unto you, that I do know that Christ shall come among the children of men, to take upon him the transgressions of his people, and that he shall atone for the sins of the world; for the Lord God hath spoken it. 9 For it is expedient that an atonement should be made; for according to the great plan of the Eternal God there must be an atonement made, or else all mankind must unavoidably perish; yea, all are hardened; yea, all are fallen and are lost, and must perish except it be through the atonement which it is expedient should be made. 10 For it is expedient that there should be a great and last sacrifice; yea, not a sacrifice of man, neither of beast, neither of any manner of fowl; for it shall not be a human sacrifice; but <u>it must be an infinite and eternal sacrifice.</u>

11 Now there is not any man that can sacrifice his own blood which will atone for the sins of another. Now, if a man murdereth, behold will our law, which is just, take the life of his brother? I say unto you, Nay. 12 But the law requireth the life of him who hath murdered; therefore <u>there can be nothing which is short of an infinite atonement which will suffice for the sins of the world</u>.

13 Therefore, it is expedient that there should be a great and last sacrifice, and then shall there be, or it is expedient there should be, a stop to the shedding of blood; then shall the law of Moses be fulfilled; yea, it shall be all fulfilled, every jot and tittle, and none shall have passed away. 14 And behold, this is the whole meaning of the law, every whit pointing to that great and last sacrifice; and that great and last sacrifice will be the Son of God, yea, infinite and eternal.

15 And thus he shall bring salvation to all those who shall believe on his name; this being the intent of this last sacrifice, to bring about the bowels of mercy, which overpowereth justice, and bringeth about means unto men that they may have faith unto

repentance. 16 And thus mercy can satisfy the demands of justice, and encircles them in the arms of safety, while he that exercises no faith unto repentance is exposed to the whole law of the demands of justice; therefore only unto him that has faith unto repentance is brought about the great and eternal plan of redemption." (Book of Mormon: Alma 34:8-16)

c) He was a sinless substitute

Jesus was our sinless substitute, who took upon himself the punishments for our sins:

"God showed his love towards us by sending his only Son into the world so that we might live through him. 10 This is real love: Not that we loved God, but because he loved us—and sent his Son to be the substituting sacrifice for our sins! . . . 14 And we have seen and testify that the Father sent his Son to be the Savior of mankind." (Holy Bible: 1 John 4:9-10,14)

"For it is I that taketh upon me the sins of the world; for it is I that hath created them; and it is I that granteth unto him that believeth unto the end a place at my right hand." (Book of Mormon: Mosiah 26:23)

d) He paid our ransom and freed us

Christ paid our ransom by substituting himself and setting us free from bondage:

"He gave himself as a ransom for all, and is witnessed to all the world at the right time." (Holy Bible: 1 Timothy 2:6)

"And now, because of the covenant which ye have made ye shall be called the children of Christ, his sons, and his daughters; for behold, this day he hath spiritually begotten you; for ye say that your hearts are changed through faith on his name; therefore, ye are born of him and have become his sons and his daughters. 8 And under this head ye are made free, and there is no other head whereby ye can be made free. There is no other name given whereby salvation cometh; therefore, I would that ye should take upon you the name of Christ, all you that have entered into the covenant with God that ye should be obedient unto the end of your lives. 9 And it shall come to pass that whosoever doeth this shall be found at the right hand of God, for he shall know the name by which he is called; for he shall be called by the name of Christ." (Book of Mormon: Mosiah 5:7-9)

e) He died for mankind

Christ died for all of mankind:

"For while we were powerless, Christ died at the appointed time for us sinners. 7 It is rare for someone to give up his life for a righteous person except, perhaps, for an especially good man. 8 But God proved his great love for us—although we were sinners, Christ died for us!" (Holy Bible: Romans 5:6-8)

"Behold, thus saith the Lord, even Alpha and Omega, the beginning and the end, even he who was crucified for the sins of the world." (Doctrine and Covenants: Section 54:1)

f) His sacrifice/blood reconciles us to God

Christ's sacrifice reconciles us to God:

"And through Jesus, God reconciled the universe to himself, whether things on earth or in the heavens—by making peace through Jesus' blood on the cross. 21 You were once alienated from God, with a hostile mind because of your evil actions. 22 But now, Jesus has reconciled you in his flesh through his death, to present you to God, holy, unblemished, and beyond reproach." (Holy Bible: Colossians 1:20-22)

"Behold, he created Adam, and by Adam came the fall of man. And because of the fall of man came Jesus Christ, even the Father and the Son; and because of Jesus Christ came the redemption of man. 13 And because of the redemption of man, which came by Jesus Christ, they are brought back into the presence of the Lord; yea, this is wherein all men are redeemed, because the death of Christ bringeth to pass the resurrection, which bringeth to pass a redemption from an endless sleep, from which sleep all men shall be awakened by the power of God when the trump shall sound; and they shall come forth, both small and great, and all shall stand before his bar, being redeemed and loosed from this eternal band of death, which death is a temporal death." (Book of Mormon: Mormon 9:12-13)

g) His blood forgives sins

Christ's blood forgives our sins:

"But if we walk in the light, as he is in the light, we participate with one another, and the blood of his Son, Jesus, cleanses us from all sin." (Holy Bible: 1 John 1:7)

"That by reason of transgression cometh the fall, which fall bringeth death, and inasmuch as ye were born into the world by water, and blood, and the spirit, which I have made, and so became of dust a living soul, even so ye must be born again into the kingdom of heaven, of water, and of the Spirit, and be cleansed by blood, even the blood of mine Only Begotten; that

ye might be sanctified from all sin, and enjoy the words of eternal life in this world, and eternal life in the world to come, even immortal glory." (Pearl of Great Price: Moses 6:59)

h) We participate with him

Christ's true follower participates in his death and resurrection. Somehow, Christ's Incarnation into human flesh allows us to become one with Christ's death and resurrection so that the effects of those actions apply to us:

"Don't you know that we who are baptized into Jesus Christ are baptized into his death? 4 We were buried with him by baptism into death, and just as Christ rose from the dead by the Father's glory, so too we rise and live a new life. 5 Since we've been united with him in his death; so too will we be in his resurrection.

6 We know that our old self was crucified with him, so that the body of sin will be annulled and free us from slavery to sin, 7 because those who are dead have been freed from sin. 8 If we died with Christ, we also believe that we will live with him." (Holy Bible: Romans 6:3-8)

"Here's a saying we can trust: "If we die together with him; we will live together with him!" (Holy Bible: 2 Timothy 2:12)

Clarification of the "6. The Resurrection of Jesus" Stanzas

a) He preached to the spirits in prison

Where did Jesus go and what did he do during the three days between his death and resurrection? He preached to the dead:

> "Because Christ suffered a single time for sins, the righteous for the unrighteous, to bring you to God. He was put to death in the body but made alive in the Spirit. 19 <u>He then went and preached to the spirits in prison</u>, 20 who were disobedient from long ago, when God waited patiently while Noah was building an ark, so that a few, just eight people, were saved through water." (Holy Bible: 1 Peter 3:18-20)

> "As I pondered over these things which are written, the eyes of my understanding were opened, and the Spirit of the Lord rested upon me, and <u>I saw the hosts of the dead, both small and great</u>. 12 And there were gathered together in one place an innumerable company of the spirits of the just, who had been faithful in the testimony of Jesus while they lived in mortality; 13 And who had offered sacrifice in the similitude of the great sacrifice of the Son of God, and had suffered tribulation in their Redeemer's name. 14 <u>All these had departed the mortal life, firm in the hope of a glorious resurrection, through the grace of God the Father and his Only Begotten Son, Jesus Christ</u>. 15 I beheld that they were filled with joy and gladness, and were rejoicing together because the day of their deliverance was at hand. 16 They were assembled awaiting the advent of the Son of God into the spirit world, to declare their redemption from the bands of death. 17 Their sleeping dust was to be restored unto its perfect frame, bone to his bone, and the sinews and the flesh upon them, the spirit and the body to be united never again to be divided, that they might receive a fulness of joy. 18 While this vast multitude waited and conversed, rejoicing in the hour of their deliverance from the chains of death, <u>the Son of God appeared, declaring liberty to the captives who had been faithful</u>;

> 19 And there he preached to them the everlasting gospel, the doctrine of the resurrection and <u>the redemption of mankind from the fall</u>, and from individual sins on conditions of repentance. 20 But unto the wicked he did not go, and among the ungodly and the unrepentant who had defiled themselves while in the flesh, his voice was not raised; 21 Neither did the rebellious who rejected the testimonies and the warnings of the ancient prophets behold his presence, nor look upon his face. 22 Where

these were, darkness reigned, but among the righteous there was peace; 23 And the saints rejoiced in their redemption, and bowed the knee and acknowledged the Son of God as their Redeemer and Deliverer from death and the chains of hell. 24 Their countenances shone, and the radiance from the presence of the Lord rested upon them, and they sang praises unto his holy name." (Doctrine and Covenants: Section 138:11-24)

The gospel is preached not just to the living but also to the dead (1 Peter 4:6) who are currently in Hades. This heaven/hell or paradise/prison is where all humans go upon death as disembodied spirits until we are all resurrected into immortal, physical bodies to stand and be judged by Jesus Christ before the Father at Judgment Day.

b) Angels announced his resurrection

Christ's Atonement was the most significant event in the history of the universe. It was at that pivotal moment that sealed the fate of the universe, mankind, all life, and Satan and his angels.

Christ's resurrection was the conclusion of the Atonement and destroyed death's control over all living things. His rising from the dead showed the futility of Satan's rebellion. That empty tomb became evidence that Jesus did what the Father asked and is just waiting for the appointed time to receive his inheritance and recognition. There is now _no_ risk that God's plan can be thwarted by Jesus failing in his task.

> *"But when they entered the tomb, they didn't find the body of the Lord Jesus. 4 While they stood there confused, suddenly, two men wearing dazzling robes appeared in their midst!*
>
> *5 Terrified, the women prostrated themselves before the men, who then told them, 'Why are you looking among the dead for someone who is alive? 6 <u>He is not here—he is risen from the dead!</u> Remember when he told you back in Galilee, 7 that the Son of Man needs to be handed over to sinful men to be crucified to death only to rise again after three days?'*
>
> *8 Then the women remembered Jesus told them these things were going to happen." (Holy Bible: Luke 24:3-8)*

c) He rose from the dead

The most amazing news: Jesus Christ came back to life after being dead for three days!

"Remember Jesus Christ, the descendant of David, was raised from the dead! This is the good news I am preaching!" (Holy Bible: 2 Timothy 2:8)

"And it came to pass, as they understood they cast their eyes up again towards heaven; and behold, they saw a Man descending out of heaven; and he was clothed in a white robe; and he came down and stood in the midst of them; and the eyes of the whole multitude were turned upon him, and they durst not open their mouths, even one to another, and wist not what it meant, for they thought it was an angel that had appeared unto them.

9 And it came to pass that he stretched forth his hand and spake unto the people, saying: 10 Behold, <u>I am Jesus Christ</u>, whom the prophets testified shall come into the world. 11 And behold, I am the light and the life of the world; and I have drunk out of that bitter cup which the Father hath given me, and have glorified the Father in taking upon me the sins of the world, in the which I have suffered the will of the Father in all things from the beginning.

12 And it came to pass that when Jesus had spoken these words the whole multitude fell to the earth; for they remembered that it had been prophesied among them that Christ should show himself unto them after his ascension into heaven.

13 And it came to pass that the Lord spake unto them saying: 14 Arise and come forth unto me, that ye may thrust your hands into my side, and also that ye may feel the prints of the nails in my hands and in my feet, that ye may know that I am the God of Israel, and the God of the whole earth, and have been slain for the sins of the world.

15 And it came to pass that the multitude went forth, and thrust their hands into his side, and did feel the prints of the nails in his hands and in his feet; and this they did do, going forth one by one until they had all gone forth, and did see with their eyes and did feel with their hands, and did know of a surety and did bear record, that it was he, of whom it was written by the prophets, that should come. 16 And when they had all gone forth and had witnessed for themselves, they did cry out with one accord, saying: 17 Hosanna! Blessed be the name of the Most High God! And they did fall down at the feet of Jesus, and did worship him." (Book of Mormon: 3 Nephi 11:8-17)

d) Many eyewitnesses saw, interacted with, and felt the resurrected Jesus

Over 500 eyewitnesses saw Jesus after his resurrection (1 Corinthians 15:6), and their testimony was the foundation of the early church's credibility. Christ's resurrection was a physical one – his body could be felt. It was a "spiritual" body because it was no longer subject to the vulnerabilities of the mortal body (he couldn't get killed again or feel pain or discomfort of any kind), but there's no doubt it was a material resurrected body of some kind.

> "As they hastily left the tomb with fear and great joy, and were rushing to tell the disciples what the angel instructed; 9 Jesus met them and said, "Greetings!" They then prostrated themselves before him and <u>held on to his feet</u>, and worshiped him." (Holy Bible: Matthew 28:8-9)

> "While they were talking about these things, Jesus suddenly appeared in their midst and said, 'May you have peace.' 37 They then jumped in terror and feared they saw a ghost. 38 He said to them, 'Why are you frightened? Why are your hearts filled with doubt? 39 <u>Look at my hands and my feet. It is me! Touch me and confirm it is me. A ghost does not have a body of flesh and bone that you see I have.</u>'

> 40 He then showed them his hands and feet, 41 and while they still couldn't believe it was him out of sheer joy and amazement, he asked them, 'Do you have anything to eat?' 42 They then handed him some broiled fish, 43 which he then ate in front of them.

> 44 He then said, 'This is what I told you before—everything about me that is written in the law of Moses, the prophets, and psalms need to be fulfilled.' 45 He then opened their minds so that they could completely understand the scriptures, 46 and told them, 'This is what was written: The Messiah needs to suffer and rise from the dead after three days. 47 Repentance and forgiveness of sins are proclaimed in his name, starting in Jerusalem. 48 You are witnesses of these things. 49 And now, I am going to send to you what my Father has promised; so stay in the city, until you are clothed with power from heaven.'

> 50 He then led them close to Bethany, when he then lifted up his hands towards heaven and blessed them. 51 While he was blessing them, he started rising up into the air, and was then carried off into heaven." (Holy Bible: Luke 24:36-51)

e) He was first to resurrect from the dead as an immortal body

While the Bible describes cases of people coming back to life before Christ's resurrection (such as those brought back to life by Elijah and Elisha, the Nain widow's son, the daughter of Jairus, and Lazarus); Christ's resurrection was different because he was the first to be resurrected as an *immortal* body. All others who were brought back to life were still mortal – at some point, they died again.

> "In reality, Christ truly rose from the dead and was the very first person to ever come back to life after dying. . . 23 But each according to their place in line: Christ is the very first one to live again, followed by those who belong to him when he comes again." (Holy Bible: 1 Corinthians 15:20,23)

> "Wherefore, how great the importance to make these things known unto the inhabitants of the earth, that they may know that there is no flesh that can dwell in the presence of God, save it be through the merits, and mercy, and grace of the Holy Messiah, who layeth down his life according to the flesh, and taketh it again by the power of the Spirit, that he may bring to pass the resurrection of the dead, being the first that should rise." (Book of Mormon: 2 Nephi 2:8)

f) He will destroy death and Hades

Jesus was dead but came back to life. In so doing, he destroyed death and Hades' control over all humans. He possesses their "keys" and controls who comes in and who goes out. After death and hell are "emptied," they will be destroyed, never again to contain deceased humans – since there will never again be any dead humans.

> "I am the living one. I was dead, but look at me now—I am alive and will be for all eternity. I hold the keys of Death and Hades." (Holy Bible: Revelation 1:18)

> "The last enemy he will annul is death." (Holy Bible: 1 Corinthians 15:26)

> "The sea gave up the dead who were in it and Death and Hades gave up the dead that were in them—and each person was judged according to what they've done. 14 Then Death and Hades were thrown into the lake of fire. The second death is the lake of fire." (Holy Bible: Revelation 20:13-14)

"And if Christ had not risen from the dead, or have broken the bands of death that the grave should have no victory, and that death should have no sting, there could have been no resurrection. 8 But there is a resurrection, therefore the grave hath no victory, and the sting of death is swallowed up in Christ." (Book of Mormon: Mosiah 16:7-8)

"Know ye that ye must come to the knowledge of your fathers, and repent of all your sins and iniquities, and believe in Jesus Christ, that he is the Son of God, and that he was slain by the Jews, and by the power of the Father he hath risen again, whereby he hath gained the victory over the grave; and also in him is the sting of death swallowed up. 6 And he bringeth to pass the resurrection of the dead, whereby man must be raised to stand before his judgment-seat." (Book of Mormon: Mormon 7:5-6)

g) He can never die again

Jesus can never experience death again, which means he can never become a mortal human once more, again subject to pain and death:

"Know that Christ was resurrected from the dead—he can never experience death again! Death can never again have power over him. 10 When he died; he died once for all time to conquer sin. And the life he lives, he lives for God." (Holy Bible: Romans 6:9-10)

h) He makes everyone immortal

Jesus Christ's resurrection gives all humans a free gift, regardless of their righteousness and belief in him or lack thereof. He will make all humans immortal, with physical, material bodies that can never die:

"In Adam, everyone dies; in Christ, everyone will live again." (Holy Bible: 1 Corinthians 15:22)

"Therefore the wicked remain as though there had been no redemption made, except it be the loosing of the bands of death; for behold, the day cometh that all shall rise from the dead and stand before God, and be judged according to their works. 42 Now, there is a death which is called a temporal death; and the death of Christ shall loose the bands of this temporal death, that all shall be raised from this temporal death. 43 The spirit and the body shall be reunited again in its perfect form; both limb and joint shall be restored to its proper frame, even as we now are at this time; and we shall be brought to stand before God, knowing

even as we know now, and have a bright recollection of all our guilt. 44 Now, this restoration shall come to all, both old and young, both bond and free, both male and female, both the wicked and the righteous; and even there shall not so much as a hair of their heads be lost; but every thing shall be restored to its perfect frame, as it is now, or in the body, and shall be brought and be arraigned before the bar of Christ the Son, and God the Father, and the Holy Spirit, which is one Eternal God, to be judged according to their works, whether they be good or whether they be evil. 45 Now, behold, I have spoken unto you concerning the death of the mortal body, and also concerning the resurrection of the mortal body. I say unto you that this mortal body is raised to an immortal body, that is from death, even from the first death unto life, that they can die no more; their spirits uniting with their bodies, never to be divided; thus the whole becoming spiritual and immortal, that they can no more see corruption." (Book of Mormon: Alma 11:41-45)

Clarification of the "7. The Glorification of Jesus" Stanzas

a) He is glorified and exalted above all

The triumphant Son of God is glorified by the Father – Jesus did what no other entity could do: perform an infinite Atonement. By doing so, he reconciled us to God and freed us from our slavery to sin and death.

> *"Jesus was temporarily made lower than angels. He is now crowned with glory and honor because he subjected himself to death. By God's grace, he died for everyone!" (Holy Bible: Hebrews 2:9)*

> *"These are they who are cast down to hell and suffer the wrath of Almighty God, until the fulness of times, when Christ shall have subdued all enemies under his feet, and shall have perfected his work; 107 When he shall deliver up the kingdom, and present it unto the Father, spotless, saying: I have overcome and have trodden the wine-press alone, even the wine-press of the fierceness of the wrath of Almighty God. 108 Then shall he be crowned with the crown of his glory, to sit on the throne of his power to reign forever and ever." (Doctrine and Covenants: Section 76:106-109)*

b) His name is above all names/he is Lord

Jesus Christ's actions of becoming human flesh, becoming our sinless substitute who died for us, and coming back from the dead (the Incarnation, Atonement, and Resurrection) are so enormous, so vital, and so integral to our ultimate fate and happiness that every one of us, will acknowledge our debt and gratitude towards him.

> *"This is why God elevated him higher than anything possible and made his name more exalted than any other name. 10 And at the mention of Jesus' name, every knee in heaven, on earth, and in the underworld shall bend, 11 and everyone will concede that Jesus Christ is Lord, to the glory of God the Father." (Holy Bible: Philippians 2:9-11)*

> *"And moreover, I say unto you, that there shall be no other name given nor any other way nor means whereby salvation can come unto the children of men, only in and through the name of Christ, the Lord Omnipotent." (Book of Mormon: Mosiah 3:17)*

Even those who will be eternally condemned due to their evil works will still concede that Jesus Christ is Lord because they didn't remain as disembodied spirits, but will be resurrected with immortal bodies thanks to Christ's gift to all of material immortality.

c) He is exalted to God's right-hand side

Jesus is now at the Father's right-hand side to rule over all beneath the Father's authority.

> "Who is ascended into heaven, and sitting at God's right-hand side and rules over the angels, authorities, and powers." (Holy Bible: 1 Peter 3:22)

> "And may the grace of God the Father, whose throne is high in the heavens, and our Lord Jesus Christ, who sitteth on the right hand of his power, until all things shall become subject unto him, be, and abide with you forever. Amen." (Book of Mormon: Moroni 9:26)

d) He is the only way to God/he is the only way for us to be saved

The world does not want to hear it; but there is no ambiguity. There are not many ways to heaven. There is only one way: Through Jesus Christ.

> "Jesus said to them, 'I am the Way, and the Truth, and the Life. <u>No one can come unto the Father except through me.</u>'" (Holy Bible: John 14:6)

> "And now, my son, I have told you this that ye may learn wisdom, that ye may learn of me that there is no other way or means whereby man can be saved, only in and through Christ. Behold, he is the life and the light of the world. Behold, he is the word of truth and righteousness." (Book of Mormon: Alma 38:9)

> "Take upon you the name of Christ, and speak the truth in soberness. 22 And as many as repent and are baptized in my name, which is Jesus Christ, and endure to the end, the same shall be saved. 23 Behold, Jesus Christ is the name which is given of the Father, and there is none other name given whereby man can be saved." (Doctrine and Covenants: Section 18:21-23)

It does not matter if this message is offensive. It is irrelevant if it's not politically correct. It is immaterial if popular culture, the media, politicians, the government, or other religions punish those who unapologetically say this out loud. All will know this truth when we die and stand to be judged.

e) He is given the universe as an inheritance and reigns over it

This inconceivably vast universe belongs to Christ as an inheritance from Heavenly Father.

> "And now, God has spoken to us through his Son in these last days. God has given the universe to him as an inheritance, and created it through him." (Holy Bible: Hebrews 1:2)
>
> "The Father loves the Son and has given him the universe." (Holy Bible: John 3:35)
>
> "Jesus knew that the Father gave him dominion over the entire universe and that he came from God and will return to God." (Holy Bible: John 13:3)
>
> "Behold, I am from above, and my power lieth beneath. I am over all, and in all, and through all, and search all things, and the day cometh that all things shall be subject unto me." (Doctrine and Covenants: Section 63:59)

f) He will return to earth with great power and glory

All the survivors on earth will see Jesus returning while he's accompanied by a throng of angels. Suddenly, his righteous followers who are dead will be resurrected and will float up to meet him while he's still above the earth. After this occurs, his followers who are still mortal will abruptly become immortal, where their mortal bodies change to a glorified one, and they too will ascend to meet the returning Christ.

> "And then the sign of the Son of Man will appear in heaven, and all nations shall mourn and will see the Son of Man arrive on the clouds, with great power and glory." (Holy Bible: Matthew 24:30)
>
> "To you who are being oppressed, rest assured that you will find relief together with us when the Lord Jesus appears from heaven with his mighty angels." (Holy Bible: 2 Thessalonians 1:7)
>
> "For if we believe that Jesus died and rose again, we also believe that when Jesus returns, God will have those who've died having faith in Jesus, accompany him. 15 We tell you this directly from the Lord, his followers who will still be alive when the Lord comes will not precede those who've already died. 16 For the Lord himself will descend from heaven and will command, using the voice of an archangel and a blaring trumpet, for his dead

> followers to rise and meet him first. 17 After this happens, those of us who are still alive will rise up into the air to meet the Lord among the clouds, and we will be with the Lord forever." (Holy Bible: 2 Thessalonians 4:14-17)
>
> "And then they shall look for me, and, behold, I will come; and they shall see me in the clouds of heaven, clothed with power and great glory; with all the holy angels; and he that watches not for me shall be cut off.
>
> 45 But before the arm of the Lord shall fall, an angel shall sound his trump, and the saints that have slept shall come forth to meet me in the cloud. 46 Wherefore, if ye have slept in peace blessed are you; for as you now behold me and know that I am, even so shall ye come unto me and your souls shall live, and your redemption shall be perfected; and the saints shall come forth from the four quarters of the earth. 47 Then shall the arm of the Lord fall upon the nations.
>
> 48 And then shall the Lord set his foot upon this mount, and it shall cleave in twain, and the earth shall tremble, and reel to and fro, and the heavens also shall shake. 49 And the Lord shall utter his voice, and all the ends of the earth shall hear it; and the nations of the earth shall mourn, and they that have laughed shall see their folly. 50 And calamity shall cover the mocker, and the scorner shall be consumed; and they that have watched for iniquity shall be hewn down and cast into the fire.
>
> 51 And then shall the Jews look upon me and say: What are these wounds in thine hands and in thy feet? 52 Then shall they know that I am the Lord; for I will say unto them: These wounds are the wounds with which I was wounded in the house of friends. I am he who was lifted up. I am Jesus that was crucified. I am the Son of God.
>
> 53 And then shall they weep because of their iniquities; then shall they lament because they persecuted their king.
>
> 54 And then shall the heathen nations be redeemed, and they that knew no law shall have part in the first resurrection; and it shall be tolerable for them. 55 And Satan shall be bound, that he shall have no place in the hearts of the children of men." (Doctrine and Covenants: Section 45:44-55)

g) He will resurrect and judge mankind

The scriptures describe Jesus Christ's resurrection as a complete triumph over death itself, and he gives a gift to all mankind—the gift of immortality—where all humans will receive immortal, perfected physical bodies, irrespective of their belief or unbelief in him and regardless of their good or evil works. These "spiritual" bodies are to be somewhat identical with his resurrected body, which could be touched, can eat and drink, and so forth.

A "spiritual" body means a physical, material body that isn't subject to death and harm and can do things that normal mortal bodies cannot do. It is not something immaterial or insubstantial (which would negate the whole point of Christ's resurrection and triumph over "death").

After we are resurrected as immortal physical bodies, we will all stand before God and be judged by Jesus Christ:

> "Don't be so surprised, because the time is coming when all those who are dead will hear his voice, 29 and will come out of the grave. Those who've lived righteously will receive a resurrection of life while those who've been evil will receive a resurrection where they'll be condemned." (Holy Bible: John 5:28-29)

> "I have the same hope in God that these men have—that there will be a resurrection of both the righteous and unrighteous." (Holy Bible: Acts 24:15)

> "If it is being preached that Christ rose from the dead, how is it possible some of you are claiming there's no such thing as the resurrection of the dead? 13 But if there's no resurrection of the dead, then Christ did not rise from the dead either. 14 And if Christ didn't rise, then our preaching is pointless, and your faith is pointless as well. 15 Not just that, but we would also be exposed as liars because we've testified that God raised up Christ when in fact he didn't—if the dead are not resurrected. 16 For if the dead are not resurrected, neither has Christ been resurrected. 17 And if Christ has not been raised from the dead, then your faith is pointless, and you are still in your sins. 18 Furthermore, those who have already died while having faith in Christ are irretrievably gone. 19 If it is only in this life that we can have hope in Christ; we are the most pitiful of men.

> 20 In reality, Christ truly rose from the dead and was the very first person to ever come back to life after dying. 21 Since death came because of a man; it is necessary for the resurrection of the dead to also come from a man.

> 22 In Adam, everyone dies; in Christ, everyone will live again.

23 But each according to their place in line: Christ is the very first one to live again, followed by those who belong to him when he comes again.

24 Then the end will come, when he hands over the kingdom to God the Father (after he annuls all rulers, authorities, and powers). 25 He must reign until he puts all his enemies under his feet. 26 <u>The last enemy he will annul is death</u>. 27 For he has dominion over all things. However, when it says, "All things," it is obvious that that excludes God, who gave Jesus dominion over the universe. 28 After all things are put under the Son's authority; he then is put under the Father's authority, so that God may have dominion over all.

29 Finally, if there is no resurrection, why are those who are baptized for the dead doing it? If the dead are not going to rise, why then are they baptized for them? 30 And why are we in constant danger from others?" (Holy Bible: 1 Corinthians 15:12-30)

"For the Son of Man is going to come in his Father's glory and will be accompanied by his angels. He will judge all men according to their works." (Holy Bible: Matthew 16:27)

"We must all stand before the judgment-seat of Christ, so that each of us will be judged based on what we've done in our lives, whether good or bad." (Holy Bible: 2 Corinthians 5:10)

"O how great the goodness of our God, who prepareth a way for our escape from the grasp of this awful monster; yea, that monster, death and hell, which I call the death of the body, and also the death of the spirit.

11 And because of the way of deliverance of our God, the Holy One of Israel, this death, of which I have spoken, which is the temporal, shall deliver up its dead; which death is the grave. 12 And this death of which I have spoken, which is the spiritual death, shall deliver up its dead; which spiritual death is hell; wherefore, death and hell must deliver up their dead, and hell must deliver up its captive spirits, and the grave must deliver up its captive bodies, and the bodies and the spirits of men will be restored one to the other; and it is by the power of the resurrection of the Holy One of Israel.

13 O how great the plan of our God! For on the other hand, the paradise of God must deliver up the spirits of the righteous, and the grave deliver up the body of the righteous; and the spirit and the body is restored to itself again, and all men become incorruptible, and immortal, and they are living souls, having a

perfect knowledge like unto us in the flesh, save it be that our knowledge shall be perfect. 14 Wherefore, we shall have a perfect knowledge of all our guilt, and our uncleanness, and our nakedness; and the righteous shall have a perfect knowledge of their enjoyment, and their righteousness, being clothed with purity, yea, even with the robe of righteousness.

15 And it shall come to pass that when all men shall have passed from this first death unto life, insomuch as they have become immortal, they must appear before the judgment-seat of the Holy One of Israel; and then cometh the judgment, and then must they be judged according to the holy judgment of God." (Book of Mormon: 2 Nephi 9:10-15)

h) He will replace heaven and earth

Regardless of our attachment to material things, this earth will not last in its present state. Just as humans are going to be changed from mortal to immortal; so too will the earth:

"And I saw a new earth and sky, for the earlier earth and sky had disappeared, and the sea disappeared as well." (Holy Bible: Revelation 21:1)

"The day of the Lord will come unexpectedly, like a thief in the night. The sky will disappear with a terrible roar, and the earth's materials will be burned off, exposing all its secrets and evil deeds.

11 Since these things are going to disappear, what type of person should you then be? You should be righteous and godly, 12 looking forward to the day of God, and pushing for it to come sooner, where the sky burns, and the earth's materials melt from the heat. 13 This is so that his promise of a new heaven and new earth will finally occur, <u>where only righteousness dwells</u>." (Holy Bible: 2 Peter 3:10-13)

"All of creation eagerly awaits the unveiling of the Sons and Daughters of God! 20 Creation became corrupted, not through its own fault, but because God subjected it so that there may be hope, 21 that <u>after creation is freed from corruption</u>, it will share in the freedom and glory of the Children of God." (Holy Bible: Romans 8:19-21)

"And the end shall come, and the heaven and the earth shall be consumed and pass away, and there shall be a new heaven and a new earth. 24 For all old things shall pass away, and all things shall become new, even the heaven and the earth, and all the fulness thereof, both men and beasts, the fowls of the air, and

the fishes of the sea; 25 And not one hair, neither mote, shall be lost, for it is the workmanship of mine hand.

26 But, behold, verily I say unto you, before the earth shall pass away, Michael, mine archangel, shall sound his trump, and then shall all the dead awake, for their graves shall be opened, and they shall come forth—yea, even all. 27 And the righteous shall be gathered on my right hand unto eternal life; and the wicked on my left hand will I be ashamed to own before the Father." (Doctrine and Covenants: Section 29:23-27)

Clarification of the "8. Jesus Creates the Children of God" Stanzas

a) Belief in him brings salvation

Those who believe in Jesus Christ and strive to follow him will be rewarded with "eternal life." This is different from becoming immortal:

- Immortality – Having a perfected physical body that can never die or be subject to discomfort, damage, or pain

- Eternal Life – Living with God for all eternity in a state of happiness

Christ's followers receive both rewards while the wicked and those who reject him only receive immortality.

> *"So that whoever believes in him shall not perish but have eternal life. 16 God loved mankind so much, that he gave up his only Son, so that whoever believes in him shall not perish but have eternal life. . . Whoever believes in the Son has eternal life. Whoever does not obey him will never experience eternal life and God's wrath remains on him." (Holy Bible: John 3:15-16,36)*

> *"For behold he judgeth, and his judgment is just; and the infant perisheth not that dieth in his infancy; but men drink damnation to their own souls except they humble themselves and become as little children, and believe that salvation was, and is, and is to come, in and through the atoning blood of Christ, the Lord Omnipotent." (Book of Mormon: Mosiah 3:18)*

> *"And behold, this is the whole meaning of the law, every whit pointing to that great and last sacrifice; and that great and last sacrifice will be the Son of God, yea, infinite and eternal. 15 And thus he shall bring salvation to all those who shall believe on his name; this being the intent of this last sacrifice, to bring about the bowels of mercy, which overpowereth justice, and bringeth about means unto men that they may have faith unto repentance." (Book of Mormon: Alma 34:14-15)*

> *"And this is my doctrine, and it is the doctrine which the Father hath given unto me; and I bear record of the Father, and the Father beareth record of me, and the Holy Ghost beareth record of the Father and me; and I bear record that the Father commandeth all men, everywhere, to repent and believe in me.*

> *33 And whoso believeth in me, and is baptized, the same shall be saved; and they are they who shall inherit the kingdom of*

> God. 34 And whoso believeth not in me, and is not baptized, shall be damned.
>
> 35 Verily, verily, I say unto you, that this is my doctrine, and I bear record of it from the Father; and whoso believeth in me believeth in the Father also; and unto him will the Father bear record of me, for he will visit him with fire and with the Holy Ghost. 36 And thus will the Father bear record of me, and the Holy Ghost will bear record unto him of the Father and me; for the Father, and I, and the Holy Ghost are one.
>
> 37 And again I say unto you, ye must repent, and become as a little child, and be baptized in my name, or ye can in nowise receive these things. 38 And again I say unto you, ye must repent, and be baptized in my name, and become as a little child, or ye can in nowise inherit the kingdom of God." (Book of Mormon: 3 Nephi 11:32-38)

b) We must obey him

The condition for true discipleship is obedience to Jesus Christ's commands. Since none of us can obey perfectly, we must then <u>strive</u> to obey, repent when (not if, when) we fail, make restitution when we can, but always have faith in him and continually make an effort to improve and obey.

> "If you keep my commandments, you will stay in my love; even as I keep my Father's commandments and stay within his love." (Holy Bible: John 15:10)
>
> "And being perfected; he became the source of eternal salvation for all who obey him." (Holy Bible: Hebrews 5:9)
>
> "But is now revealed in accordance with the scripture prophecies, so that all nations will know that God commands them to obey and have faith in Jesus." (Holy Bible: Romans 16:26)
>
> "I give unto you these sayings that you may understand and know how to worship, and know what you worship, that you may come unto the Father in my name, and in due time receive of his fulness. 20 For if you keep my commandments you shall receive of his fulness, and be glorified in me as I am in the Father; therefore, I say unto you, you shall receive grace for grace." (Doctrine and Covenants 93:19-20)
>
> "There is a law, irrevocably decreed in heaven before the foundations of this world, upon which all blessings are predicated— 21 And when we obtain any blessing from God, it

is by obedience to that law upon which it is predicated." (Doctrine and Covenants: Section 130:20-21)

"And there stood one among them that was like unto God, and he said unto those who were with him: We will go down, for there is space there, and we will take of these materials, and we will make an earth whereon these may dwell; 25 And we will prove them herewith, to see if they will do all things whatsoever the Lord their God shall command them;

26 And they who keep their first estate shall be added upon; and they who keep not their first estate shall not have glory in the same kingdom with those who keep their first estate; and they who keep their second estate shall have glory added upon their heads for ever and ever." (Pearl of Great Price: Abraham 3:24-26)

c) He enables his followers to be adopted by God

Christ enables his true followers to be adopted by God:

"You've received a Spirit that does not enslave you and make you afraid once more. You've received a Spirit of divine adoption as sons and daughters. We can now call him "Abba! Father!" . . . 22 We know that all of creation has been continually groaning as if it's experiencing the pain of childbirth. 23 Not just creation—despite we've received the first portions of the Spirit; we are also groaning while we eagerly wait for our adoption as sons and daughters, and the redemption of our bodies." (Holy Bible: Romans 8:15,22-23)

"You are the Sons and Daughters of God through faith in Christ Jesus. 27 All of you who've been baptized into Christ have become enveloped by Christ. 28 There is no Jew or Gentile, slave or free, or male or female: You are all one in Christ Jesus. 29 And if you are Christ's, then you are Abraham's descendants and heirs of the divine promise.

4:1 What I'm saying is that as long as the heir is still a child, it is as if he's a slave despite he actually owns the estate. 2 He is still under the authority of his guardians and trustees until reaching the age his father set for him.

3 Similarly, while we were still children, we were enslaved under the control of the world's principles, 4 but when the appointed time arrived, God sent his Son, born of a woman, born under the law, 5 to redeem those enslaved to the Law and adopt us as his Sons and Daughters.

6 Because you are Sons and Daughters, God sent the Spirit of his Son into our hearts so that we may be able to cry out loud: "Abba! Father!" 7 As a result, you are no longer a slave, but a Son or Daughter, and if so, then an heir of God." (Holy Bible: Galatians 3:26-4:7)

"Just as God chose us to be within Jesus since before the world was created (for us to be holy, and blameless within "love" when we're in front of God); 5 We were predestined to be divinely adopted as God's children through Jesus Christ, in accordance with his pleasure and desire." (Holy Bible: Ephesians 1:4-5)

d) His true followers become the Children of God and God's heirs

Christ's true followers become the exalted "Children of God" and his "Heirs":

"If you know that he is righteous, you then know that all who do righteousness are his children.

3:1 See how much the Father loves us: We shall be called the "Children of God" and that is precisely what we are! Because of this, the world does not recognize us because it does not know him.

2 Dear friends, we are already the Children of God, but he has not yet revealed to us what exactly we will be, only that when Jesus appears, we will become like him, for we will see him as he truly is, 3 and all who have this hope within them, purifies themselves, even as Jesus is pure." (Holy Bible: 1 John 2:29-3:3)

"For those who are led by the Spirit of God are the Children of God. 15 You've received a Spirit that does not enslave you and make you afraid once more. You've received a Spirit of divine adoption as sons and daughters. We can now call him 'Abba! Father!'

16 The Spirit himself testifies with our spirit that we are the Children of God. 17 If we are children, then we are heirs—heirs of God and fellow-heirs with Christ, provided we suffer with him, so that we may be glorified together. 18 I do not consider our current sufferings to be anywhere comparable to the coming glory that will be revealed to us.

19 All of creation eagerly awaits the unveiling of the Sons and Daughters of God!

20 Creation became corrupted, not through its own fault, but because God subjected it so that there may be hope, 21 that after creation is freed from corruption, it will share in the freedom and glory of the Children of God." (Holy Bible: Romans 8:14-21)

"They who overcome will inherit these things. I will be their God, and they will be my son or daughter." (Holy Bible: Revelation 21:7)

"Behold, I am Jesus Christ the Son of God. I created the heavens and the earth, and all things that in them are. I was with the Father from the beginning. I am in the Father, and the Father in me; and in me hath the Father glorified his name. 16 I came unto my own, and my own received me not. And the scriptures concerning my coming are fulfilled. 17 And as many as have received me, to them have I given to become the sons of God; and even so will I to as many as shall believe on my name, for behold, by me redemption cometh, and in me is the law of Moses fulfilled." (Book of Mormon: 3 Nephi 9:15-17)

"But verily, verily, I say unto you, that as many as receive me, to them will I give power to become the sons of God, even to them that believe on my name. Amen." (Doctrine and Covenants: Section 11:30)

e) The Children of God share oneness and mutual indwelling with God

The "Children of God" will share oneness and mutual indwelling with God:

" 'On that day, you will understand that I am in my Father, and you are in me, and I am in you.' . . . 23 Jesus replied, 'Those who love me will keep my teachings, and my Father will love them. We will come to them and will dwell within them.' " (Holy Bible: John 14:20,23)

"Holy Father, I'm about to leave this world and go to you, but they are staying in this world. Protect them by the power of your name so that they may be one as we are one. . . 21 That they may be one just as you are in me and I in you. May they be one in us so that the world may believe that you sent me. 22 I gave them the glory you gave me so that they may be one just as we are one. 23 I in them and you in me, so that they may become perfectly united. The world will then know that you sent me and loved them just as you loved me." (Holy Bible: John 17:11,21-23)

"Whoever is joined to the Lord is one spirit." (Holy Bible: 1 Corinthians 6:17)

"I am Jesus Christ, the Son of God, who was crucified for the sins of the world, even as many as will believe on my name, that they may become the sons of God, even one in me as I am one in the Father, as the Father is one in me, that we may be one." (Doctrine and Covenants: Section 35:2)

"And the Father and I are one. I am in the Father and the Father in me; and inasmuch as ye have received me, ye are in me and I in you." (Doctrine and Covenants: Section 50:43)

"The light shineth in darkness, and the darkness comprehendeth it not; nevertheless, the day shall come when you shall comprehend even God, being quickened in him and by him. 50 Then shall ye know that ye have seen me, that I am, and that I am the true light that is in you, and that you are in me; otherwise ye could not abound." (Doctrine and Covenants: Section 88:49-50)

f) The Children of God share the divine nature

The Children of God share in the divine nature, the very nature of God:

"His divine power has given us all things relating to life and godliness, through the knowledge of the one who called us by his own glory and virtue; 4 through which, he has given us precious and magnificent promises: After we've escaped from the corruption of the sinful desires of the world, we can share in the divine nature!" (Holy Bible: 2 Peter 1:3-4)

"The veil has been removed from our face, and we can see the glory of the Lord as if it's reflected in a mirror. Thanks to the Lord's Spirit, we are undergoing metamorphosis into the same image." (Holy Bible: 2 Corinthians 3:18)

"Until we achieve the unity of the faith and knowledge of the Son of God, and grow up until finally measuring up to the dimensions of the fulness of Christ's nature. . . 15 Rather, we speak the truth in love: We should grow up into him in all things, who is the head, Christ. . . 24 And to put on the new nature, which is after God's, created in righteousness and holy truth." (Holy Bible: Ephesians 4:13,15,24)

"Wherefore, my beloved brethren, pray unto the Father with all the energy of heart, that ye may be filled with this love, which he hath bestowed upon all who are true followers of his Son, Jesus Christ; that ye may become the sons of God; that when he shall

appear we shall be like him, for we shall see him as he is; that we may have this hope; that we may be purified even as he is pure. Amen." (Book of Mormon: Moroni 7:48)

g) The Children of God share glory

The Children of God receive incredible glory – and share in the glory of God:

"I gave them the glory you gave me so that they may be one just as we are one." (Holy Bible: John 17:22)

"Through whom we have access to this grace we're currently standing in because of our faith, and we boast of our hope in sharing the glory of God." (Holy Bible: Romans 5:2)

"If we are children, then we are heirs—heirs of God and fellow-heirs with Christ, provided we suffer with him, so that we may be glorified together." (Holy Bible: Romans 8:17)

"Our troubles are minor and momentary—but will result in us obtaining an incredible glory that lasts forever!" (Holy Bible: 2 Corinthians 4:17)

"And again we bear record—for we saw and heard, and this is the testimony of the gospel of Christ concerning them who shall come forth in the resurrection of the just—

51 They are they who received the testimony of Jesus, and believed on his name and were baptized after the manner of his burial, being buried in the water in his name, and this according to the commandment which he has given— 52 That by keeping the commandments they might be washed and cleansed from all their sins, and receive the Holy Spirit by the laying on of the hands of him who is ordained and sealed unto this power; 53 And who overcome by faith, and are sealed by the Holy Spirit of promise, which the Father sheds forth upon all those who are just and true. 54 They are they who are the church of the Firstborn.

55 They are they into whose hands the Father has given all things— 56 They are they who are priests and kings, who have received of his fulness, and of his glory; 57 And are priests of the Most High, after the order of Melchizedek, which was after the order of Enoch, which was after the order of the Only Begotten Son.

58 Wherefore, as it is written, they are gods, even the sons of God— 59 Wherefore, all things are theirs, whether life or death, or things present, or things to come, all are theirs and they are

Christ's, and Christ is God's. 60 And they shall overcome all things. 61 Wherefore, let no man glory in man, but rather let him glory in God, who shall subdue all enemies under his feet.

62 These shall dwell in the presence of God and his Christ forever and ever. 63 These are they whom he shall bring with him, when he shall come in the clouds of heaven to reign on the earth over his people. 64 These are they who shall have part in the first resurrection. 65 These are they who shall come forth in the resurrection of the just. 66 These are they who are come unto Mount Zion, and unto the city of the living God, the heavenly place, the holiest of all. 67 These are they who have come to an innumerable company of angels, to the general assembly and church of Enoch, and of the Firstborn. 68 These are they whose names are written in heaven, where God and Christ are the judge of all. 69 These are they who are just men made perfect through Jesus the mediator of the new covenant, who wrought out this perfect atonement through the shedding of his own blood.

70 These are they whose bodies are celestial, whose glory is that of the sun, even the glory of God, the highest of all, whose glory the sun of the firmament is written of as being typical." (Doctrine and Covenants: Section 76:50-70)

h) The Children of God share rule and everything he has

Jesus shares everything he has with the Children of God. This includes sharing rule over the universe since he received it as an inheritance from the Father:

"We have become entitled to share everything Christ has – if we keep our initial belief, by staying faithful until the end." (Holy Bible: Hebrews 3:14)

"If we endure, we will reign together with him; if we deny him, he will deny us." (Holy Bible: 2 Timothy 2:12)

"I will give those who overcome, the right to sit with me on my throne—just as I overcame, and sat down with my Father on his throne." (Holy Bible: Revelation 3:21)

"He has made us kings and priests for God his Father. To him be glory and dominion forevermore! Amen." (Holy Bible: Revelation 1:6)

"Even while dead in sin, we came back to life together with Christ (you are saved by grace) 6 and rose up together, and are to be seated together in the heavenly realms in unity with Christ Jesus; 7 so that God may show all future ages how incalculably

rich his grace is, because of his kindness towards us in Christ Jesus." (Holy Bible: Ephesians 2:5-7)

"For he that receiveth my servants receiveth me; 37 And he that receiveth me receiveth my Father; 38 And he that receiveth my Father receiveth my Father's kingdom; therefore all that my Father hath shall be given unto him." (Doctrine and Covenants: Section 84:36-38)

The stupendous gift Jesus shares with those who will become the "Children of God" is so enormous, so magnificent, that it will be everlasting evidence to all creatures in the universe of just how "incalculably rich his grace is."

CONCLUSION

Reading these hymns gives me a lot of comfort and I feel the Holy Spirit confirming that the phrasings are accurate depictions of our Lord and Savior and of issues relating to him.

Jesus Christ is the most important person in history. He created the universe and Earth and then became human two millennia ago. He performed the infinite Atonement whereby we can be saved and even become exalted as immortal rulers of the universe if we just truly follow him.

The Holy Bible contains within itself the evidence of its credibility – *the New Testament is a frameless, unharmonized, correlative anthology*. This is such a powerful witness that when I saw its single coherent cosmology, I instantly lost my atheism and regained my faith in Jesus Christ. This is because it is demonstrably impossible for nine people to write books whose contents blend to create a single large picture without following a common frame such as author guidelines or have their deliverables harmonized by a common editor.

The Book of Mormon claims it was written so that the world may believe that "**Jesus is the Christ, the Eternal God**" and so that we may believe the Holy Bible's teachings are true. This means if the Book of Mormon is true, then the Holy Bible is also true.

Like the Holy Bible, the Book of Mormon has internal evidence that it is true – *the Book of Mormon contains argumentative and persuasive essays despite it was "dictated from imagination."* The presence of this logical structure type of literature within a dictated work is an objective fact that challenges the firsthand experience of anyone who's had to create them in college. And yet over 22 of them exist in the Book of Mormon – something millions know from experience is impossible to create from imagination.

The New Testament has *four* eyewitnesses that testified of Jesus Christ and his ministry. The Book of Mormon has *twelve* eyewitnesses (including Joseph Smith) who testified that they had seen the gold plates, and four of them stated they had seen an angel and heard God's voice commanding them to witness to the world. All these eyewitnesses affirmed their testimonies until their deaths, even those who were no longer within the Church. These eyewitnesses cannot be honestly ignored.

The Church of Jesus Christ of Latter-day Saints is definitely Christian in theology while at the same time is such an outlier that it is a separate branch of Christianity (the fifth branch).

My decades of firsthand experience analyzing complex documentation confirms to my mind that the empirical evidence for the New Testament and Book of Mormon are credible and likely. This validation provides intellectual support to the much more important subjective witness from the Holy Spirit telling me that Jesus is truly God made flesh who suffered and died for our sakes so that we may become one with him and his Father and share in their very nature.

I am so grateful for regaining my faith in Christ in 2016 and for not dying while an atheist and while willfully disobeying his will.

> *I want to become one of the Children of God – one of those who will be adopted by God to share in his divine nature, oneness, and mutual indwelling. It is such an overwhelming gift to such an unworthy being that it is next to impossible to grasp the enormous significance of that adoption.*

Here we are, mere specks, but subject to a divine promise that can only be fulfilled by obedience to the Son of God. Let us follow him wherever he leads us and endure to the end.

In the name of Jesus Christ, my Savior and God. Amen.

APPENDIX:
PROOF THE BOOK OF MORMON CONTAINS ARGUMENTATIVE AND PERSUASIVE ESSAYS

This appendix contains analysis forms of some of the argumentative or persuasive essays found within the Book of Mormon. They prove these types of literary styles exist within a book that was "dictated from imagination" (Joseph Smith dictated the words to Oliver Cowdery).

But since it is demonstrable that a person like Joseph Smith within his circumstance cannot create coherent argumentative essays from "dictation from imagination" (as anyone who's had to create them in college knows); what then explains their presence in the Book of Mormon except the power of God?

We cannot pretend they do not exist – they do – we've had the Book of Mormon since 1830. We have the entirety of the Printer's Manuscript and 28% of the Original Manuscript that show no major rewrites or layout changes were done to the text after they left Joseph's mouth. We've always known he dictated the book to Oliver Cowdery and all claims to the contrary have consistently failed validation. (Even South Park made fun of the translation process since Joseph had his face in a hat to cut off outside light while dictating most of the book.)

The Church of Jesus Christ of Latter-day Saints has been condemned for nearly two centuries because of *how* the book was created but the book's contents are always ignored. But now, the dictation from imagination methodology becomes the smoking gun that shows the impossibility of the contents.

Alma 32

Argumentative/Persuasive Writing Analysis

Title	Alma's Preaching to the Zoramites (1 of 2)			
Subject	Salvation	Reference	Alma 32:8-43	
Author Name	Alma	Audience	Zoramites	
Perspective	Those who believe in and live the word of God are blessed.			
Background	Alma was the high priest over the Nephites and was the former chief judge (Alma 8:11-12) who led a mission to the Zoramites around 74 BC. The Zoramites were dissenters from the Nephites and functioned as an autonomous group within the Nephite nation. They were apostates who rejected the belief of the coming Christ and believed they were guaranteed salvation without needing to repent. They also only prayed once a week and only in their houses of worship. The audience was comprised of poor Zoramites who were prohibited from entering the synagogues to worship God. While it is never stated, it appeared their concern was they couldn't be saved because they couldn't worship God in the synagogues.			
Purpose/Goal	Alma led a delegation of missionaries to preach to the Zoramites so that they will return to Christ.			
Form	☒ Rebuttal		☐ One-Sided	

1) Thesis Claim/Position

Salvation comes from having faith in the word of God and living it (v. 16).

2) Frame of Argument

Argument 1	You are not worthless ("esteemed as filthiness/dross" – v. 3) because of your poverty; you are actually blessed because your poverty has made you humble (v. 13).

Evidence	Your humility has made you receptive to learning wisdom (v. 12) [Logic: Deductive Reason, Experience]. You are blessed because when some men are forced to become humble, they repent and obtain mercy. And those who find mercy and endure to the end will be saved (v. 13) [Emotion: Anticipation].
Argument 2	Asking for a sign to obtain surety before believing is useless (vv. 17-18).
Evidence	Those who know God's will and do not do it are cursed much more than those who only have faith who then fall into sin (v. 19) [Logical: Deductive Reason]. Faith is to not have a perfect knowledge [Logical: Facts]. If you have faith, you hope for things that are not seen but are true (v. 21) [Logical: Deductive Reason]. Faith is not perfect knowledge. This is also the case with my words - you cannot know of their surety at first anymore than faith is a perfect knowledge (v. 26) [Logical: Facts]. Feeling the seed of the word of God grow within your chest increases your faith but it has not yet grown into a perfect knowledge (v. 29) [Logical: Facts].
Argument 3	One can know the truth concerning the word of God by conducting an experiment where only a particle of faith, even just a desire to believe, is used (v. 27).
Evidence	Imagine that the word is a **seed** that you plant in your heart [Note: vv. 28-43 is a thought experiment using the deductive process]. If it is a true or good seed and you do not pluck it out due to your unbelief whereby you resist the Spirit of the Lord, then you will feel it growing inside your chest. You will then tell yourself that "*It must needs be that this is a good seed, or that the word is good, for it beginneth to enlarge my soul; yea, it beginneth to enlighten my understanding, yea, it beginneth to be delicious to me.*" This will then increase your faith (vv. 28-29) [Logic: Inductive Reason and Experience; Emotion: Joy]. It now becomes possible to say you "know" the seed is good because you felt it grow (vv. 30-33) [Logic: Inductive Reason and Experience].

You now have perfect knowledge in the goodness of the seed and your faith is now <u>dormant</u> because you know that the word has swelled your soul and you also know that your understanding has started to be enlightened and your mind has started to expand (v. 34) [Logic: Experience; Emotion: Joy]. This knowledge is real because it is "light" and whatever is light is good because it is discernable which means you know that it is good (v. 35) [Logic: Experience].

However, this does not mean your knowledge is now perfect and you can now abandon your faith because your experiment was to only plant the seed to determine whether it is good. As the tree begins to grow, you will say that you want to take care of the tree so that it may grow up and produce fruit. Thus you will take care of the tree (vv. 35-37) [Logic: Experience].

But if you neglect it and ignore its need for nourishment, then it will not take root. When the heat of the sun bears down on it, it will wither away and you will then throw it out. The loss wasn't because the seed wasn't good or its fruit wasn't desirable but was solely due to your ground being barren and your refusal to nourish the tree. Because of this neglect, you will not be able to have the fruit. (vv. 38-39) [Logic: Facts].

And thus, if you will not nourish the word, looking forward with an eye of faith to its fruit; then you will never be able to pluck the fruit of the tree of life (v. 40) [Logic: Authority, Facts; Emotion: Fear].

But if you nourish the word, yea, nourish the tree as it starts to grow with your faith, diligence, and patience, looking forward to its coming fruit, then the tree will take root and will become a tree springing up unto everlasting life (v. 41) [Logic: Authority].

And because of your diligence and your faith and your patience with the word in nourishing it so that it may take root in you, *in just a little* while, you will pluck the fruit, which is the most precious and sweetest, and whitest, and purest thing imaginable! You will feast upon the fruit until you are full and no longer hunger or thirst. Then, my brethren, you shall reap the rewards of your faith, diligence, patience, and long-suffering, waiting for the tree

APPENDIX 153

	to bring forth fruit unto you (vv. 42-43) [Emotion: Anticipation, Joy].				
The author claimed to be credible because	Alma did not claim to be credible, but he was likely recognized to be the most famous person in the Nephite nation as the former chief judge and current high priest.				
The author appealed to		☒	Logic	☒	Emotion
If logic, used	☒	Authority	☐ Examples	☒	Deductive Reason
	☐	Precedent	☒ Experience	☒	Inductive Reason
	☒	Facts	☐ Competence	☐	Statistics
If emotion, used	☒	Joy	☐ Trust	☐	Surprise
	☐	Anger	☒ Fear	☒	Anticipation
	☐	Awe	☐ Yearning	☐	Envy
	☐	Dread	☐ Disgust	☐	Sadness
If rebuttal, opposition's position	1. We have no place to worship our God because we are cast out of our synagogues because of our poverty (v. 5). 2. There are many who demand a sign from heaven so that they will know for sure before they will believe (v. 17).				
Was concession made of opposition's valid points?			☐ Yes	☒	No
Counter-arguments	1. Do you think the synagogue is the only place where you can worship God? Also, what makes you think you must only worship God once a week? It is well that you were cast out of your synagogues				

	because of your poverty for it made you humble and open to learning wisdom (vv. 10-12). 2. Demanding a sign from heaven before believing is not faith because if a man knows something, then he does not need to believe because he knows it (v.18). Try an experiment. Imagine the word is a seed that you plant inside you. If you feel it grow, you know that it is a good seed even though you do not have perfect knowledge (vv. 28-43) [see Argument 3].
Form of counterarguments	☐ Removal of the opponent's support ☒ Exposure of the opponent's faulty logic ☐ Demonstration that the opponent has no support

3) Conclusion

If you nourish the word, yea, nourish the tree as it starts to grow with your faith, diligence, and patience, looking forward to its coming fruit; then the tree will take root and will become a tree springing up unto everlasting life. In just a little, you will then pluck the fruit, which is the most precious and sweetest, and whitest, and purest thing imaginable! You will feast upon the fruit until you are full and no longer hunger or thirst. Then, my brethren, you shall reap the rewards of your faith, and diligence, patience, and long-suffering, waiting for the tree to bring forth fruit unto you (vv. 41-43).

Was the thesis restated?	☒ Yes	☐ No

The word of God (the tree) will produce fruit that gives eternal life (vv. 41-43).

Was there a call to action?	☒ Yes	☐ No

Become humble without being compelled to be humble because those who voluntarily become humble are much more blessed (vv. 14-16).

Exercise a particle of faith, even if you can no more desire to believe (v. 27).

APPENDIX 155

Nurture the seed (the word of God) so that it will grow and produce fruit that gives eternal life (vv. 37-42).	
Did the essay intend to make the audience think or look at the world or themselves in a different way?	☒ Yes ☐ No
The poor Zoramites are not worthless but are actually blessed because their poverty has forced them to be humble (vv. 12-14). They are now much more receptive to accepting the truth of the word of God so that they will enjoy true eternal life.	

4) Performance Assessment

What was the author's persuasion strategy?	☒	Ethos (Author's credibility)	☒	Pathos (Audience's emotions)
	☒	Logos (Audience's mind)	☐	Kairos (Sales pressure)
In your opinion, was the author credible to *the target audience*, given their worldview?		☒ Yes		☐ No
Why?	As the high priest over the Nephite nation and former chief judge, Alma couldn't help but be credible to the poor Zoramites. He wouldn't need to state his credibility – they automatically would find him credible.			
Did the author address *the target audience's* needs or concerns?		☒ Yes		☐ No
Why?	The poor Zoramites had a terrible self-image – they were "esteemed as filthiness/dross" by the wealthier Zoramites (v. 3) and priests who cast them out of the synagogues (v. 5) – the only place where they could worship God (v. 10). The unsaid implication is because they were prohibited from worshiping God in their places of worship, they would be excluded from those who are guaranteed salvation (Alma 31:17).			

	Alma counteracted their negative self-image by telling them repeatedly that they are actually "blessed" (vv. 8,13,14) and built on this by telling them they'll be even more blessed if they accept the word or the word of God (vv. 14-16). He then segued into his prepared speech concerning faith and the seed as the word.		
Was the author credible *to you*, given your worldview?	☒ Yes	☐ No
Why?	The evidence of Alma's three arguments are all valid because they are logically coherent: Argument 1: People who are forced to become humble are much more receptive to receiving new ideas or return to God. Argument 2: Knowledge and belief are not the same with the former being much more credible (e.g., "I know Mr. Jones was at the scene of the crime because I saw him" versus. "I believe Mr. Jones was at the scene of the crime because someone told me"). Faith – belief allows repentance whereas it's very hard to be forgiven when one knowingly violates the law. Argument 3: Alma skillfully blended the persuasion strategies of Logos and Pathos within a deductive thought experiment. He started with logical implications and ended with emotional confirmation. Given the premise (one can know that a seed is good if it grows) the conclusion (one can eat the fruit of the tree if one nurtures a seed) is valid.		

5) Is it a Genuine Argumentative or Persuasive Essay?				
a.	Does the reference text contain a Thesis Claim/Position?	☒ Yes	☐ No
b.	Does the reference text contain arguments supported by evidence?	☒ Yes	☐ No
c.	Does the reference text contain counter-arguments?	☒ Yes	☐ No

APPENDIX 157

d.	Does the reference text restate the thesis?	☒	Yes	☐	No
e.	Does the reference text contain a call to action or give the recipient a different perspective?	☒	Yes	☐	No

CONCLUSION

ALMA 32:8-43 is a genuine argumentative essay and can be proven empirically since it contains all the components and structure of an argumentative essay. The #2 counter-argument shows preparation was made prior to preaching concerning faith and the seed as the word of God. Argument 1 was unrehearsed but Arguments 2 and 3 were written and refined before preaching.

It is easy to see Alma's prepared speech (vv. 17-43) which he added personalization in vv. 24-25 using both Logos and Pathos. Verses 8-16 were unprepared text that specifically addressed the concerns of the newly-arrived second group of Zoramites (vv. 4-5). Because that portion was unprepared, it contains an argument without support or evidence (vv. 14-16).

The organized structure of Alma 32:8-43 cannot be "dictated from imagination" by someone like Joseph Smith without extensive rewrites and layout changes.

Alma 33

Argumentative/Persuasive Writing Analysis

Title	**Alma's Preaching to the Zoramites (2 of 2)**

Subject	Scripture authority	Reference	Alma 33:2-23
Author Name	Alma	Audience	Zoramites

Perspective	If we believe in the scriptures then we must believe in the Son of God who was prophesied in the scriptures.
Background	Alma was the high priest over the Nephites and was the former chief judge (Alma 8:11-12) who led a mission to the Zoramites around 74 BC. The Zoramites were dissenters from the Nephites and functioned as an autonomous group within the Nephite nation. They were apostates who rejected the belief of the coming Christ and believed they were guaranteed salvation without needing to repent. They also only prayed once a week and only in their houses of worship. The audience was comprised of poor Zoramites who were prohibited from entering the synagogues to worship God. While it is never stated, it appeared their concern was they couldn't be saved because they couldn't worship God in the synagogues. This chapter is the second half of Alma's preaching to the Zoramites.
Purpose/Goal	Alma led a delegation of missionaries to preach to the Zoramites so that they will return to Christ.
Form	☒ Rebuttal ☐ One-Sided

1) Thesis Claim/Position

[Since the scriptures are authoritative,] one should believe what they say concerning worshiping God (v. 2).

2) Frame of Argument

Argument 1	The Scriptures teach one can pray to God anywhere (vv. 3-11).

APPENDIX 159

Evidence	The prophet Zenos prayed to God while in the wilderness, field, in his house, closet, and in the midst of the congregations (vv. 4-9) [Logic: Authority].
Argument 2	The prophets in the scriptures prophesied of the Son of God (vv. 12-14).
Evidence	The prophets Zenos and Zenock mention the Son of God (vv. 11-17) [Logic: Authority].
Argument 3	The scriptures say we receive mercy because of the Son of God (vv. 11,13,16).
Evidence	The prophets Zenos and Zenock said we receive mercy because of the Son of God (vv. 11,16) [Logic: Authority]. Moses raised up a type of him (per Numbers 21:8-9) where people are saved just by looking at the brass serpent. Those who refused to look did so because they did not believe it would heal them (vv. 19-20) [Logic: Precedent]. Cast your eyes upon the Son of God and believe in him to be saved (vv. 21-22) [Emotion: Trust].
The author claimed to be credible because	Alma did not claim to be credible, but he was likely recognized to be the most famous person in the Nephite nation as the former chief judge and current high priest.

The author appealed to	☒ Logic		☒ Emotion	
If logic, used	☒ Authority	☐ Examples	☐ Deductive Reason
	☒ Precedent	☐ Experience	☐ Inductive Reason
	☐ Facts	☐ Competence	☐ Statistics
If emotion, used	☒ Joy	☒ Trust	☐ Surprise
	☐ Anger	☐ Fear	☒ Anticipation
	☐ Awe	☐ Yearning	☐ Envy
	☐ Dread	☐ Disgust	☐ Sadness

If rebuttal, opposition's position	1. We have no place to worship our God because we are cast out of our synagogues because of our poverty (Alma 32:5).

160 A LATTER-DAY SAINT ODE TO JESUS

	2. There is no Christ (Alma 31:16-17).		
Was concession made of opposition's valid points?		☐ Yes	☒ No

| Counter-arguments | 1. The prophet Zenos said in the scriptures that God listens to our prayers regardless of where we are (vv. 2-12). |
| | 2. The prophet Zenos, Zenock, and Moses in the scriptures all spoke of the Son of God [Christ] (vv. 11-20). |

| Form of counterarguments | ☐ Removal of the opponent's support | ☒ Exposure of the opponent's faulty logic |
| | ☒ Demonstration that the opponent has no support | |

3) Conclusion

Believe in the Son of God and that he will come to redeem his people, and that he shall suffer and die to atone for their sins; and that he shall rise again from the dead, which shall bring to pass the resurrection, that all men shall stand before him, to be judged at the last and judgment day, according to their works. Plant this word in your hearts, and as it beginneth to swell even so nourish it by your faith. And behold, it will become a tree, springing up in you unto everlasting life. And then may God grant unto you that your burdens may be light, through the joy of his Son. And even all this can ye do if ye will (vv. 22-23) [Emotion: Joy, Anticipation].

Was the thesis restated?	☒ Yes	☐ No

Believe the scriptures (v. 12).
Read the scriptures / it is written (vv. 14-19).

Was there a call to action?	☒ Yes	☐ No

Cast your eyes upon the Son of God and be saved (vv. 21-22).
Plant this word in your hearts (v.23).

Did the essay intend to make the audience think or look at the world or themselves in a different way?	☒ Yes	☐ No

If you plant the word in your heart and nourish it by your faith, then it will become a tree, springing up in you unto everlasting life. Your burdens will become light through the joy of God's Son (v. 23).

APPENDIX

4) Performance Assessment

What was the author's persuasion strategy?	☒	Ethos (Author's credibility)	☒	Pathos (Audience's emotions)
	☒	Logos (Audience's mind)	☐	Kairos (Sales pressure)

In your opinion, was the author credible to *the target audience*, given their worldview?	☒ Yes	☐ No

Why?	As the high priest over the Nephite nation and former chief judge, Alma couldn't help but be credible to the poor Zoramites. He wouldn't need to state his credibility – they automatically would find him credible. We can already see at the beginning of chapter 33 that they were impacted by Alma's speech in chapter 32 by wanting to know more information on what they must do to get the seed planted in them. Alma's citations of scripture quotations that directly refuted what they've been taught concerning praying to God and the Son would've been devastating to the theology their believed in. Alma then closed his speech by an emotional appeal immediately after the Gospel definition in v. 32. It is hard to overstate the impact this would have had to the poor Zoramites given their worldview: They started in a "No-Win" religious situation believing their priests who claimed their poverty prohibits them from entering their places of worship which would've prevented them from being saved. But now, if they did what Alma suggested, they will end up in a "No-Lose" situation – they do not need the synagogues to be saved. In fact, they now possess the true salvation—the Son of God. Also, these poor would've applied vv. 10-11 to themselves. Like Zenos, they too were cast out and despised by their enemies. Like Zenos, they too could find mercy because of the Son of God.

Did the author address *the target audience's* needs or concerns?	☒ Yes	☐ No

Why?	The poor Zoramites had a terrible self-image – they were "esteemed as filthiness/dross" by the wealthier Zoramites (Alma

	32:3) and priests who cast them out of the synagogues (Alma 32:5) – the only place where they could worship God (Alma 32:10). The unsaid implication is because they were prohibited from worshiping God in their places of worship, they would be excluded from those who are guaranteed salvation (Alma 31:17). The Zoramites asked Alma some questions in v. 1 that Alma wisely ignored because he wanted to steer the message to what the scriptures said concerning praying to God and on the Son of God. Alma provided the logical foundation for justifying the poor Zoramites' abandonment of their elitist theology. He focused on their belief in the prophets of the scriptures and then used that source of authority to demonstrate the Zoramite theology directly contradicts the scriptures. They then have nothing to fear from being prohibited from entering the synagogues.
Was the author credible *to you*, given your worldview?	☒ Yes ☐ No
Why?	While Alma's preaching in Alma 33 is nowhere near as well developed as what exists in Alma 32, his summary in v. 22 of the Gospel is one of the best passages in all the scriptures. It not only captured nearly all key points concerning the Savior, but it also mentioned the flip side of the coin – where we must believe on the Son and we will be judged according to our works. Also, Alma's pieces of evidence address the arguments making them valid even though my preference would be to provide more references from at least four figures. These make him credible to me.

5) Is it a Genuine Argumentative or Persuasive Essay?		
a. Does the reference text contain a Thesis Claim/Position?	☒ Yes	☐ No
b. Does the reference text contain arguments supported by evidence?	☒ Yes	☐ No
c. Does the reference text contain counter-arguments?	☒ Yes	☐ No

d.	Does the reference text restate the thesis?	☒	Yes	☐	No
e.	Does the reference text contain a call to action or give the recipient a different perspective?	☒	Yes	☐	No

CONCLUSION

Alma 33:2-23 is a genuine argumentative essay and can be proven empirically since it contains all the components and structure of an argumentative essay.

However, the structure of the two dominant thoughts – the scriptures teach we can pray to God anywhere and the scriptures mention the Son of God are not as developed as Alma's preaching in Alma 32:17-43 or Amulek's preaching in Alma 34:9-16 and Alma 34:32-41. This shows Alma lacked time to refine the logic and possibly didn't have additional written resources to enhance the references by the time of his speech. His summary of the Gospel in v. 22 is something that appears to have gone through numerous revisions to explain how such a broad topic was summarized so succinctly and brilliantly [see a comparable passage about the Gospel from the Savior in 3 Nephi 27:13-18].

The organized structure of Alma 33:2-23 cannot be "dictated from imagination" by someone like Joseph Smith without extensive rewrites and layout changes. As an example, it is a near-certainty that even someone highly knowledgeable in the scriptures will not be able to summarize the gospel in the same manner Alma did in v. 22 without first reading the passage.

Alma 34

	**Argumentative/Persuasive Writing Analysis**
Title		**Amulek's Preaching to the Zoramites**
Subject	The Atonement of Jesus Christ	Reference	Alma 34:2-41
Author Name	Amulek	Audience	Zoramites
Perspective		Salvation can only come from Jesus Christ
Background		Alma was the high priest over the Nephites and was the former chief judge (Alma 8:11-12) who led a mission to the Zoramites around 74 BC. The Zoramites were dissenters from the Nephites and functioned as an autonomous group within the Nephite nation. They were apostates who rejected the belief of the coming Christ and believed they were guaranteed salvation without needing to repent. They also only prayed once a week and only in their houses of worship. The audience was comprised of poor Zoramites who were prohibited from entering the synagogues to worship God. While it is never stated, it appeared their concern was they couldn't be saved because they couldn't worship God in the synagogues. Amulek's preaching immediately followed Alma's preaching (Alma 32-33) in convincing the Zoramites of the errors of their teachings concerning prayer and on the reality of Jesus Christ as the Savior.
Purpose/Goal		Alma and Amulek were missionaries and went to preach to the Zoramites so that they will return to Christ.
Form		☒ Rebuttal ☐ One-Sided
	**1) Thesis Claim/Position**
	Jesus Christ is the source of salvation (vv. 5-6).
	**2) Frame of Argument**
Argument 1		Christ was foretold by the prophets (v. 7).
Evidence		The prophets testified of the coming Savior, Jesus Christ (vv. 7,33) [Summation of Alma words in Alma 33:11-19: Logic: Appeal to Authority].

APPENDIX 165

Argument 2	Christ will come and atone for humanity (v. 8).
Evidence	The Lord God said so (v. 8) [unelaborated but Logic: Appeal to Authority].
Argument 3	Mankind must perish unless the Son of God performs an infinite Atonement (v. 9).
Evidence	Only an infinite Atonement by the Son of God may save humanity (vv. 9-16) [Logic: Deductive Argument]. The law of the nation, which is just, will not kill the brother of a murderer (vv. 11-12) [Logic: Appeal to Experience and Facts]. The sacrifices of the Law of Moses will be fulfilled (vv. 13-14) [Logic: Appeal to Precedent]. The Atonement allows Mercy to satisfy the demands of Justice [Logic: Deductive Reason in v. 16].
Argument 4	This life is the time for mankind to repent. If one postpones repenting, that person cannot be saved (v. 32).
Evidence	When we're dead, we keep the same spirit or attitude that we have in life (v. 34) [Logic: Deductive Reason]. If we procrastinated our repentance until death, we become subject to the devil (v. 35) [Emotion: Fear]. God said he does not dwell in unholy temples (v. 36) [Logic: Appeal to Facts]. The righteous have God dwelling in them and they will sit down in his kingdom (v. 36) [Emotion: Anticipation]. Work out your salvation with fear and trembling (v. 37) [Emotion: Fear].
The author claimed to be credible because	Only implied because he claimed to know Christ shall come because the Lord God said so (v. 8) and because he was part of Alma's delegation (Alma was the high priest over the Nephites).

The author appealed to	☒ Logic		☒ Emotion
If logic, used	☒ Authority	☒ Examples	☒ Deductive Reason
	☒ Precedent	☐ Experience	☐ Inductive Reason
	☒ Facts	☐ Competence	☐ Statistics
If emotion, used	☒ Joy	☒ Trust	☐ Surprise
	☐ Anger	☒ Fear	☒ Anticipation

	☐ Awe		☐ Yearning		☐ Envy	
	☐ Dread		☐ Disgust		☐ Sadness	
If rebuttal, opposition's position	1. There is no Christ (Alma 31:16). 2. The Zoramites do not need to repent because they are guaranteed salvation (Alma 31:17). 3. They only need to pray once a week and can only worship God in the synagogues (Alma 31:12-23; 32:5,11).					
Was concession made of opposition's valid points?			☐ Yes		☒ No	
Counter-arguments	1. The prophets (that the Zoramites believed in) testified of Christ (vv. 6-7,33). 2. Logic tells us that Christ must come since only an infinite Atonement can save all of humanity (vv. 9-16). Both of these mean the Zoramites must repent and accept Christ or else they cannot be saved. 3. The Zoramites can worship God anywhere (vv. 17-27 cf. Alma 33:2-11).					
Form of counterarguments	☒	Removal of the opponent's support	☒		Exposure of the opponent's faulty logic	
	☒	Demonstration that the opponent has no support				

3) Conclusion

Repent and accept Christ. Do not harden your heart, for now is the time and day of your salvation (vv. 30-31). Do not delay because if you do, you will become subject to the devil instead of dwelling with God forever (vv. 35-36). Humble yourselves and worship God wherever you are (v. 38). Pray continually and patiently bear your afflictions for if you do, you shall one day rest from all your afflictions (vv. 39-41).

Was the thesis restated?	☒ Yes	☐ No

The Scriptures testify of Christ (v. 30).

There are many witnesses that testify of Christ (v. 33).

Christ's sacrificial blood will make the garments of his followers white (v. 36).

Christ will come (v. 37).

Was there a call to action?	☒ Yes	☐ No

Exercise your faith unto repentance and cry unto the Lord (vv. 17-30).

Become charitable otherwise, your prayers will be in vain and you will be cast out (vv. 28-29).

Now is the time to repent – do not procrastinate until it is too late (vv. 31-37).

Accept the Holy Spirit and the name of Christ. Repent and pray continually. Be patient and do not revile others (v. 38-41).

Did the essay intend to make the audience think or look at the world or themselves in a different way?	☒ Yes	☐ No

Only the infinite Atonement of Jesus Christ can cause Mercy to satisfy the demands of Justice. Those who refuse to repent are exposed to the whole punishment that Justice imposes (v. 16).

Pray continually and everywhere (vv. 17-27) instead of once a week and only in the synagogues (per Alma 31:12,23; 32:5,9-11).

Have hope that you will one day rest from all your afflictions (v. 41) [Emotion: Joy, Trust].

4) Performance Assessment

What was the author's persuasion strategy?	☒ Ethos (Author's credibility)	☒ Pathos (Audience's emotions)
	☒ Logos (Audience's mind)	☒ Kairos (Sales pressure)

In your opinion, was the author credible to *the target audience*, given their worldview?	☒ Yes	☐ No

Why?	Amulek was part of Alma's party, which association would've automatically made him credible since Alma was the high priest over the nation (a prominence comparable to today's Catholic pope or the Latter-day Saint prophet) and was the former chief judge (like today's president or prime minister). Amulek reinforced Alma's arguments in a way that conformed to the worldview of the poor Zoramites. Since they believed in the prophets, then they must accept what the prophets taught. He preached to a multitude that

	likely numbered in the high hundreds or low thousands and the audience would most probably be illiterate and unsophisticated who would've been in awe that such prominent figures were speaking directly to them. They definitely considered the arguments of Amulek and Alma to be credible since they then converted to the Church
Did the author address *the target audience's* needs or concerns?	☒ Yes ☐ No
Why?	The poor Zoramites' main concern was that they were prohibited from entering their synagogues to worship God. Why would this matter if their religion taught only the Zoramites were saved? The implication is no, not all Zoramites will be saved, only those Zoramites who can worship God in the synagogues. This is why they were so troubled – their own theology taught that they couldn't be saved because of their poverty. Amulek (and Alma) pointed out that the same prophets they honored taught that not only can they worship God anywhere, they also taught that Christ was going to come someday. Amulek then focused on what was truly important: The coming Savior, Jesus Christ, who will perform an infinite Atonement. That was the message the Zoramites needed to hear – their repentance and acceptance of Jesus Christ will result in their salvation instead of praying in their synagogues.
Was the author credible *to you*, given your worldview?	☒ Yes ☐ No
Why?	Since I believe in the legitimacy of the Old Testament and Book of Mormon prophets who lived before the birth of Christ, I then accept their teaching concerning the coming of Christ in the first century who performed an infinite Atonement. However, the arguments Amulek phrased could be improved. His Argument 2 needed evidence more than "God said so." His Argument 3 is definitely valid but the provided evidence lacked the valuation justification (i.e., Jesus as God is infinitely more valuable than sinful humans, making his substitutionary sacrifice validly infinite in scope and duration). His Argument 4 was excellent and skillfully blended the Pathos, Logos, and Kairos modes of persuasion. This means that while I view Amulek's essay to be credible for his audience; it could be improved when in a discussion with an educated person of today who has the modern scientific worldview.

APPENDIX 169

> However, Amulek's thoughts in vv. 9-16 and vv. 32-35 show a brilliant mind that was already visible in Alma 11 (which was comparable to Lehi's in 2 Nephi 2 and even deeper than Alma's).

5) Is it a Genuine Argumentative or Persuasive Essay?

a.	Does the reference text contain a Thesis Claim/Position?	☒ Yes	☐ No
b.	Does the reference text contain arguments supported by evidence?	☒ Yes	☐ No
c.	Does the reference text contain counter-arguments?	☒ Yes	☐ No
d.	Does the reference text restate the thesis?	☒ Yes	☐ No
e.	Does the reference text contain a call to action or give the recipient a different perspective?	☒ Yes	☐ No

CONCLUSION

Alma 34:2-41 is a genuine argumentative essay and can be proven empirically since it contains all the components and structure of an argumentative essay. The counter-arguments show preparation was made prior to preaching concerning prayer and the infinite Atonement. Arguments 1 and 2 were unrehearsed and appear to be impromptu reinforcement statements to Alma's words in Alma 33 but the contents and structure of Arguments 3 and 4 show they were written and refined before preaching.

In fact, it appears Amulek's preaching in Alma 34:9-16 and Alma 34:32-41 were originally combined and Amulek inserted vv. 17-31 after learning what the Zoramites believed and what Alma was going to say about it in Alma 33:2-11. He then edited v. 33 to harmonize the insert. He specifically used the word "dross" in v. 29 as a counterpoint to its use in Alma 32:2 (the poor are not dross because of their poverty, they will be dross if they do not remember to be charitable).

The ideas found in Amulek's writings show he was one of the most profound thinkers in the Book of Mormon and was comparable to Lehi in 2 Nephi 2.

Amulek quickly picked up highly complex ideas from Alma since their first contact in Alma 8:19-22. He became Alma's companion and his first recorded preaching occurred in Alma 10-11. His exchange with Zeezrom (Alma 11:21-46) reveals a very sharp mind but lacked the persuasion strategy that Alma possessed which is shown by the absence of an argumentative essay in that passage. He obviously learned persuasion from Alma after that incident since Alma 34 is a master example of an argumentative essay. Another factor in believing he was a better writer than Alma is in the quality of the "prayer" verses in vv. 17-27 which were obviously written after Alma's "prayer" passages in Alma 33:2-11 but were significantly better written. Not only did he insert it in the middle of his prepared text, but he also added vv. 28-31 to bridge the very different thoughts and rewrote v. 33 to make all four text blocks flow better together. It was an amazing accomplishment.

The organized structure of Alma 34:2-41 cannot be "dictated from imagination" by someone like Joseph Smith at a pace of 4000 words per day without extensive rewrites and layout changes. The contents of Alma 34 are so well developed and advanced that it is ludicrous to allege anyone could dictate Alma 34 from one's imagination.

Alma 36

Argumentative/Persuasive Writing Analysis

Title	**Alma's Commandment to His Son, Helaman (1 of 2)**

Subject	Keep the commandments of God	Reference	Alma 36
Author Name	Alma	Audience	Helaman

Perspective	Those who keep God's commandments will prosper.
Background	At the twilight of Alma's life and 18-26 years after his conversion to Christ stemming from a supernatural appearance of an angel, Alma the high priest gave a commandment to his son Helaman who accompanied him on his recent mission to the Zoramites. The angelic appearance to Alma and the sons of King Mosiah was the most impactful event in the five hundred year history of the Nephite nation. It resulted in the dissolution of the monarchy and weakening of the central authority of the state to such an extent that the Amlicites tried to re-establish a monarchy and the rulers of the provinces of Ammonihah and Zoram tried to break away, causing tens of thousands of deaths. It also established the office of the chief judges and substantially increased individual freedom and responsibility.
Purpose/Goal	Alma wanted his son to always keep God's commandments and maintain strong faith and loyalty to Jesus Christ.

Form	☐	Rebuttal	☒	One-Sided

1) Thesis Claim/Position

If you keep the commandments, you will prosper in the land. (v.1)

	2) Frame of Argument
Argument 1	Whoever trusts in God shall be supported in their trials, troubles, and afflictions and shall be lifted up at the last day (v.3).
Evidence	**I) Objective Evidence** Do what I do, remember the captivity of our fathers. Our fathers, the Israelites, were in bondage and captivity and God delivered them [because they trusted God] (v.2) [Logic: Precedent – believed to be a factual event by the audience]. My knowledge of this truth comes from God. If I haven't been born of God, I wouldn't know these things. But God made them known to me by the mouth of his holy angel (vv.4-5) [Logic: Experience; Authority – the angel was trustworthy and other trustworthy eyewitnesses saw him]. God's holy angel appeared to me and to the sons of King Mosiah to stop us while we were trying to destroy God's church (vv.6-11) [Logic: Experience – includes other trustworthy eyewitnesses]. **II) Subjective Evidence** **A) Negative Experience** "I was struck with such great fear and amazement lest perhaps that I should be destroyed ..." (v.11) [Emotion: Fear]. "I was racked with eternal torment" and "tormented with the pains of hell" because "I had rebelled against my God, and that _I had not kept his holy commandments_" (vv.12-13) [Emotion: Fear]. "... So great had been my iniquities, that the very thought of coming into the presence of my God did rack my soul with inexpressible horror." (v.14) [Emotion: Dread]. I wish I could become extinct in both soul and body so that I wouldn't be brought to stand in the presence of my God, to be judged of my deeds (v.15) [Emotion: Fear]. I was racked with the pains of a damned soul for three days and for three nights (v.16) [Emotion: Fear]. **B) Transition** While I was in torment and harrowed up by the memory of my sins, I remembered that my father prophesied that one Jesus Christ, a son of God, was going to come "to atone for the sins of the world." While my mind caught hold of this

	thought, I cried within my heart: "**O Jesus, thou Son of God, have mercy on me, who am in the gall of bitterness.**" (vv.17-18) [Emotion: Fear; **Trust**]. "When I thought this, I could remember my pains no more; yea, I was harrowed up by the memory of my sins no more." (v.19) **Positive Experience** "And oh, what joy, and what marvelous light I did behold; yea, my soul was filled with joy as exceeding as was my pain." "there could be nothing so exquisite and so bitter as were my pains" "and nothing so exquisite and sweet as my joy." (vv.20-21) [Emotion: Joy]. Methought I saw "God sitting upon his throne, surrounded with numberless concourses of angels ... singing and praising their God ... and my soul did long to be there." (v.22) [Emotion: Awe, Yearning]. [Argument 2 insert] **III) Objective Evidence** Many have also been born of God and have tasted what I tasted, and have seen as I have seen, and know as I know that the knowledge I have is of God (v.26) [Logic: Examples; Authority – other eyewitnesses exist who can confirm that Alma's knowledge is from God]. God has consistently delivered me from trials, troubles, and afflictions because I put my **trust in him** (v.27) [Logic: Experience; Fact – can be confirmed by others]. "And I know that [God] will raise me up at the last day, to dwell with him in glory" because he brought our fathers out of bondage and captivity. I have always remembered their captivity and you should as well (vv.28-29) [Logic: Precedent – believed to be a factual event by the audience].
Argument 2	I am born of God (v.23)
Evidence	From that time until now, I have labored without ceasing that I might bring souls unto repentance so that they may also taste of the same great joy I tasted so that they may also be born of God and be filled with the Holy Spirit (v.24) [Logic: Facts – Alma's ministry is confirmable by others].

174 A LATTER-DAY SAINT ODE TO JESUS

	The Lord gives me great joy in the fruit of my labor (v.25) [Emotion: Joy]. Many have also been born of God and have tasted what I tasted, and have seen as I have seen, and know as I know that the knowledge I have is of God (v.26) [Logic: Examples; Authority – other eyewitnesses exist who can confirm that Alma's knowledge is from God].				
The author claimed to be credible because	He saw an angel and was born of God (vv.3-24). Others who are also born of God can confirm his words (v.26).				
The author appealed to	☒ Logic			☒ Emotion	
If logic, used	☒	Authority	☒ Examples	☐	Deductive Reason
	☒	Precedent	☒ Experience	☐	Inductive Reason
	☒	Facts	☐ Competence	☐	Statistics
If emotion, used	☒	Joy	☒ Trust	☐	Surprise
	☐	Anger	☒ Fear	☐	Anticipation
	☒	Awe	☒ Yearning	☐	Envy
	☒	Dread	☐ Disgust	☐	Sadness
If rebuttal, opposition's position	N/A				
Was concession made of opposition's valid points?			☐ Yes	☐	No
Counter-arguments					

APPENDIX 175

Form of counterarguments	☐ Removal of the opponent's support	☐ Exposure of the opponent's faulty logic
	☐ Demonstration that the opponent has no support	

3) Conclusion

You need to know just as I know that provided you keep the commandments of God, you shall prosper in the land. And if you refuse to keep his commandments, you will be cut off from God's presence (v.30).

Was the thesis restated?	☒ Yes	☐ No

If you keep the commandments of God, you shall prosper in the land. And if you refuse to keep his commandments, you will be cut off from God's presence (v.30)

Was there a call to action?	☒ Yes	☐ No

Remember the bondage and captivity of our fathers just as I remember them (v.29).

Know even as I know that if you keep God's commandments you will prosper (v.30)

Did the essay intend to make the audience think or look at the world or themselves in a different way?	☒ Yes	☐ No

Obedience to God's commandments brings rewards that are unimaginably glorious (v.30 cf. vv.20-22) while disobedience brings unimaginable horror (v.30 cf. vv.12-16).

4) Performance Assessment

	☒ Ethos (Author's credibility)	☒ Pathos (Audience's emotions)

What was the author's persuasion strategy?	☒ Logos (Audience's mind)	☐ Kairos (Sales pressure)		
In your opinion, was the author credible to *the target audience*, given their worldview?		☒ Yes	☐ No	
Why?	Alma was Helaman's father and was highly credible. Helaman knew firsthand of the truthfulness of Alma's claims of his effort to bring people to Christ and of his deliverance from "trials, troubles, and afflictions." However, Helaman was not the original audience of this speech – it would be those Alma was preaching to since Alma 36 is a Conversion Story speech that was customized for Helaman.			
Did the author address *the target audience's* needs or concerns?		☒ Yes	☐ No	
Why?	Alma gave Helaman a simple rule to follow: keep God's commandments and trust Christ.			
Was the author credible *to you*, given your worldview?		☒ Yes	☐ No	
Why?	I agree with Alma's perspective on the need to trust God and keep his commandments to obtain true happiness. There's no doubt that the transition or core of the chiasmus (Jesus Christ a/the Son of God and his atonement) is the center or fulcrum of the speech.			

5) Is it a Genuine Argumentative or Persuasive Essay?

a. Does the reference text contain a Thesis Claim/Position?	☒ Yes	☐ No	
b. Does the reference text contain arguments supported by evidence?	☒ Yes	☐ No	
c. Does the reference text contain counter-arguments?	☐ Yes	☒ No	

d.	Does the reference text restate the thesis?	☒	Yes	☐	No
e.	Does the reference text contain a call to action or give the recipient a different perspective?	☒	Yes	☐	No

CONCLUSION

Alma 36 is a persuasive essay instead of an argumentative essay since it is designed to be spoken to an audience without the need to use counterarguments. It is a *refined* "Conversion Story" speech that has seen continuous improvement from hundreds of retellings to maximize its persuasion impact to an audience. This explains why it contains the ethos, pathos, and logos persuasion strategies within the chiasmus inverted parallelism writing style that the ancient Hebrews used to help illiterate people retain information (which wouldn't be needed with his own son who helped him in his ministry).

I initially thought the chiasmus claim was confirmation bias due to what was excluded from the outline, but the analysis shows it was an existing speech that Alma personalized for his son, Helaman. His actual command is in Alma 37.

It is easy to conclude it is a conversion story because it is structured in such a way that it would've been used whenever Alma spoke to people, including immediately after the experience. The idea that a missionary-minded person like Alma would let around 20 years lapse before writing it within a year before his departure from earth is ludicrous.

Alma had an amazing story to tell and he knew it. And everyone he encountered would've wanted to hear it:

An angel of God appeared to him and to the sons of King Mosiah. (Mosiah 27)

The reason for the public interest is that supernatural event triggered the most impactful change in the over 500 years of the Nephite nation's history that directly affected everyone's lives. It shattered the stability of the Nephite nation that was ruled by a powerful monarch but gave the Nephites their first real taste of freedom to live their lives as they pleased.

The monarchy was abolished because Mosiah's sons refused the crown and left to become missionaries to the Lamanites (Mosiah 28). The office of Chief Judge was created, with Alma himself becoming the first to hold the public office (Mosiah 29:42-44) until his resignation after a tumultuous eight years in office (Alma 4:17-20). The nation became decentralized with different provinces becoming autonomous and functioning as quasi-independent states which severely impacted national unity. The Amlicite rebellion and Lamanite invasions (Alma 2-3,28) were existential threats that resulted in tens of thousands of casualties (Alma 3:26; 28:2). The rulers of the city of Ammonihah were so confident in their ability to withstand the central government that not only did they imprison and assault Alma (Alma 14:4,14,17-25), they actually had the wives and children of their citizens who believed Alma be burned alive (Alma 14:8-15). This same city was later destroyed by the Lamanites with all its inhabitants slaughtered (Alma 16:2-3,9-11). The Anti-Nephi-Lehi Lamanite converts of the sons of Mosiah recently showed up at the border and requested to join the Nephite nation and were granted the land of Jershon (Alma 27:14-15,20-27). The Zoramite province dissented from the Nephite nation (Alma 31) and expelled those who believed Alma (Alma 35:6).

In light of the chaos and bestowal of personal responsibility caused by the angelic visitation, what would people be asking Alma whenever they met him for the first time since the other eyewitnesses, the sons of Mosiah, were gone and no one knew what happened to them?

***Of course*, they would want to know details concerning the appearance of the angel that overturned their world!** And Alma, as the high priest, whose goal was to bring people to Christ and keep God's commandments, would use the story of the angel within a context of his actions as an evil man who found redemption and immense joy in trusting God. That speech would've been his *first* tool in strengthening and enlarging the church.

Given most of the audience he would encounter in his ministry would be illiterate, he would then frame his speech in a manner that would be the most impactful to the greatest number. Thus the presence of the persuasion strategies within a chiasmus.

I suspect Alma customized his conversion story speech for Helaman so that his young son would have his own copy to refer to for the remainder of his days since Alma's time on earth was over. The presence of chiasmus was for the illiterate public and not for Helaman since his involvement in Alma's ministry means there would be no reason to use chiasmus just for him.

Speaking of a complex chiasmus, they can only be created if the author first outlines the "ribs" that he or she builds the meat around with the central thought as the first built and the surrounding ribs built outward (both backwards and forwards). After the rib outline is completed, then textual "meat" is built around each rib. This is a conscious, three-step process and takes time and *cannot be created from front to back* without complete mastery over the subject. The over a dozen point and counterpoint chiasmic ribs in Alma 36 is astonishing to those of us who know how to create complex documentation since we know it is a process that cannot be dictated from imagination off the top of one head in a couple of hours (which would've been the case if Joseph Smith made Alma 36 up).

APPENDIX

> Alma 36 is likely the single greatest example of a complex chiasmus in ancient literature.
> See below for Alma 36's chiasmus (taken from https://byustudies.byu.edu/charts/132-chiasmus-alma-36).
> Note: Argument 2 is self-contained in its entirety within Argument 1.

Chiasmus in Alma 36

My son give ear to my *words* (v. 1)
  Keep the commandments and ye shall *prosper in the land* (v. 1)
    Do *as I* have done (v. 2)
      Remember the captivity of our fathers (v. 2)
        They were in *bondage* (v. 2)
          He surely did *deliver* them (v. 2)
            Trust in God (v. 3)
              Support in *trials, troubles, and afflictions* (v. 3)
                Lifted up at the *last day* (v. 3)
                  I know this not myself but *of God* (v. 4)
                    Born of God (v. 5)
                      I sought to destory the church (vv. 6-9)
                        My *limbs* were paralyzed (v. 10)
                          Fear of being in the *presence of God* (vv. 14-15)
                            Pains of a damned soul (v. 16)
                              Harrowed up by the memory of sins (v. 17)
                                I remembered *Jesus Christ, a son of God* (v. 17)
                                I cried, *Jesus Christ, son of God* (v. 18)
                              Harrowed by the memory of sins no more (v. 19)
                          Joy as exceeding as was the *pain* (v. 20)
                      Long to be in the *presence of God* (v. 22)
                  My *limbs* received strength again (v. 23)
              I labored to bring souls to repentance (v. 24)
            Born of God (v. 26)
          Therefore *my knowledge* is *of God* (v. 26)
        Supported under *trials, troubles, and afflictions* (v. 26)
      Trust in him (v. 27)
      He will *deliver* me (v. 27)
        And *raise me up at the last day* (v. 28)
      As God brought our fathers out of *bondage* and captivity (vv. 28-29)
    Retain a *remembrance of their captivity* (v. 29)
  Know *as I* do know (v. 30)
Keep the commandments and ye shall *prosper in the land* (v. 30)
This according to his *word* (v. 30)

These four examples (Alma 32, 33, 34, 36) are proof that the Book of Mormon contains argumentative and persuasive essays despite it was "dictated from imagination." What explains their presence since they are demonstrable impossibilities?

SCRIPTURE REFERENCE GUIDE

Old Testament

Genesis
Gen 2:4 96

Exodus
Ex 3:14 .... 57, 96
Ex 13:21-22 97

Numbers
Num 35:30 31

Deuteronomy
Deut 6:16 97
Deut 10:17 96
Deut 17:6 31
Deut 19:15 31
Deut 32:3-4 97
Deut 32:39 .... 57, 96
Deut 32:43 97
Deut 33:2 97

2 Kings
2 Kg 17:13 96

1 Chronicles
1 Chr 16:33 96

2 Chronicles
2 Chr 36:15-16 96

Nehemiah
Neh 9:6 97

Job
Job 4:9 97
Job 9:8 97
Job 38:1-4 96

Psalms
Ps 8:1-3 96
Ps 9:7 96
Ps 23:1 96
Ps 31:5 97
Ps 31:20 97
Ps 32:7 97
Ps 45:6-7 97
Ps 47:5 97
Ps 50:6 96
Ps 57:1 97
Ps 62:6-7 97
Ps 65:5-8 97
Ps 91:1-10 97
Ps 96:13 96
Ps 97:7 97
Ps 99:6 96
Ps 102:24-27 97
Ps 102:25 96
Ps 116:13,17 96
Ps 118:22 97
Ps 136:3 96
Ps 148:5-6 97

Isaiah
Isa 2:12 97

Isa 6:1-10 96
Isa 8:13-14 97
Isa 11:4 97
Isa 12:4 96
Isa 31:5 97
Isa 40:3-9 96
Isa 41:4 .... 57, 96
Isa 43:10 .... 57, 96
Isa 43:11 .... 57, 96
Isa 43:14 96
Isa 43:14-15 97
Isa 44:6 96
Isa 44:24 96
Isa 45:11-12 96
Isa 45:23 96
Isa 46:4 .... 57, 96
Isa 48:12 96
Isa 49:26 96
Isa 54:5 96
Isa 62:5 96
Isa 66:2 96

Jeremiah

Jer 3:1-2 96
Jer 23:5-6 97
Jer 46:10 97

Ezekiel

Ezek 30:3 97
Ezek 34:11-16 96

Hosea

Hos 2:16 96
Hos 11:9 97
Hos 13:4 .... 57, 96
Hos 13:14 96

Joel

Joel 1:15 97
Joel 2:32 96

Obadiah

Obad 1:15 97

Habakkuk

Hab 1:12 97

Zephaniah

Zeph 1:7,14 97
Zeph 3:9 96

Zechariah

Zech 12:10 96
Zech 13:8-9 96
Zech 14:5 97

Malachi

Mal 3:1 96
Mal 4:5 97

New Testament

Matthew

Matt 3:3,11-12 96
Matt 3:16-17 39
Matt 3:17 57
Matt 4:1,7 63
Matt 4:7 97
Matt 5:48 10
Matt 7:7 18
Matt 7:12 4
Matt 8:23-27 97
Matt 11:10 96
Matt 11:27 69
Matt 14:25-33 97
Matt 16:27 ... 69, 70, 96, 134
Matt 17:5 57
Matt 18:16 31
Matt 19:27-29 73
Matt 19:28 .... 69, 70
Matt 20:28 65
Matt 23:34 96
Matt 23:37-38 97
Matt 24:30 .... 69, 131
Matt 25:31 69
Matt 25:31-34,41,46 70
Matt 25:40,45 4
Matt 26:28 65
Matt 26:64 69
Matt 28:5-7 67
Matt 28:8-9 125
Matt 28:9 .... 42, 67
Matt 28:18 69
Matt 28:19 39

Mark

Mark 1:24 97
Mark 1:34 63
Mark 3:11-12 63
Mark 6:48-51 97
Mark 8:34 61
Mark 12:31 4
Mark 13:13 74
Mark 14:62 69
Mark 15:34 102
Mark 16:9 67
Mark 16:19 69

Luke

Luke 1:76 96
Luke 2:11 96
Luke 3:4-6 96
Luke 3:22 39
Luke 4:41 .... 63, 116
Luke 5:34-35 96
Luke 7:27 96
Luke 12:32 74
Luke 12:40 69
Luke 12:44 74
Luke 13:34-35 97
Luke 22:15-16,19-20,
    42-44 65
Luke 22:29-30 74
Luke 22:42-44 .... 65, 117
Luke 22:69 69
Luke 24:3-8 .... 67, 123
Luke 24:36-51 ....42, 67, 125

John

John 1:1 .... 39, 57, 63, 103
John 1:1,3,10,14 96
John 1:1-3,10,14 57
John 1:3 61
John 1:3,10,14 ..... 7, 61, 109
John 1:6-8,15-36 96
John 1:10 .... 61, 109

John 1:12-13 .... 10, 61, 73
John 1:14 .... 57, 63, 112
John 1:18 96
John 3:13,31-32 57
John 3:15-16,36 .... 73, 137
John 3:16 .... 63, 99
John 3:16,18,35 57
John 3:16-17 57
John 3:35 .... 69, 131
John 5:17-18 ..... 39, 59, 105
John 5:22 96
John 5:22-30 70
John 5:23 .... 39, 59, 105
John 5:28-29 .... 67, 133
John 6:19-21 97
John 6:32,38-40,44,46, 57 57
John 6:33,38 93
John 6:33,38,41-42,50-51,58,62 57
John 6:40,47, 51,54-58 73
John 6:56 .... 38, 73
John 7:33-34 .... 57, 94
John 8:16-18 31
John 8:18,42 57
John 8:23 57
John 8:24, 28 96
John 8:24,28,58 57
John 8:42 94
John 8:58 96
John 8:58-59 95
John 10:14-16 96
John 10:15 63
John 10:15,17-18 65
John 10:28 73
John 10:30 59
John 10:30,38 39
John 10:33 .... 39, 59
John 10:36 57
John 10:38 .... 59, 101
John 12:34 4
John 12:39-41 96
John 12:41-50 57
John 12:45 .... 39, 59
John 13:3 .... 57, 69, 131
John 13:19 .... 57, 96
John 13:31-32 .....39, 59, 69, 104
John 14:6 .... 69, 130
John 14:7-12 59
John 14:7-12,20 39
John 14:9-11 106
John 14:10-11,20 ....59, 101, 103
John 14:16 .... 39, 59, 105
John 14:20,23 ....38, 73, 141
John 15:1-11 .... 38, 73
John 15:7 18
John 15:10 .... 73, 138
John 16:5 57
John 16:15 69
John 16:26 .... 39, 59, 105
John 16:28 57
John 17:1-2,5,24 69
John 17:2-3 73
John 17:3,8,21,23,25 57
John 17:5,22,24 .... 57, 92
John 17:9,15,20 .... 39, 59
John 17:10 69
John 17:11,21-22 59
John 17:11,21-23 ..... 38, 73, 104, 141
John 17:19 65
John 17:21,23 ....59, 101
John 17:21-23 39
John 17:22 ....74, 143
John 18:5-8 .... 57, 96
John 19:34-37 96
John 20:19-20 .... 42, 67
John 20:21-22 39
John 20:25-29 .... 42, 67

Acts

Acts 1:1-11 .... 42, 67
Acts 1:9-11 69
Acts 2:20 97
Acts 2:32-33 69
Acts 3:14 97
Acts 3:20 .... 57, 93
Acts 4:10-12 .. 57, 69, 96, 97
Acts 5:3-4 39
Acts 7:55-56 ...... 38, 69, 102
Acts 7:59 .... 96, 97
Acts 9:5,13-14,17,21 96
Acts 10:36 69
Acts 10:42 70
Acts 13:37 67
Acts 17:31 .... 67, 70
Acts 20:32 .... 10, 73
Acts 24:15 .... 67, 70, 133
Acts 26:18 .... 10, 73
Acts 26:23 .... 65, 67

Romans

Rom 1:3 63
Rom 1:5 73
Rom 3:23-25 65
Rom 5:2 .... 74, 143
Rom 5:6-8 .... 65, 120
Rom 5:9-11 65
Rom 5:15-18 67
Rom 5:21 73
Rom 6:3-8 121
Rom 6:3-11 65
Rom 6:9-10 .. 42, 63, 67, 127
Rom 6:10 63
Rom 6:16 73
Rom 6:23 73
Rom 7:4 65
Rom 8:3 ..... 57, 63, 112, 114
Rom 8:3,32 99
Rom 8:9-11 .... 38, 73
Rom 8:14-21 ...... 10, 73, 141
Rom 8:15,22-23 .... 10, 73, 139
Rom 8:16-17 .... 38, 73
Rom 8:17 .... 65, 143
Rom 8:17-21,28-30 74
Rom 8:19-21 .... 70, 135
Rom 8:28-30 73
Rom 8:32 .... 65, 74
Rom 8:34 .... 42, 63, 67, 69
Rom 9:5 69
Rom 9:23-24 74
Rom 9:33 97
Rom 10:9,13 96
Rom 10:9-10 61
Rom 16:26 .... 73, 138

1 Corinthians

1 Cor 1:2 96
1 Cor 1:7-8 97
1 Cor 1:9 73
1 Cor 1:30 97
1 Cor 3:16-17 .... 38, 73
1 Cor 3:21-23 74
1 Cor 5:5 97
1 Cor 6:17 .... 38, 73, 142
1 Cor 8:6 ...... 7, 61, 107, 110
1 Cor 10:1-4 97
1 Cor 10:9 97
1 Cor 12:3 39
1 Cor 15:4,12-26 67
1 Cor 15:5-8 .... 42, 67
1 Cor 15:6 125
1 Cor 15:12-30 ...67, 70, 134
1 Cor 15:20,23 ....67, 126
1 Cor 15:20-22 96
1 Cor 15:21 ....63, 114
1 Cor 15:22 127
1 Cor 15:23 69

1 Cor 15:25-28 69
1 Cor 15:26 .... 67, 126
1 Cor 15:35,40-57 67
1 Cor 15:47 57
1 Cor 15:48-49 73

2 Corinthians

2 Cor 1:14 97
2 Cor 3:18 .... 73, 142
2 Cor 4:4-6 .... 39, 59
2 Cor 4:14 65
2 Cor 4:17 .... 74, 143
2 Cor 5:10 .... 70, 96, 134
2 Cor 5:14-15 65
2 Cor 5:15 .... 42, 63, 67
2 Cor 5:19 .... 39, 59
2 Cor 5:21 63
2 Cor 6:10 74
2 Cor 8:9 73
2 Cor 9:7 61
2 Cor 13:1 31

Galatians

Gal 1:4 65
Gal 2:20 .... 38, 73
Gal 2:20-21 65
Gal 3:13 .... 65, 96
Gal 3:26-29 .... 38, 73
Gal 3:26-4:7 .... 10, 73, 140
Gal 3:28 4
Gal 4:4 .... 57, 63
Gal 5:1,13 61

Ephesians

Eph 1:4 .... 38, 73
Eph 1:4-5 .... 10, 73, 140
Eph 1:7 .... 65, 96
Eph 1:10,20-23 69
Eph 1:11-18 .... 10, 73, 74
Eph 1:20 .... 67, 69
Eph 1:21 69
Eph 2:5-6 65
Eph 2:5-7 ....74, 145
Eph 2:13-16 65
Eph 3:19 73
Eph 4:9-10 57
Eph 4:13,15,24 .... 73, 142

Philippians

Phil 2:5-7 .... 39, 57
Phil 2:5-11 114
Phil 2:6-8 57
Phil 2:7-8 63
Phil 2:9-11 .... 69, 129
Phil 2:10-11 96
Phil 3:10 65

Colossians

Col 1:12-13 .... 10, 73
Col 1:13-14 96
Col 1:13-17 .... 7, 61, 96
Col 1:15 .... 39, 59, 103
Col 1:15-16 108
Col 1:15-17 .... 57, 86
Col 1:16 61
Col 1:16-17 79
Col 1:16-20 69
Col 1:17 .... 61, 97, 109
Col 1:18 67
Col 1:19 ..... 39, 59, 105, 112
Col 1:20-22 .... 63, 65, 120
Col 1:27 .... 38, 73, 74
Col 2:9 .... 39, 59, 105, 112
Col 2:9-10 73
Col 2:14 65
Col 3:1 69

Col 3:4 .... 69, 74
Col 3:10 73
Col 3:24 .... 10, 73

1 Thessalonians

1 Thes 2:12 74
1 Thes 3:13 .... 69, 97
1 Thes 4:14 67
1 Thes 4:14-17 69
1 Thes 4:16 97
1 Thes 5:2 97
1 Thes 5:9-10 .... 65, 69

2 Thessalonians

2 Thes 1:7 131
2 Thes 1:7-10 69
2 Thes 2:8 .... 69, 97
2 Thes 2:13-14 74
2 Thes 4:14-17 132

1 Timothy

1 Tim 2:5 69
1 Tim 2:6 .... 65, 119
1 Tim 5:19 31
1 Tim 6:14 .... 69, 97
1 Tim 6:14-15 96

2 Timothy

2 Tim 1:9-10 57
2 Tim 1:10 67
2 Tim 2:8 .... 67, 124
2 Tim 2:10 74
2 Tim 2:11 65
2 Tim 2:12 .... 74, 121, 144
2 Tim 4:1 .... 70, 97
2 Tim 4:1,8 69
2 Tim 4:7-8 74

Titus

Tit 2:13 .... 69, 97
Tit 2:13-14 96
Tit 2:14 65
Tit 3:7 .... 10, 73

Hebrews

Heb 1:2 .... 69, 131
Heb 1:2-3 .... 7, 39, 57, 59, 61, 63, 103
Heb 1:3 ...... 61, 97, 105, 109
Heb 1:5 57
Heb 1:6 97
Heb 1:8-9 97
Heb 1:8-10 .... 7, 61
Heb 1:10 96
Heb 1:10-12 .... 70, 97
Heb 1:13 69
Heb 1:14 .... 10, 73
Heb 2:9 .... 69, 129
Heb 2:9-10 .... 65, 118
Heb 2:10 .... 7, 61, 69, 74
Heb 2:10-17 .... 10, 73
Heb 2:14-18 63
Heb 2:18 63
Heb 3:14 .... 73, 74, 144
Heb 4:15 .... 63, 115
Heb 5:7-9 65
Heb 5:9 .... 73, 138
Heb 7:25-28 65
Heb 7:26 .... 63, 69
Heb 7:27 63
Heb 8:1 69
Heb 9:11-14 65
Heb 9:11-28 65
Heb 9:12,25-28 63
Heb 9:14 63
Heb 9:15 .... 10, 73

Heb 9:15,26-28 65
Heb 9:28 69
Heb 10:10-14 .... 63, 116
Heb 10:10-20 65
Heb 10:12 69
Heb 12:2 69
Heb 12:9-10 73

James

Jas 1:5-6 18
Jas 1:12 74
Jas 2:5 .... 10, 73, 74
Jas 2:26 42

1 Peter

1 Pet 1:2 73
1 Pet 1:3-5 .... 10, 73
1 Pet 1:11,18-20 ...... 65, 118
1 Pet 1:13-14,22-23 73
1 Pet 1:18-20 65
1 Pet 1:19-20 57
1 Pet 1:20 .... 57, 93
1 Pet 2:21-24 .... 65, 117
1 Pet 2:22 63
1 Pet 2:24 65
1 Pet 2:25 96
1 Pet 2:4-8 97
1 Pet 3:18 .... 63, 65
1 Pet 3:18-20 .... 67, 122
1 Pet 3:21 67
1 Pet 3:22 .... 69, 130
1 Pet 4:5-6 70
1 Pet 4:6 123
1 Pet 5:4 .... 69, 96
1 Pet 5:10 73

2 Peter

2 Pet 1:3-4 .... 73, 74, 142
2 Pet 1:17 .... 57, 69
2 Pet 3:10 97
2 Pet 3:10-13 .... 70, 135

1 John

1 Jn 1:1-2 .... 57, 63
1 Jn 1:2 73
1 Jn 1:3-7 73
1 Jn 1:7 .... 65, 120
1 Jn 2:13 57
1 Jn 2:20 97
1 Jn 2:25 73
1 Jn 2:29-3:3 ...... 10, 73, 140
1 Jn 3:5 63
1 Jn 3:9 .... 10, 73
1 Jn 4:2-3 .... 42, 63, 112
1 Jn 4:9-10 .... 57, 99
1 Jn 4:9-10,14 .... 57, 65, 119
1 Jn 4:14 57
1 Jn 4:14-15 96
1 Jn 5:1-5 .... 10, 73
1 Jn 5:3 73
1 Jn 5:7 37
1 Jn 5:9-13,20 73
1 Jn 5:13-15 18
1 Jn 5:20 .... 38, 73

2 John

2 Jn 1:4,6 73
2 Jn 1:7 .... 42, 63, 112

Jude

Jude 1:14 .... 69, 97
Jude 1:21 73

Revelation

Rev 1:5 .... 65, 67
Rev 1:6 .... 74, 144
Rev 1:7 96
Rev 1:8,17-18 96
Rev 1:18 .... 67, 70, 126
Rev 3:14 .... 7, 61
Rev 3:20 61
Rev 3:21 .... 74, 144
Rev 5:5,9,12 63
Rev 5:5,9,12-13 69
Rev 5:9 65
Rev 5:10 74
Rev 5:13-14 69
Rev 7:17 69
Rev 17:14 .... 57, 96
Rev 19:7-8 96
Rev 19:13-16 .... 57, 96
Rev 20:4 74
Rev 20:10-15 70
Rev 20:11 70
Rev 20:13-14 .... 67, 126
Rev 21:1 135
Rev 21:1,5 70
Rev 21:7 ...... 10, 73, 74, 141
Rev 21:8 36
Rev 21:9 96
Rev 22:5 74
Rev 22:12 .... 69, 70
Rev 22:12-16 96
Rev 22:15 36
Rev 22:20 96

Book of Mormon

1 Nephi

1 Ne 10:11	67
1 Ne 11:32-33	65
1 Ne 12:10-11	65
1 Ne 13:38-40	20
1 Ne 13:40	19, 37, 57, 69
1 Ne 19:7-10	36
1 Ne 19:7-10,13	57
1 Ne 19:9-10	63
1 Ne 19:10	98
1 Ne 22:24	69

2 Nephi

2 Ne 1:10	19, 36
2 Ne 2:4	63
2 Ne 2:6-9	19
2 Ne 2:6-10	65
2 Ne 2:8	67, 126
2 Ne 2:26-27	61
2 Ne 6:9	19, 36, 63, 98, 112
2 Ne 6:9,14-18	57
2 Ne 6:14-15	69
2 Ne 9:4-7	19
2 Ne 9:5	63
2 Ne 9:5,20-21	36
2 Ne 9:7,20-21	65
2 Ne 9:7,20-22	65
2 Ne 9:7-13,22	67
2 Ne 9:10-12,26	67
2 Ne 9:10-15	135
2 Ne 9:10-15,22	70
2 Ne 9:20-21	19, 36
2 Ne 9:41	19, 37, 69
2 Ne 10:3	65
2 Ne 10:3-4	19, 36, 57
2 Ne 10:23	61
2 Ne 10:24	65
2 Ne 25:12-13	37, 57, 63
2 Ne 25:12-19	19
2 Ne 25:13-14	67
2 Ne 25:16	65
2 Ne 25:20,26,28-29	37, 69
2 Ne 30:2	19, 37, 69
2 Ne 30:10	69
2 Ne 31:7	63, 115
2 Ne 31:19-21	37, 69
2 Ne 31:21	19, 37
2 Ne 32:6	63
2 Ne 33:10-11	35

Jacob

Jac 4:5,11	37
Jac 4:11	57, 63, 65
Jac 6:2-3	69

Enos

Enos 1:8	63

Mosiah

Mosi 3:5-8	57, 65, 92
Mosi 3:5-12	19, 36
Mosi 3:8	19, 61, 109
Mosi 3:10	67
Mosi 3:11,16	65
Mosi 3:12,17	19, 37, 69
Mosi 3:17	129
Mosi 3:18	137
Mosi 4:2	61, 73
Mosi 4:6-7	57
Mosi 4:8	19, 37, 69

Mosi 5:7 73
Mosi 5:7-9 .... 65, 119
Mosi 5:8 .... 19, 37, 69, 73
Mosi 5:15 61
Mosi 7:27 .... 19, 36, 57, 63
Mosi 13:28 65
Mosi 13:28,34-35 36
Mosi 13:34-35 .... 19, 57
Mosi 15:1-14 19
Mosi 15:5 63
Mosi 15:5-7 65
Mosi 15:8,23 67
Mosi 15:10-13 73
Mosi 16:7-8 .... 67, 127
Mosi 16:7-11 .... 67, 70
Mosi 16:13 .... 37, 69
Mosi 17:8 36
Mosi 18:2 67
Mosi 18:22 73
Mosi 26:21-23 73
Mosi 26:23 .... 61, 65, 119
Mosi 26:23-26 .... 19, 36
Mosi 27:25-26 73
Mosi 27:30 61

Alma

Alma 5:48 .... 37, 57
Alma 5:50 .... 57, 69, 92
Alma 6:8 19
Alma 7:9-13 19
Alma 7:9-14 65
Alma 7:11-13 65
Alma 7:12-13 .... 63, 114
Alma 9:26 .... 37, 57
Alma 11:38-40 36
Alma 11:40 73
Alma 11:41-45 ... 67, 70, 128
Alma 11:44 .... 19, 37
Alma 12:25-35 57
Alma 12:33-34 37

Alma 13:5 37
Alma 13:8-14 65
Alma 16:19 65
Alma 18:39 57
Alma 21:9 .... 37, 65, 69, 70
Alma 22:13 57
Alma 22:14 .... 19, 65, 67
Alma 30:7-11 111
Alma 30:7-12 61
Alma 33:22 ..... 19, 65, 67, 70
Alma 34:2 19
Alma 34:8 65
Alma 34:8-12 19
Alma 34:8-16 119
Alma 34:9,15 .... 37, 69
Alma 34:14-15 137
Alma 34:15 73
Alma 34:34 43
Alma 34:36 65
Alma 36:17-18 19
Alma 38:9 ..... 19, 37, 69, 130
Alma 40:2-25 70
Alma 42:15 36
Alma 42:23 65
Alma 42:26 57

Helaman

Hel 3:28 .... 19, 37, 57
Hel 3:28-30 .... 19, 37, 69
Hel 5:9 .... 19, 37, 69
Hel 5:12 19
Hel 8:15 .... 37, 69
Hel 14:8 .... 37, 69
Hel 14:12 .... 19, 61
Hel 14:13 73
Hel 14:14-16 65
Hel 14:15-16 67
Hel 14:17 65
Hel 14:30-31 61

3 Nephi

3 Ne 9:15 ...... 19, 37, 57, 59, 61, 86, 101, 104, 108, 110
3 Ne 9:15-17 .... 73, 141
3 Ne 11:1-17 ...... 37, 57, 100
3 Ne 11:7,11 59
3 Ne 11:8-17 .... 67, 124
3 Ne 11:14 .... 19, 36, 65
3 Ne 11:27 .... 37, 59, 101, 104
3 Ne 11:27,36 .... 19, 37
3 Ne 11:32-38 .... 73, 138
3 Ne 12:44-45 73
3 Ne 15:1-5 .... 57, 98
3 Ne 19:18 .... 19, 36
3 Ne 19:23,29 ..... 37, 38, 59, 73, 101, 103
3 Ne 20:35 .... 19, 37, 59
3 Ne 23:9 59
3 Ne 26:4-5 67
3 Ne 26:5 57
3 Ne 27:13-14 ...... 19, 57, 95
3 Ne 27:14 70
3 Ne 28:7-8 69
3 Ne 28:10 .... 59, 73, 105

4 Nephi

4 Ne 1:17 73

Mormon

Morm 3:21 19
Morm 6:21 .... 67, 70
Morm 7:5 .... 19, 67
Morm 7:5-6 127
Morm 7:5-7 .... 70, 73
Morm 7:7 .... 19, 37
Morm 7:9 20
Morm 9:2 69
Morm 9:6 65
Morm 9:12-13 .... 65, 120
Morm 9:13-14 70
Morm 9:22 19
Morm 9:26 73
Morm 9:29 .... 37, 57

Ether

Eth 3:6-18 .... 36, 57
Eth 3:13 65
Eth 3:14 .... 57, 73, 93
Eth 3:14-15 61
Eth 3:14-16 .... 61, 111
Eth 3:16,21 63
Eth 4:7 19
Eth 4:9 69
Eth 4:12 57
Eth 12:7-8 59
Eth 13:9 70
Eth 13:10-11 65

Moroni

Moro 7:19,26,48 73
Moro 7:27 69
Moro 7:48 .... 73, 143
Moro 8:8 .... 19, 36
Moro 9:26 .... 69, 130
Moro 10:3-5 17
Moro 10:23 65

Doctrine and Covenants

D&C 5:19 69	D&C 42:52 73
D&C 10:57 .... 37, 57	D&C 43:27,34 36
D&C 10:70 .... 36, 69	D&C 43:32 70
D&C 11:28 .... 37, 57	D&C 45:1-3 61
D&C 11:30 .... 73, 141	D&C 45:1-4 .... 61, 110
D&C 14:9 61	D&C 45:4 .... 59, 63
D&C 17:9 .... 36, 69	D&C 45:8 73
D&C 18:11 65	D&C 45:44-55 .... 69, 132
D&C 18:11-12 67	D&C 45:51-53 .... 37, 57
D&C 18:21-23 130	D&C 49:5 37
D&C 18:23 .... 37, 69	D&C 49:6 69
D&C 18:33,47 36	D&C 50:26-28 74
D&C 19:1-4,16-19,24 36	D&C 50:43 ....37, 38, 59, 73,
D&C 19:2 69	102, 142
D&C 19:16-19,24 ..... 65, 117	D&C 51:1,20 36
D&C 20:21 .... 37, 57	D&C 51:20 69
D&C 20:22 63	D&C 52:13 74
D&C 20:24 69	D&C 53:1-2 36
D&C 20:28 37	D&C 54:1 .... 65, 120
D&C 20:29 73	D&C 56:3 73
D&C 21:9 65	D&C 58:4 74
D&C 25:1 73	D&C 58:22 69
D&C 27:1 36	D&C 59:2 74
D&C 27:2 65	D&C 59:21 73
D&C 29:11-26 69	D&C 6:21 .... 37, 57
D&C 29:23-27 .... 70, 136	D&C 61:38-39 69
D&C 29:26-28 70	D&C 62:1 36
D&C 29:42 .... 37, 57	D&C 63:59 .... 69, 131
D&C 33:1,17-18 36	D&C 63:66 74
D&C 34:3 73	D&C 66:12 74
D&C 34:7-9 69	D&C 66:13 36
D&C 35:1 69	D&C 66:2 74
D&C 35:1-2 36	D&C 70:8 73
D&C 35:2 .... 73, 142	D&C 72:8 36
D&C 35:2,18 .... 38, 73	D&C 76:5-6 74
D&C 38:1-3 .... 61, 110	D&C 76:13,25,39 .... 37, 59
D&C 38:8 69	D&C 76:13-14,20,23,
D&C 39:1 .... 36, 57	25,35 57
D&C 39:1-4 73	

D&C 76:13-14,20,23,25,35,57 37
D&C 76:20,23,106-109 69
D&C 76:23-24 61
D&C 76:23-24,58 73
D&C 76:40-43 59
D&C 76:41 65
D&C 76:50-70 144
D&C 76:55-59 74
D&C 76:55-59,94-95 74
D&C 76:58-59 73
D&C 76:61,106 69
D&C 76:73-74 67
D&C 76:76-77 43
D&C 76:106-109 ...... 69, 129
D&C 78:1,20 36
D&C 78:5-6,22 74
D&C 81:1,6-7 36
D&C 82:8-10 73
D&C 84:36-38 .... 74, 145
D&C 88:6 .... 63, 115
D&C 88:17-20 74
D&C 88:49-50 .... 38, 73, 142
D&C 88:91-98 69
D&C 88:97-102 67
D&C 88:107 .... 73, 74
D&C 93:3 .... 59, 103
D&C 93:3-4,17,20 ..... 37, 59, 102
D&C 93:3-9 .... 36, 57
D&C 93:4-6,16 .... 59, 106
D&C 93:7,21 57
D&C 93:7-11 .... 61, 109
D&C 93:1,20-22 73
D&C 93:19-20 .... 73, 138
D&C 93:20-22 .... 73, 74
D&C 95:17 69
D&C 98:8 65
D&C 98:8,18,38 36
D&C 98:22 73
D&C 101:23-25 69
D&C 101:25 70

D&C 103:4-5 36
D&C 104:7 74
D&C 109:4 .... 37, 69
D&C 110:4 67
D&C 117:6 61
D&C 121:29,46 74
D&C 122:8 ....63, 115
D&C 128:22 57
D&C 130:20-21 ....73, 139
D&C 132:12 .... 37, 69
D&C 132:19-23,37, 49,57 74
D&C 132:2,11-12 36
D&C 132:28 57
D&C 133:1-2,74 36
D&C 133:53 65
D&C 133:57 74
D&C 137:1-10 43
D&C 138:4 73
D&C 138:6-52 67
D&C 138:11-24 123
D&C 138:14,57 37
D&C 138:17 67
D&C 138:51 67
D&C 138:60 69

Pearl of Great Price

Moses

Mos 1:3-8,27-38	61, 108
Mos 1:10-13	73
Mos 1:32	37
Mos 2:26	57
Mos 5:9	57
Mos 5:15	73
Mos 5:57	37, 57
Mos 6:52	37, 57, 69
Mos 6:59	65, 121
Mos 6:68	73
Mos 7:1	73
Mos 7:30	61
Mos 7:50	37, 57
Mos 7:54	63
Mos 7:59	74
Mos 7:62	67
Mos 8:13	73

Abraham

Abr 3:11-13	61
Abr 3:22-24	36, 57
Abr 3:22-27	57, 94
Abr 3:23-25	57
Abr 3:24	59, 103, 105
Abr 3:24-26	139
Abr 3:26	74

Joseph Smith-Matthew

JS-M 1:1	69
JS-M 1:49-50	74

Joseph Smith-History

JS-H 1:17	38, 57, 100
JS-H 1:35	21

INDEX

Abiogenesis............ 81, 110
Anglicanism/Independent
 Catholicism 44
Aristotle 3
Athanasius of Alexandria . 40
Atheism 42, 81
Basic Trinitarianism ... 39, 40
Big Bang.............. 60, 81, 86
Book of Mormon, The
 Objective evidence for its
  credibility 21
 Only external evidence for
  the credibility of the
  Holy Bible 35
 Subjective evidence for its
  credibility 17, 18
Catholicism...................... 44
Children of God, The .. 7, 46,
 72, 77, 114, 135, 137,
 140, 141, 142, 143, 144,
 145, 148
 Are adopted by the
  Father.... 7, 10, 46, 139,
  140, 148
 Become God's heirs and
  joint-heirs with
  Christ... 10, 46, 72, 139,
  140, 143, 144
 Share God's glory 46
 Share in God's nature as
  "God"....... 7, 38, 46, 72,
  142, 148
 Share oneness with
  God . 6, 46, 58, 72, 104,
  141, 148
Christian ethics 3, 4, 5
Cicero 3
Civil Law 3

Common Law................... 3
Dark energy 81
Dark matter 81
David Whitmer 31, 32, 34
Eastern Christian 44
Expanded
 Trinitarianism..........40, 41
Fall, The...............6, 1, 7, 93
Father, Son, and Holy Spirit
 Are One God 19, 37, 39
Fine-tuned universe 109
Five Branches of
 Christianity................... 44
Four sigma level of
 evidence...........12, 30, 84
Greek philosophy 40
Holy Bible, The
 Objective evidence for its
  credibility......12, 13, 14,
  16, 45
 Subjective evidence for
  its credibility 11, 12
Holy Spirit, The
 Dwells within the
  Christian.....6, 9, 11, 50,
  52
 Provides a subjective
  witness of the
  Truth 11, 12, 17, 19,
  20, 21, 35
Homo sapiens sapiens... 82,
 83, 86
Jesus Christ
 "God" by nature 6, 7, 36
 Annulled the Fall....... 1, 7,
  121

Atonement of..... 7, 66, 93, 114, 115, 117, 123, 129
Atonement was infinite .. 7, 64, 76, 81, 117, 118, 129, 137
Became human flesh 6, 1, 76, 112, 113, 114, 121, 129
Conjoined the God and human natures together 7
Created the universe 6, 7, 54, 56, 60, 76, 79, 80, 86, 103, 107, 108, 109, 110, 114
Gives the free gift of physical immortality to all 6, 67, 127, 128, 130, 132, 137
Has an immortal physical body 116, 125, 126
Humility of 114
Infinite Atonement annuls the Fall 6, 10
Inherits the universe 46, 92, 103, 117, 131, 134, 144
Is our God ... 7, 19, 36, 46, 52, 64, 134
Judges all humanity 7
Keeps the forces of the universe together 6, 60, 103, 105, 109
One-time sacrifice of .. 115
Only way to the Father .. 7, 37, 45
Resurrection of 7, 114, 116, 122, 123, 125, 129
Second Coming of 68, 131, 132, 134
Single incarnation 115, 127

Son of God .. 1, 16, 37, 45, 60, 66, 76, 86, 92, 94, 98, 101, 104, 108, 109, 114, 116, 118, 122, 123, 127, 129, 132, 137, 141, 142, 148
Source of the West's ethics 2, 84
Suffered infinite pain. 6, 7, 117, 118
Taught empathetic morality and human equality 3, 5
The Father's Only Begotten Son 1, 12, 17, 37, 42, 45, 98, 107, 148
World's debt to ... 5, 1, 2, 3, 4, 6, 12, 52, 55, 84, 85
Jesus is Jehovah 95
Joseph Smith 20, 38, 42, 69, 74, 100, 147, 149
Latter-day Saints ... 1, 36, 38, 39, 40, 42, 43, 44, 45, 46, 47
Martin Harris 31
Moses 3
Mutual indwelling .. 6, 37, 38, 42, 46, 101, 102, 104, 141, 148
Natural Rights 2, 4, 84
Neoplatonic 40
New Testament, The
  Did not have a common frame nor harmonizing editor 13, 16, 45, 55, 83, 84
  Has a single coherent cosmology 5, 3, 7, 12, 13, 84

Is a correlative anthology. 5, 12, 13, 83, 84
Nontrinitarian 96
Oliver Cowdery 31, 149
Prebiotic Earth 81, 110
Protestantism 44
Quantum fluctuation 81
Science, Technology, Engineering, & Mathematics (STEM) Modern 3
Son of Jehovah 95
Synthetic chemists 81
Testimony of the Eight Witnesses 33
Testimony of the Three Witnesses 31, 33
Three Cappadocians 40
Trinitarian 40
Trinity 39, 40, 41, 42, 102
Western civilization 3
YHWH 95

ABOUT THE AUTHOR

Edward K. Watson has over 70,000 hours in writing, editing, and analyzing complex documents such as RFPs, proposals, and project execution plans for very large projects, including nearly a dozen in the billion dollar range. He is the author of **The God Who Washes Feet**: *Assessing Christianity's Credibility in Light of Objective Facts and Empirical Evidence.* The book details the only empirical evidence that anyone can use to justify the belief that the Holy Bible is inspired by God (the New Testament is a frameless, unharmonized, correlative anthology). The book also provides three additional pieces of evidence that support belief in God and demolishes atheism.

He published his first book in 1998 (**Mormonism**), but lost interest in Latter-day Saint apologetics and discontinued the series. After a decade as an atheist, he is, once again, a devout member of the Church of Jesus Christ of Latter-day Saints and has enormous appreciation for the teachings in the Book of Mormon concerning our God, Jesus Christ and of his infinite Atonement.

Ed is awestruck by the Prophet Joseph Smith, by what that uneducated farmer accomplished in a mere 15 years before his death in 1844 at just 38 years of age. Ed points out that it does not matter whether one thinks Joseph Smith was a true prophet of God or a con man – his stacked accomplishments in over a dozen areas shows he was a genius without peer. People do themselves a disservice by dismissing this *supernova* without thought because his "fruits" are objective and empirical (such as the Book of Mormon containing dozens of coherent argumentative essays despite being "dictated from imagination"—a demonstrable impossibility as anyone who's had to write them in university can attest). If he wasn't a true prophet of God, then what was he since no one has been able to do what he did in similar circumstances?

Made in the USA
San Bernardino, CA
07 September 2019